A NIGHT ON THE GROUND
A DAY IN THE OPEN

DOUG ROBINSON

Mountain N' Air Books
P. O. Box 12540
La Crescenta, CA 91224

A Night on the Ground, a Day in the Open©
Copyright in 1996 by Doug Robinson
First Edition, 1996 - Paperback

Dedicated to my mother and father, who understood and encouraged.

Published in the United States of America by
Mountain N' Air Books - P.O. Box 12540, La Crescenta, CA 91224
Phone: (818) 951-4150, fax: (818) 951-4153

Cover art: *Lake Basin in the High Sierra*, 1930, by Chiura Obata. Color woodblock print, 11 x 15 3/4 in. Photograph by Brian Grogan. Courtesy of Yosemite Association, Yosemite National Park, California.

Cover and general book design and lay-out by Gilberto d' Urso
Photographs by the author, unless otherwise indicated.

Library of Congress Cataloging-in-Publication Data

Robinson, Doug, 1945-
    A night on the ground, a day in the open / Doug Robinson. -- 1st ed.

      p.   cm.
    Includes bibliographical references and index.
    ISBN 1-879415-14-3 (pbk.)
    1. Sierra Nevada (Calif. and Nevada)–Description and travel.
    2. Mountain life–Sierra Nevada (Calif. and Nevada) 3. Robinson,
    Doug, 1945- –Home and haunts–Sierra Nevada (Calif. and Nevada)
    I. Title.
    F868 . S5R55   1996
      917.94'40453–dc20   96-887
                                       CIP

ISBN: 1-879415-14-3

Table of Contents

Further Afield

Return

Introduction

"Tenaya Lake" - *Helen Robinson photo*

Doug Robinson

Want what?
More than
A night on the ground,
And a day in the open?

Bringing Light out of Stone

This collection of articles, poems and photos springs from a lifetime spent in the mountains, mainly California's High Sierra, climbing and skiing. Beginning from the drama of alpine settings and the full focus of action, these pieces often turn inward to heightened perceptions and overflowing feeling. In the wake of action I sit, back against a boulder or on top of my pack on a snowy col, scribbling about what it might all mean—or at least how the associations of the moment came about. Trying, yet again, to wring light out of stone.

It's such a simple idea, this *night on the ground,* really more of an urge. To get out and stay there. To go out and play and not come back till late. For me it has made all the difference.

When I came down from early trips to the Sierra the idea of sleeping out forgot to go away. I was still very young when I started dragging my sleeping bag out onto my parents lawn—which was really just a wild meadow mowed short where the Santa Clara Valley rose into the California Coast Range. My first sleeping bag had a light canvas cover, so I could forget a ground sheet and pad and sleep right on the irregular adobe. An owl kept vigil over my right shoulder, and sometimes deer came down. The feelings that surfaced out there seemed more vivid, and the night thoughts more expansive when held under no canopy but the stars, stretching to the edges of the universe.

Weekends I would sometimes backpack over the coast range to the sea, and hitchhike home. Once when joining a Sierra Club trip to try a winter ascent of Pyramid Peak up near Tahoe, the adventure began with a long walk across the nascent Silicon Valley in the wee hours of the morning, carrying pack and skis to meet my ride.

I stayed home to start college, and often walked the four miles to the new Foothill College campus, arriving at Henry Rink's poetry lecture with dew glistening on the rough leather of my mountain boots. Or ran, with the book bag chafing my back. I was a conscientious objector to gasoline and refused to have a drivers license. That part, at least, changed. Later I found myself living out of a car for long periods, driving around the west or across the country to guide. But I would always return—to the Sierra, to wandering on foot. The two introductory pieces here reflect that. *Five* recalls the dawning of perception when the stone and the light coming out of it were still one. And *Wanderers of the Range of Light* revolves around an impulse deeper than the passion for either climbing or skiing. Those activities are after all just channels for applying yearning to landscape. At their best they serve to intensify contact with the mountains, which remain as a direct, primeval source. The piece traces how going to the Sierra has realigned so many lives.

The writing part never changed. To write meant then and still does, catching sparks of thought in a hard-backed notebook balanced on my knees. Being on the move seemed to make thoughts come tumbling out in a rush, perfectly formed, so that the real challenge was for my pencil to keep up. The thrill of receiving ideas was always accompanied by a rush of excitement that often spilled over into physical shudders and shouts. It continues to amuse me that having "flights of ideas" is taken as a psychiatric symptom instead of a source of inspiration. Even the name seems poetic, and, if you happen to like ideas, intriguing. The twentieth century isn't always as wise as it imagines itself.

Intellectual winnowing took place later, and while some of those passages were stomped on the threshing floor, a surprising number survived to meet the rewrite editor. There I noticed that, after any amount of re-formulating and tinkering, most of these wild jottings returned to the original form in which they were taken down, white hot, like dictation. It made me admire all over again that original process of putting it on paper which I was far from either controlling or creating, one in which I felt simply privileged to serve as a scribe.

When I moved away from home it was to pitch a tent in Windmill Pasture, perched above Foothill College up on Black Mountain. My climbing partner John Fischer moved up there too. One pup tent held the library and portable typewriter, in the other were vats of peanut butter and jam, a tiny gasoline stove and our climbing ropes. We slept outside and showered in the gym.

By then family vacations in the mountains had given way to summers up there on my own. Graduating from college I moved into the Sierra for good, and my life ever since has revolved around the mountains: climbing and skiing; guiding and writing; shooting video and designing equipment. All punctuated by plenty of time to just stand and stare.

As the pieces collected here began to sort into periods and grow introductions, my publisher, Gilberto d'Urso, urged me to write more about the mountain people I encountered along the way. So I began adding thumbnail sketches to the introductions or postscripts, and I soon realized what a good idea he had: very little of the lore of these historic periods in American climbing has been written down. As that effort expanded this book, I was glad to hear that Steve Roper, who was one of my first editors at *Ascent*, was also writing a book about life in "Camp 4" during Yosemite's golden age in the Sixties.

"Never lose your contact with the earth," I remember my mother saying at Tenaya Lake in Yosemite. We were sitting on an achingly smooth granite slab that ran down into the lake. I was eight or nine. Now she allows that "I might have overdone it..." But she says it with a sly smile.

Decades later I am still enjoying the privilege of nights on the ground, days in the open. That thought, among many other words in these pages, continues to feel almost too simple to say. But that's the way it really gets out there. Reduced, finally, to a clarity, a simplicity that is perilously close to wordless, and feels alternately profound and silly. Either way, it draws me back and reinforces the feeling that this is the

> Best of vantage points,
> Those high mountain days.

Five

For me, Yosemite was the first wilderness. From the age of
five on, my family went to Tenaya Lake at the end of every August and camped in the Tuolumne high country. That was a
far more remote place in the early Fifties, when the Tioga Road
was one lane wide with turnouts and the drive took two hours
from Crane Flat. Although written much later (1989), *Five* reflects the drive to return to the freshness of that first vision,
something that I am seeing all over again through the eyes of
my young son Tory, looking over my shoulder at his first summers in the Sierra.

I was five years old that first Sierra day, running on pure whim.
From the tent down over bright sand to the lapping edge of Tenaya Lake,
deliciously cold. Over to a rock. Slap that rock. Laugh and run to a pine tree.
Roots. Sap. Rub that sap into the sand. The sand is sharp. It's all bright,
brighter than the coast hills of home. Breathe in the brightness, everything
quickens. The lake shatters the sun, scattering it up under my Cape Cod hat.

Granite domes ring the lake, to keep it from spilling into the sky. I burn off the first of many noses.

We come back every summer. I have a feather sleeping bag, army surplus, nestled just under the eaves of the tent, outside with the stars. In the morning I button my maroon wool shirt right up to the collar, throw chips into the fire, smell coffee. Now I have a brother. Charlie and I hike in the cool woods; we lash rafts to paddle out to each of the rock islands, and fish. I snag a fishhook in my brother's scalp, so we drive all the way down to the hospital in Yosemite Valley.

As my legs get stronger, the Sierra grows. Longer trails lead away from Tenaya Lake to the High Sierra Camps, big tents with wooden floors and steel beds. Then I have another brother, and our mother coaxes Bruce's feet all the way up to Vogelsang by reciting the deaths of Presidents. Up there is another threshold, timberline, opening onto an wider, peak-spattered horizon. Step over and run alpine tundra gardens in Indian moccasins.

Now I am at home in the Sierra, dwelling in the light. I climb up the flanks of Pywiack, the granite dome across Tenaya, still on the edge of the world. Exhale and focus, balancing my self onto crystals. Such concentration brightens even that light.

In the spring I come back to Tenaya Lake, skiing four days over the crest from Mammoth. I step out onto its frozen, drifted surface and spread my parka like a sail. The wind skates me along. Like the cirrus passing overhead, I slide south toward summer....

Wanderers of The Range of Light

How old *is* the tradition of Sierra vagabonds?

Maybe we can approach the Sierra best through the lives of the obsessed, who have been consumed by a fascination with the place. This attempt ranges broadly, sweeping together decades and ideas into a kind of grand design. A little wild and sporting a mystical bent, it made editors shy and had a tough time getting published in magazines; perhaps it is better suited to this context.

The last part of this piece lapses into fiction. My only excursion in that direction, it has generated some interesting responses. For years now a number of Outward Bound instructors and guides at NOLS, the National Outdoor Leadership School, have been passing along xeroxed copies and reading them to students around campfires.

The first summer that I guided in the Sierra, Bob Swift was the chief guide at the Palisades climbing school. Bob was a Himalayan veteran, having climbed twice in Pakistan and just returned from Nepal. The students were awed by such experience. So was I. Once a week came the question. It was always around the campfire as dusk settled that someone would ask him for tales of adventure in the Great Ranges. Bob would sit back, light his pipe and check the alpenglow on Mt. Sill to let the moment lengthen before answering. He never mentioned the expeditionary fever that once drove him to buy a one-way ticket to the East, leaving the problem of getting home until after the climb. "You know," he said instead, "going to any mountain range in the world is an appreciation course in the Sierra Nevada."

That was decades ago. I was young and *assumed* that I should get around too. So now I'm a Himalayan veteran myself, not to mention forays into the Alps of Europe and New Zealand, and many of the major ranges of North America. I had to go see, but the further I traveled, the more I realized that Bob Swift was right.

Coming home to the Sierra is always a treat. Best of all is to drive in from Nevada, cresting the White Mountains at dawn to be suddenly confronted full in the face by the eastern wall of the range. The weather will be perfect, as usual: western blue sky, hundred-mile visibility. Alpenglow shoots across the summit snowfields, then just as suddenly goes incandescent white—reach for the shades. Light crawls down the face of the range, etching in ridgelines. Some of them drop two vertical miles from summit to sage. Yard lights wink out at alfalfa ranches down along the Owens River. Going west, it is nearly a hundred miles to the next plowed land, and the sun will take some time yet to climb over the roof of the Sierra and crawl down over miles of rolling forests and manzanita thickets before falling on those Central Valley farms. Either side, the Golden State greens its fields with water wrung from the westerly trades by that four-hundred-mile-long spine, the Sierra.

What is it about this range? A glimpse into the lives of the Sierra fanatics who will live nowhere else leads toward an answer. Once, after two months away, I came back to Bishop, the high desert town that sits at the eastern base of the Sierra, to find local guide Mike Graber showing Everest slides. Nearly a hundred people crowded into Wheeler & Wilson's boot shop. This wasn't the Rotary Club, nor the crowd from down at Waterhole #3. Don Lauria was there, whose second ascent of El Capitan's North American Wall had broken a spell by showing that someone besides the 'Big Four' could climb that hard. He sold a thriving business in L.A. to move here. And Duane Raleigh, who had wandered out from Oklahoma in the spring to climb Zenyata Mondata, the latest and hardest of all forty El Cap routes, in an amazing seven and a half days, solo. Now Duane is washing dishes at a ski touring lodge. Will Crljenko was there, who has probably done more backcountry skiing than anyone else in the Sierra, usually alone. No one outside of this room has heard a word about it. There were extreme skiers and ice acrobats and timberline ramblers. Each of them ekes out a living in a thin desert economy just to be in the Sierra at every opportunity.

Graber was in fine form, and soon had us in stitches. But halfway through the show his voice faltered: "I'd be slogging up some snow slope high on the west ridge of Everest and find myself thinking about Mount Humphreys," he said gesturing west, "or of warm granite, short pants, the people here that I love." An electric rustle ran through the room. Two miles straight above town the chisel summit of Mt. Humphreys glowed under fresh snow and new moon.

Maybe it was just another storefront evening. Outside was the redneck Main Street of a town that liked to think of itself as "the mule capitol of the world," with Rexall Drugs next door and the new McDonald down the block. Yet for this ragged band, bound together by the visionary fact that they could see beyond the western false-fronts to the Sierra beyond, feelings ran high. When Mike Graber got home from Asia he had burned his passport.

Clearly something is going on here, realigning lives to follow the ragged axis of the Sierra crest. Bob Swift was nowhere near the first. In fact, the tradition of Sierra wanderers goes at least as far back as John Muir.

When he got off the Panama boat in San Francisco on a spring day in 1869, Muir was making just a brief stopover on his way to Alaska. Nonetheless, he "soon inquired the quickest way out of town"—and was pointed to the Oakland ferry. Really? Perhaps he got directions from Mark Twain. John Muir wandered with delight that spring, through shoulder-high wildflowers in a place that would be reborn a hundred years later as Silicon Valley, and up to Pacheco Pass over the inner Coast Range. There he had his famous epiphany on the first view eastward, seeing: "...not the Sierra Nevada, or snowy range, but the Range of Light."

In an era of cool, Muir's writing can seem overwrought. Sure, it first brought the Sierra to public attention and managed to save most of the high country from commercial destruction. But that Victorian prose—even those who love it can sometimes take no more than a sentence at a time. By July 11, Alaska forgotten, Muir was deep into Yosemite backcountry and penned a sentence that kept me pumped up during weeks on the East Coast one fall:

> "Having greatly enjoyed all this huge day, sauntering and seeing, steeping in the mountain influences, sketching, noting, drinking ozone and Tamarack water."

Drinking Ozone? Sometimes John Muir manages to sound more like Hunter S. Thompson than his contemporaries Wordsworth and Thoreau. Anyway, the man who had been on his way somewhere else fell into the orbit of the Sierra, and lingered for the rest of his life.

Muir rambled the Sierra for no other reason than just being there. Of course the fur-trapping "mountain men" had been passing through for fifty years before that, but they still saw the range as a barrier. Blaze a trail over to the coast, then hurry on back to the Green River rendezvous. They didn't stop and they didn't look back, not even for a chance first sighting of Yosemite Valley. The 49'ers couldn't see the light of the crest for the glitter in the foothill streams. Muir came and stayed. His extravagant ravings brought others. Now there are whole communities of Sierrans throughout the range, brotherhoods of saunterers and seers.

In 1914, the year that John Muir died, Norman Clyde spent his first summer in the Sierra. Over the next fifty years, living mostly in the high country, Clyde made more first ascents of peaks and ridges and walls than anyone had managed before. When he died at 87 in 1972, Clyde was just two years beyond his last climb. Jules Eichorn wrote his obituary in the usually staid American Alpine Journal, and it spoke of an enormous single-mindedness:

> "He had lived as every alpinist wants to live, but as none of them dare to, and so he had a unique life... He was the only man I know who gave himself up completely to a passionate love of the mountains."

When Clyde lived for months in the high Sierra, his pack became his home. Those who sometimes laughed at Clyde's hundred-pound pack failed to consider that it contained all the fly rods, spare cameras, night-stand reading and canned goods that the next fortnight might require. The mode has come to be known as Clyde-style.

Norman Clyde was still going strong in 1971 at a party in Bishop for the appearance of his last book. "The next speaker will be strictly limited to twenty minutes" intoned the emcee. Clyde got up and ambled toward the microphone. He was notorious for rambling stories that lost their point by drifting on to other topics. He talked a little about sheep, then touched on his reputation as a camp mooch—"there were some college girls up there, though, and they thought I looked hungry"—before getting around to the main topic: "Speaking of mountaineering, I did have a little mania...."

The emcee got up and began edging toward Clyde. Norman looked around, then quickly summed it up: "Well, I guess that ends my fool stories, as I call 'em." It seemed rude. Clyde never spoke in public again; within a year

Norman Clyde

he was dead. But anyone who heard out his "fool" stories and miscellaneous ramblings soon found that after he had five of them in the air, Clyde would finish off the last one, then return to the next, finish it, and so on, until he had knitted them all together so that each fit. By then it might be an hour later. A life spent among alpine rhythms had simply stretched his sense of time past the restless attention span now considered normal. He had the clearest eyes I have ever seen on an eighty-year-old man, sparkling with alpine light.

Fool Stories. When I got home that night—a borrowed cabin— there was my favorite poster on the wall. It showed the Tarot card of The Fool—the wanderer, innocent and amazed, swinging his bindle on a stick over his shoulder and smelling a rose. Behind him, sun poured onto a profusion of mountains. Alongside ran an illuminating inscription:

> "It is all too often forgotten that the ancient symbol of the prenascence of the world is a fool, and that foolishness, being a divine state, is a condition to be neither proud nor ashamed of."

Intriguingly, the quote originated from a mathematician, G. Spencer Brown. Foolishness travels in unexpected arcs.

Clyde had been winter caretaker of lodges up and down the eastern Sierra, and was among the first to recognize the skiing potential here. So when

Skiing in Rock Creek - photo by Vern Clevenger

I had the opportunity I asked him about favorite runs. He started right in talking about Rock Creek Canyon. It seems that the lodge owners always moved him out at the beginning of May to make room for early fishermen. When Clyde vacated, he would go straight up to Rock Creek for the spring skiing. At the head of that broad and gentle valley, up where the highest whitebark pines hunch their backs against the freewheeling wind blasting down off the crest, he would burrow in under one of the trees for shelter and settle into an interesting routine.

When the sun came early into the leeward side of his home, Norman would lace on his Triconi-nailed boots, lash skis to his packframe and crunch up the frozen crust to Bear Creek Spire. Stopping at the 13,000 foot notch and usually not bothering with the summit, he would wait patiently until midmorning when the crust had softened into perfect spring corn snow an inch deep before changing into ski boots and snapping on the ultra-short five foot skis he kept for "Christiania swings down the steep gullies." After a perfect run back to camp—they're so predictable in the spring—he would settle in for

Doug Robinson

an afternoon of basking and reading. Norman always carried a generous selection of classics, in half a dozen original languages.

One day while perched up on the divide waiting for the corn, Clyde got to looking west out over the voluptuous contours of the Lake Italy basin. So he skied down there instead. Then up over Gabbot Pass to the Second Recess, since that looked good too. And down that to Mono Creek, which he followed back over Mono Pass into Rock Creek again. Only by then it was three days later! On the spur of the moment Clyde had launched into a cross-country lark over the still frozen Sierra without so much as a copy of "The Odyssey" in Greek for equipment.

"Rock Creek Canyon," he said, as if deciding it right then, "is the finest skiing on the east side of the Sierra." I moved in the next winter. Into another borrowed cabin. Winter in the high Sierra is sheer pleasure, not only for the snow and the skiing but because the mountains are so empty then. Their trashing at the hands of callow tourists is mercifully obscured, leaving the closest thing to true wilderness still to be found in this country. And for stormy days, perhaps a cane chair in front of the wood stove, with maybe a view of Bear Creek Spire out the front window as it clears....

Yes, that's better already. Here was a chance to go out and play in the snow, come back in truly drenched, and stoke up the fire. And some of us were getting pretty wet that winter, a first season of experimenting with nordic skis. Beyond the thrill of exploring so graceful a technology...well, it's difficult to describe the fascination of white space and wind-blown silence. By smothering its rocky texture, snow accentuates the smooth contours of the landscape, bringing out the feminine side of terrain, and makes the wilderness more gentle even as it gets colder. Also softer to land on.

I, too, had to move out in May. So, following Clyde's lead once again, two or three of us would lug our camp up to the superb granite of the Palisades. Employment at the climbing school wouldn't start for a couple of months. But I was broke. Working was out of the question since it would cut too heavily into mountain time, and even cheaper than living out of a VW was traveling on foot and saving the 30¢ a gallon that gasoline cost. Really, any excuse would have served; with snow melting I couldn't think of anything I'd rather do than live and climb in the Palisades, free from the habits of mind that pass for civilization.

There are differences, of course, from Clyde's camps up here at Third Lake. But canvas rock shoes breathing stale sweat in a sandy corner aren't one of them—Clyde often traded his nailed boots for tennis shoes on harder

.friction climbs, like the first ascent of the "Milk Bottle," the Starlite summit of North Palisade. Cast iron frying pan, plenty of garlic and potatoes, ample library, all pretty much the same. I wouldn't be surprised if Clyde read Jung up here too. The ghetto blaster propped on a rock is new, softly playing *Dark Star* into a Sierra night; anyone who objects had better not have music in *their* living room. We're just alpine hedonists after all, trying to bring together all the good things in life at a timberline home. Sex, drugs, rock & roll—but with a definite emphasis on the rock.

Those years when we moved into the Palisades in May, pooling our poverty and pushing a retreating snowline to get at the high granite, had their own rhythm. Camp was deliberately aimed so dawn drove us out of sleeping bags. We'd brew tea and settle against a granite backrest to read, which usually inspired writing in the notebook. Laugh out loud, stand and stretch, go for a walk, climb in the afternoon. Once in a while we got disciplined and left camp at first light to hop the chill away over talus boulders on our way up to Temple Crag, there to put the moves onto smooth walls of perfect stone. No other drug got us as high as steep granite—in multi-tonnage doses.

Under the influence we dreamed of harder routes and greater glory, and sometimes we dreamed beyond that:

> Waking these early morning hours
> With mind abroad on the Sierra night,
> I have dreams of granite glory
> Consistently coming up.
> Yet they drown each time
> In return to present beauty.
>
> My head is filled and scoured
> Time upon time
> By tumbling creek
> Or trailing shooting stars to fluorescent death.
> Against fresh feelings
> Ego hasn't a chance.
>
> A perfect pentagon of stars hangs in Contact Pass.
> Ego dissolves in darkness
> Soluble in starlight.

Surely there have been other Sierra wanderers. History is thin here; the written record is barely more than a century-wide slice. Yet there are pictographs right at the base of the range waiting to be deciphered, and a few old trails over the crest were already deep grooves by the time fur trappers appeared on the eastern horizon. John Muir could hardly have been the first.

A wanderer, if anyone, can be unobtrusive, literally melting into the landscape if he chooses. Signs of his passage might take the form of subtle innuendoes, apparent only to the prepared mind. There is a saying in Eastern religion—or was it from Alchemy?—that when the student is ready, the master will appear. It suggests that the next degree of subtlety, though it may be right at hand, is always veiled from present viewpoint. So for practical purposes the ultimate Sierra vagabond is invisible. Mastery of terrain has blended him into the landscape. He can be seen only when he chooses to reveal himself, though he may well be watching me now, sprawled on a granite slab in the afternoon sun.

That ultimate form of mountaineer first came to light in, of course, China. It was some 1500 years ago, during the T'ang Dynasty, that the Senin arose. Literally "mountain madmen," they were midwives to the birth of Zen, and some of them are rumored to have been immortal. The best known of those "Zen lunatics" was one Han Shan who lived in the seventh century and left over three hundred poems scrawled on cliffsides, on bamboo and barns. They leave no doubt of his devotion to wild mountains and his ability to be anywhere at home:

> I settled at Cold Mountain long ago,
> Already it seems like years and years.
> Freely drifting, I prowl the woods and streams
> And linger watching things themselves.
> Men don't get this far into the mountains,
> White clouds gather and billow.
> Thin grass does for a mattress,
> The blue sky makes a good quilt.
> Happy with a stone underhead
> Let heaven and earth go about their changes.

Han Shan was completely unpredictable. He would appear at the local monastery, but instead of lecturing to the Zen students he would go feed the fire in the kitchen, laughing, pulling pranks and carrying on with his buddy Shih-te. When the Governor sent him a gift of new clothes, Han Shan saw the messenger coming and vanished into the cliffs yelling "Thief! Thief!" Maybe after that he came to the Sierra.

Suppose that later in life Han Shan grew tired of playing the local fool, or ... But a backwoods Zen Master doesn't need an excuse to do anything. He can just stand up and walk away if he feels like checking for mountains on the other side of the world. On just such a whim of far terrain he may have left Cold Mountain one misty day for the coast.

Han Shan built a reed raft and, with the typical abandon of a Zen Master, cast himself onto the surge of current running up the coast. He rode right on out with a sack of pine nuts and an eye toward the dawn, forty days, or twice that, of open ocean. He made landfall under mists like home, shredding on the rocks and ice of a wild, strange coast. He stopped once, for chance sunshine to dry his sodden raft, and was awed by rivers of ice running right into the sea. Back afloat he drifted south, only mindfulness keeping him off the rocks. He floated until the current warmed and the rains slackened, an old man dreaming of mountains of the sun.

Han Shan came ashore on a meadowed coastline, walking east at the season when the mud dried. The locals accepted his passage almost as if they expected it. Not many days inland he came in sight of a great range of mountains, blanketed with snow along their summits and blazing like crystallized light.

With the spring he ascended slowly into the foothills, where red-barked bushes grew thick as bamboo in chaotic ravines. Only here it was hot; his birch bark hat cracked and peeled. Upstream he came into a meadow-floored canyon with walls of smooth, bright stone. Home across the water was steep like this but all jumbled, he explained to new friends, stick-drawing in river-edge sand. They laughed, rubbed pine pitch on Han Shan's feet and took him slithering up the walls, balance-dancing along the sharp edge of life, up and down the steep slabs.

The bravest among them even took him up the back of the rock-that-is-half-gone at the head of the canyon. They danced around a fire on top that night, and in the morning re-pitched their feet. It was a breathless tiptoe back down, staring straight down on the tops of the trees, but soon they were running and laughing, down past the river-falling-through-sky, back into the canyon.

It grew hotter. Rained some afternoons, but there were rarely mists like home. When a band of rabbit-eaters came from across the mountains to trade, drink fermented acorn mush and sing around the fire, Han Shan followed them home. But their path descended steeply eastward to the huge lake with one white and one black island, so Han Shan wandered instead down the crest of the range.

Doug Robinson

Han Shan soon forgot how many seasons he had been in the Sun Mountains. An immortal doesn't care. Once for a prank he returned to the rim of the smooth-stone canyon, built a huge fire of bark right on the edge and pushed it down the cliff at dusk. Cackling with delight, he ran down the ravine to see the reaction. But his friends below had guessed him out, and met him with an ambush of water from the treetops. He left them the sign, in six broken charcoal lines on the face of a boulder: "Fire on the Mountain," symbolic of The Wanderer. They grinned and gave Han Shan dried trout to continue his journey, but the writing was lost on them.

The next season an explosion east of the range drew Han Shan's attention to a fountain of fire coming out of the ground. It cooled into a new hill, ringed by a moat of loose, grey dust; he could see a whole line of those donut-ringed cones marching along the base of the mountains. When it cooled enough to go look, Han Shan found the same black glass that the rabbit-eaters had carried across to trade for salt and seashells in the smooth-walled canyon. He took some of it south with him into the high peaks, and left pieces on top of the most inaccessible spires of the crest. He had gone from leaving poems on stone to leaving poems *of* stone. Fire on the Mountain.

Han Shan knew that neither the rabbit-eaters nor the pitch-footed trout-grabbers would ever go there to appreciate his little joke. But he also knew that in the fullness of time a few midnight ramblers out of each millennium would blow out of nameless suburbs, feeling nowhere at home until they walked these tundra gardens and moonlit slabs. By then lightning would have blasted away his dark glass messages. And even an immortal gets old, tired, and begins to wish to feed his last tricks to the coyotes. Still, he wanted to leave some sign for those future madmen of the mountains, something only a fool's rambling might find, in a place where no one but the aimless wanderer of contentment would discover—at an unexpected spring on a parched hillside overlooking the highest peaks, where he might stoop to drink of the laughing water bubbling from the eye sockets of a bleached, Oriental skull.

Coming of Age in Yosemite

Sheridan Anderson on the Royal Arches

Doug Robinson

Tuesday Morning on the Lyell Fork with Eliot's Shadow

Pivoting on "Tuesday Morning..." my life turned a corner. Not from the night walk to Mount Lyell, which was like another snowstorms pressure added to the glacier of time-in-the-wilderness that was sculpting my unconscious, but writing a story about it that—incredibly—Ascent wanted to publish. I was shy and tentative and 22 years old, an undistinguished climber with little self-confidence, and this was the first piece of writing I ventured to send to a publisher. Steve Roper and Allen Steck recalled that "Doug Robinson came to Ascents editors one afternoon in 1968 with a dog-eared manuscript in hand. An hour later, entranced with *Tuesday Morning on the Lyell Fork with Eliot's Shadow*, the editors said yes, in what was surely a record time for acceptance." If Ascent had not printed this piece, I probably would have thrown away my pencil.

Between the conception
And the creation
Between the emotion
And the response
Falls the Shadow

— T.S. Eliot

I could not sleep. Not knowing about the diesel generator which ran all night to keep the lettuce crisp and ice cream frozen at the Tuolomne Meadows Store, we had put our sleeping bags down too near. It did not bother Chris or Rick any; they were fast asleep. But I had been awake for more than an hour and was slowly deciding to take a walk. It was warm in the bag though, and even if the generator was droning, the ground was still comfortable, so it was ten minutes more before I stirred and pulled on my boots. Mountain boots running on pavement make a fine sort of ringing, especially in the quiet of the night. Such joy to be moving in the cool air.

Half a mile beyond the store an apron of granite rises out from under the north side of the road and caps off eight hundred feet above in the summit of Lembert Dome. From the road I ran onto this apron of granite and stopped where it steepens. Irregular round-edged boulders disturb the sweep of the lower granite, and moonlight glints across glacial polish like paintings of low-horizoned moons on a calm sea. When my breathing slowed I could no longer hear the generator.

From where I stopped below the south face, the Water Cracks stretched toward the summit. The deceptive geometry of domes steepens them toward the summit without appearing to, and I was wary of being lured into a tight spot by the tricks of moonlight. Anyway I had not come deliberately to climb, so I swung a wide arc to the east avoiding the abrupt south face. But I never came out onto the gentle east slope, working my way instead up cracks and friction slopes toward the summit–the climber in us dies hard when it is spared dying suddenly.

A little way down from the summit I found a large boulder which offered some mechanical sanctuary from the wind and sat down facing the river. For some minutes I took in the scene. The campground is so well hidden in the woods that only the store and the road can remind you that there are, after all, thousands of people sleeping in this wilderness tonight. There was a party in one of the meadows and the laughter occasionally reached me. I fell to thinking about my summer. It was by now late August. I had been out since early June. So early that no one else was about; I was the third or fifth person to sign the register at the entrance to this or that wilderness area, crossed trackless snow fields, dozed on granite slabs in the afternoon sun, read, wrote in my journal, walked across Lake Italy, and on the twelfth of June came down to Muir Pass out of a notch from the Ionian Basin to find

Off season. Austin Hearst climbs Lembert Dome. After Skiing

untracked snow piled around the hut and no entry in the register since October. After that I walked north to Yosemite Valley where I planned to spend a weekend doing one climb. My travels ended right there between the all-too-sunny walls of the Valley. I stayed a week, met people, made plans, stayed longer. This very trip to Tuolumne Meadows was really only a break in the round of climbing.

Looking beyond the river and the meadows toward Cathedral Peak, Mount Dana, and the great valley of the Lyell Fork, I thought of a stanza from Eliot's "The Hollow Men" concerning the crisis of action. I thought about the kind of act of will that is necessary to keep you calm on a rock wall, to fight the clutching, immobilizing fear that paralyzes motion. A similar kind of will keeps you going against fatigue on interminable snow slopes and in scree chutes without tops. When you get into a tight spot on a rock climb or when you stop to rest in the snow, you have first to make up your mind to go on, and then to do it. In this interval between the determination and the move, a belayers legs in a cramped spot can go to sleep, wake up, and go to sleep again. That is why I like to think of Eliot when pondering such things. I had had too many confrontations with this sort of indecisiveness in rock climbing lately, but none of the endurance sort. It was then that the thought of climbing Mount Lyell fell upon me with a disabling force. Suddenly I was quite tired, but it did no good. The thought had come, and the thought was binding. Still it took me ten minutes to get up from my seat against the boulder.

The moon ceased to be the illuminator of the river and guardian of silence; now it was a lamp that had only so many hours left to burn. I picked up my ice axe and rain parka and wrote a note to Chris and Rick quoting Eliot, saying where I was going, and ending it self-consciously, "love to all my friends." I also added T.E. Lawrence's "It was a hard task for me to straddle feeling and action," then anchored this to the ground by the head of my sleeping bag by stabbing a piton through one corner of the sheet. If my note seems overly dramatic, of course it was. I was aware of it before I had finished writing. We lived in a surrealistic world anyway and assumed postures experimentally and for each others benefit. But mostly it was a somewhat sheepish attempt to tell the truth. I really was walking off up the Lyell Fork in the middle of the night because it seemed to my mind a grand scheme just on the edge of my capabilities, and having conceived it I could not rest easily with myself unless I gave it a good try. And I did love those two in their sleeping bags and others besides.

I pulled my knee socks up from around my ankles and started back up the road. Immediately I began to doubt making it. Past the store and across the bridge, this time walking. Worried about expending the energy to cover that ground twice in the same night. Past the ranger station. Past the High Sierra Camp. Just beyond is the confluence of the Dana and Lyell forks of the Tuolumne River, a piece of very irregular terrain with pothole swamps and thick stands of pine. I have lost the trail here even in daylight. This jumble of islands, if that's what they really are, takes three times too long to get across. Always there is the thought of turning back. Crumple the note and put it down to the very bottom of the pack. Leave the ice axe leaning carelessly against a tree. Go to bed and sleep. If it were any easier to find my way back than ahead, I might have done it.

Finally I cross the last bridge and am clearly on the trail again. A mile further on there is a downed log, planed flat on top, crossing Rafferty Creek. Beyond that the Lyell Fork begins in earnest. It is beautiful country all the way, but there are no landmarks to reassure that you have gone 1.7 or 3.4 of the eight miles of canyon. You have to go blindly and do it all, and when the switch backs start you will know you have finished. Many a leisurely backpacker must have come this way not caring where he was or how far he had gotten, but for me, though many things passed through my mind that night, none returned as incessantly as the worry of the miles. There are short problems and lengthy problems and the virtue of the short ones, if one can be said by a peculiar sort of logic to have an advantage over the other, is that they reach their crisis quickly and then are resolved, one way or the other. It is that way on the rocks: you either make the move or you do not make the move. It is quickly over, whether or not it is resolved, for there is usually another chance. But on the Lyell Fork there is a constant, if lower level, effort of will involved. Put the next foot in front. You have gained three feet. Don't stop to rest; it is harder to start again than to keep going. The temptation shifts from turning around and going back to stopping and going to sleep. Visions of miles toiling out to the dark southeast and Mt. Lyell still out of sight around a corner at the head of the canyon and the head of the canyon still fearfully far.

The ice axe swishes through dewy grass and comes to rest in the damp ground while four inches lower the trail dust is not wet from the dew, and there is just width enough for my left foot to pass the right as the trail slants down a few feet out of a stand of pines and into a grassy backwater of the meadow. The succession of meadow and forest cycles on, never giving a view far ahead. The trail seems longer in the dark. You can mark your progress after fifteen minutes of deliberate pushing by a little gain on a small feature of the featureless ridge across the canyon. There is a little peak of excitement as I come out of the woods into yet another patch of meadow, a straining to recognize it, to reassure progress. But I cannot identify it and then I feel my legs again, not fatigued but sore from the pace without stopping, not tired with miles but with apprehension, with feeling the scope of a thing too much begun to be undone but yet too young to be sure of success.

The next few hours pass as in a dream. Meadow, forest, meadow. Subtle curving of the trail. The moonlight climbs the ridge opposite and vanishes. My little knob on the ridge creeps down the valley. Into the forest and out. There is a silvered sheet of water on a large granite outcrop somewhere on this river. I swam there with my parents when I was thirteen. Perhaps it is here, so I go down to the river but it is placid and dark. Further on I find it. This darkly silvered whir is a landmark in the walk, though I don't know where exactly it means I have gotten. It is past now and the weariness that broods on miles to come settles again. Looking back on it later the whole way from the Rafferty log to the first switchback is summarized in a stop-action moment: a meadow with a forest beyond, one foot just lifting clear of the trail, ice axe poised over the damp ground, and above all a general sense of weariness. But while it is happening the hours will not go away. Every such moment is in reality followed by five steps and five moments in the mind. So when the scenery does not hold, I dream.

Today had a beginning and a course of events before this project began, before the generator and the road. I woke up to an up sun on Long Meadow two leisurely days out of Yosemite Valley. Mostly when I wake up in the mountains I like to lie on my back and look into a pine tree or around at the peaks. Not this morning. Because Sherri's sleeping bag was not too warm she slept between Rick and me, and as I awoke I became aware of her curled up next to me. It was a wondrous thing to have a woman lying next to me. The feeling was not sexual, but as if some part of me that wanted to rest had come to rest. It lasted some minutes until they stirred, and then I went bouldering in the meadow.

Sherri took the trail to Tenaya Lake and we went on over Cathedral Pass, meeting on the way some horsemen who laughed at our bare feet and a father and son on their way out of the mountains who stopped to talk and gave us their spare food.

I like walking new trails, and this day up Long Meadow, over Cathedral Pass and down the rocky trail into the great Tuolumne Meadows could have been one of those fine days when your pack is not heavy and you do not push toward a destination but rather absorb the woods and hills as you pass by. But today Rick wanted to talk. So the wilderness, equally indifferent to any role we might cast upon it, was today not a temple to itself but a setting for human ideas. It was the beginning of our third day of talking. If you extend the intensity, the exhaustion, and perhaps the feeling of accomplishment of an evenings heavy conversation over two days and two evening's, or if you have been a tent-bound expeditioner, you will know how on this third morning I came to desire some solitude to set things in proportion. But Rick wanted more, so we talked over the saddle, past the horsemen, past Cathedral Lake, and down a long rocky grade into the meadows. We became increasingly mystical as the day went on; a stranger would no longer have seen pattern in our phrases and silences. When we came down into sight of the road we fell silent for the last time. We were reduced to shrugging our shoulders and smiling. I have never since been able to remember anything of the content of that afternoon's talk, only bringing its mood away with me. I only know that I bear its consequences within me in the same sort of way that I am marked by climbing Cathedral Peak, or by running the Dipsea Trail.

In the Coffee Shop we found Christopher, who had come up over Vogelsang. We bought bread and peanut butter and declared a camp by sitting down in a group of trees.

Recall this morning and noon, hear them and feel them, briefly again, reflect them in this moonlit night. The day passes in review but it does not cover the space of a single mile. Chris and Rick sleep behind the Coffee Shop; others bunk in their trailers. I alone along the length of this river am sentient tonight. Do those bivouacked on Sentinel Rock or the North Palisade keep this sky with me? Good. I break into a big grin to think of such company. And what of tomorrow night? Will no one walk the Lyell Fork then and feel the breezes, smell pine wood, chase silver rapids, and pull a parka tight around his throat? And what of the others, there must have been others, who tramped this way on a summer night or skied here in a crisp January? I feel very close to such walkers-out-of-season tonight. And did I not in spirit stumble out of an alpine hut this morning, follow a bobbing candle lantern up the Bossons Glacier in the dark–silent partner on an early morning rope in the Alps?

Photo by Gordon Wiltsie

The moon, my traveling companion, goes down into the ridge, sinking, probably, into Ireland Lake to feed the trout. For the first time in hours I stop walking. I lie down under a tree, curl up and fall asleep. I wake up, resist the temptation to doze off, decide absurdly that I have slept thirty-five minutes, and walk again. It is too cold to do anything else.

Little brooks emptying into the Lyell Fork become in succession the noise at last of the river tumbling down its glacial headwall. As a result of anticipating this sound without hope I almost trip over the first switchback when it arrives. The distance has been done. Mere altitude remains. I am at the foot of the peak. Uncertainty vanishes. I can get there now. I have reached a landmark. As I start up the switchbacks the sky lightens just perceptibly. The day is coming. However much we may love the night, the awakening day brings joy. At the upper Base Camp in an ashen dawn not yet turned to rose I surprise the firemaker, first up and about his duties, and we exchange silent greetings as if to speak would disturb the frost sleeping upon stones in the meadow.

Chuch Pratt at work on a first ascent on North Six Shooter Peak, Canyonlands

The morning doesn't dawn on me; I walk up into it. The sunlight coming through Donohue Pass spread out across the glacier and worked its way toward the lowland. I met it as I stepped off the moraine onto the ice. I had an easy ascent, the suncups forming a fine stairway. An impending storm hurried my already fast pace on to the summit and back; the Merced River drainage was already filled with black and gray clouds. As I was running down the glacier lightning struck the peak.

The rain started like a thick fog, edging the leaves of tiny plants with a furry cloud of droplets, but when I regained the Muir Trail it was coming in great shiny sheets. As I dropped below the tree line I began to slow down and relax a little. The thing was done and in a number of miles and hours it would be truly over. I glowed with the feeling of impending completion. Going by I hailed the fire builder. All down the Lyell Fork that morning in the intermittent sunshine and rain I met backpackers coming up. I bore down on each little party with my ice axe swinging and grinning a big foolish grin, feeling a companionship with those smiling back who also loved this wet dimension

Doug Robinson

of the wilderness. To those I passed I beamed out the joy of daylight over night, of accomplishment over uncertainty, of companionship over solitude. And in the long intervals between human encounters I was mostly tired-tired and soggy-a man on his long way home but also a man who was, in one small respect, and for the moment at least, less divided against himself.

POSTSCRIPT: A note of homage to my barely named companions of the Tuolumne campground. Chris Fredericks, who will appear again in The Climber as Visionary, was for me a great friend and mentor to my crack climbing technique through those magical summers of the sixties in Camp 4. His influence on me was second only to Chuck Pratt. Chris was reserved and contained-maybe too much so-but his climbing and a certain sly smile were conduits into his world, and would break open a twinkly, mischievous underbelly of the Zen reserve. When Chris did hard moves, and he was always pushing it, he would squeak. I ran into him recently at a crowded slide show in Berkeley, and that smile and twinkle were as ready as ever.

OK, having shamelessly mentioned Chuck Pratt I guess I owe him a word too, but its tough. For starters, he won't necessarily appreciate the attention. And he is incredibly elusive for such a solid little man. I can cobble together some sort of an image, but his spirit would slip right through its crude shell, and the whole exercise ends up feeling futile and a little embarrassing. There is no doubt that he was the finest free climber of the era, and ahead of his time in even recognizing that free climbing spelled the future. We shared a similar build, and I was flattered when people took us for brothers. I have lost women to him, even one I was married to, without it damping my respect for the man. But it was Pratt the raconteur who left us most in awe. Normally rather quiet, when he finally warmed up to a subject or an audience, the result was a brilliant rave, sustained on its own energy, internal logic and moral force. The man became possessed, caught up in inspiration and subject, with listeners fading out of his vision. Something about those monologues made them very hard to recall afterward; maybe it was the lubrication of the audience.

And Rick. Hippie Rick; I don't even recall his last name. He climbed some, but that clearly wasn't his mission in the mountains. He was extremely charismatic; in his presence a barefoot hike to Tuolumne, with the first night on top of Half Dome, seemed just the right thing. It didn't take him long to pack, since everything he owned slid easily into a canvas and leather Rebuffat guide pack. After that trip he left Yosemite. Late one night several years later a door opened in Aspen and there stood Rick. It was already well along into one of those nights of "streaks and halos" as Thomas McGuane would say, but I have a definite recollection of Rick at the focus of a large house, a harem, and a pile of cocaine. Before I left he gave me a rather nice haul bag he had designed and built, which I later passed on to Bridwell. Somehow, no doubt, we'll meet again.

Camp 4

"Yosemite climbing has produced little journalism." wrote Galen Rowell to introduce *Camp 4* in his collection "The Vertical World of Yosemite," "[This] is the kind of article that would never have been written without a request from a faraway publication [the British magazine *Mountain*]." I finished it, hastily under the pressure of a not-so-far-away deadline, while sprawled on the grass in a park in Moab, Utah, in the spring of 1969. Chuck Pratt was patient to the last handwritten paragraph, though the next day was windy which meant that we had missed a chance to climb Castleton Tower. I got $5 in exchange, and still see this piece not as journalism at all, but more like a tone poem in praise of a dusty campground at the center of the universe.

Camp 4 is the physical and spiritual home of the Yosemite climbers. It lies near the geographical center of the Valley, where the old and stable talus, long since grown over with oaks and lichen, comes down from under the north wall to merge into the river-bottom meadows. It sits under a canopy of oak and pine. In spite of the spectacular setting, it has become the most trampled and dusty, probably the noisiest, and certainly the least habitable of all Yosemite campgrounds. It is the only camp kept open all year, and was for many years the catch-all for pets, trailers, and other hard-to-classify and vaguely undesirable Yosemite visitors. Yet the Yosemite climbers will stay nowhere else.

By day and in midsummer, it is home for tourist families, with their barking dogs and self-contained camping trailers complete with television sets. Toward evening, however, as the dust is being shaken from the last unwilling child before dinner, the clanking horde begins to return. In twos and threes, talking and laughing–or with exaggerated weariness, set off by little sweat-etched lines on dusty foreheads–with their hands polished to a shiny slate color by carabiners, and with yet another pair of Granny Grundie pants hanging in tattered ribbons from their belts, they come to reclaim their campground. For, whether the tourists realize it or not, it is the climbers campground. The other campers have penetrated unaware into a magic circle; they stand undazed at the focus of a force field of tradition and emotion.

The National Park Service provides tables, and the climbers furnish them–their only vestige of home–in their own manner: oil-skin tablecloth, stove, box of pots and pans, kerosene lantern, the inevitable red cover of Roper's "A Climbers Guide to Yosemite Valley," various talismans–an onyx rain god, a broken one-and-a-half inch angle–and perhaps a battery record player with a collection of Beethoven and the Rolling Stones. An assortment of klettershoes and boots, in various stages of decay,

Doug Robinson at a Camp-4 fire, 1966. John Svenson photo

stand in a line under the table. The camp is completed by a collection of ropes, hardware and haulbags piled against a tree, a bear-proof cache hanging overhead, and an open-air bed of pine needles–a comfortable several-months home. At peak season in the spring and fall almost half the campground is furnished in this fashion.

The boulders strewn around the campground probably first attracted climbers to Camp 4. Mostly small-hold face climbing and mantles, the boulder problems are basically unsuitable as training for the abundance of crack climbing on the walls. Yet they are quite popular; an hour of bouldering, while dinner is cooking, is common. The boulders serve other functions. They are a natural meeting place, where the lone climber can find a partner for a climb the next day. Also, for some reason, bouldering brings out the curiosity in tourist girls who come around to watch, chat, and perhaps get invited to a party—thus satisfying yet another perennial need of the Valley climbers.

Camp 4 evenings follow an irregular cycle of quiet nights and parties. The balmy evenings, a welcome by-product of the blistering hot days, banish any thought of seeking shelter. The climbers live outdoors for months at a time, and their parties are always held in the open air. There have, of course, been the legendary ones—as on the twentieth anniversary ascent of the Lost Arrow, when fourteen climbed the spire. They tyroleaned off, and were joined by thirty others for beer and Teton Tea around a fire on the rim. Parties are frequent, often spontaneous, and always unpredictable. By the time a party really gets rolling, it is late enough for the tourists to complain of noise—so the revelers must move out of camp or face the inevitable ranger. I remember one such evening when I had gone to bed early. I awoke to see Chuck Pratt, carrying a lantern and loudly calling directions, leading from the campground a ragged procession of figures clutching wine bottles. Bringing up the rear of the long line, quieter and rather more sure-footed than the rest, were two figures wearing Smokey-the-Bear hats.

Half a mile away, across the waving-grass meadows, the Merced River swings a wide arc, leaving Sentinel Beach in the quiet waters of its lee. High above, Sentinel Rock watches all that transpires here, seeing without comment the climb-watching, girl-watching, dozing, swimming, and reading while toes wiggle in the sand. And sometimes at night the moon edges over Sentinel to see them—brown-tanned and wet-slick in its light—dancing naked in the river, unselfconscious at last, while part-full bottles of red wine list at crazy angles in the sand.

And the quiet evenings: a shirt sleeved group around a table; mugs of tea; endless discussions—of climbs, climbers, philosophy, religion—any and all subjects. And the silences. With the end of a thought trailing off into the lantern light, the last of the transients shut up and gone to bed, the very darkness seems to take on a new dimension, a depth and silence that thickens before you until the night becomes palpable. The spiritual attachments, the feelings of home in this dusty campground and of companionship with one another, become almost visible for a few minutes at days end, before we walk silently away to drop tired bodies onto pine needles in the dark...to wake a few hours later, shivering slightly under oak branch moon shadows, and crawl into the sleeping bag.

Morning: the sun climbs late into this deep valley, but in the morning light is already a promise of the heat of the day. The climbers are up early–not by Alpine standards, but compared to the tourists–and for a little while an expectant calm, broken only by the low familiar roar of a Primus making morning tea, hangs over the campground. Ropes, hammer and swami belt are laid out on the end of the table. The hardware is racked, and hangs from its sling on a nearby oak branch. In this expectant hour the climbers thoughts have already left Camp 4 and moved up the walls to the chosen problem of the day.

Doug and Dennis Hennek sorting gear. Photo by Galen Rowell

Gordon Wiltsie photo

The Climber as Visionary

This piece has been collected into more anthologies than I can quite recall, and translated into French, Italian, German (I think), Danish and I believe Japanese. The excitement of the idea begun here, that the physical and emotional challenges of climbing can trigger biochemical pathways in the brain leading to visionary experience in the mind, has become a lifetime project. The resulting book, titled "The Alchemy of Action," is still struggling into being and should be out—well, who really knows when. Soon, I hope, so I can get on with my life.

I finished this essay in January 1969, in a flat in the Haight Ashbury of San Francisco. That month I also completed five term papers to graduate from College. Then I

Doug Robinson

moved to the Sierra. First stop was Tahoe City, into the midst of a 32-day snowstorm where good money was to be made shoveling snow off of collapsing roofs in Squaw Valley. When *Visionary* was published, the first mail in response was a scathing letter from a renowned vitamin researcher whose political reaction seems to have upstaged his scientific curiosity. Welcome to the politics of consciousness. Others were less intimidated, and I have been greeted on the streets of Chamonix as "les visionaire."

Since writing this I have learned the language of biochemistry well enough to track a few of its disciplines to the research level. I have lugged textbooks and xeroxes of journal articles up into the Palisades and gotten sunburned studying them. I have fallen asleep by the stove in Rock Creek with stacks of books open at my feet. The puzzle is intricate in part because there is a Catch 22 in the research: you can know exact chemistry from the brains of lab rats, but it is no use asking them about the visionary tone of their experience. On the other hand, climbers can describe subtle visionary effects when their senses have been heightened by exposure to their usual and abundant challenges (some would call them stress), but we can not get inside their skulls to measure the hormonal cocktail behind their mood shift. Hence it is a circuitous path to connect up the human experience with the animal data.

I now know that two of the technical details in this original piece are wrong. My current thought is that it is extra oxygen, not carbon dioxide build-up, that fuels the breathing/chanting effect. And I mistakenly ascribed part of the visionary mood shift to adrenaline. It is a very common and popular assumption that the excitement of tense situations is due to adrenaline, but I now know that what we all mean when we say that is not adrenaline at all, but its cousin noradrenaline. The feeling of adrenaline itself is more like full panic, not something anyone would voluntarily seek or cheerfully repeat. The psychedelic transformation speculated here can happen just as easily starting from noradrenaline-the compounds are very similar, but their moods as opposite as bracing challenge and blind fear.

My evolving theories surrounding the climber's visionary experience surfaced a decade later in a piece about endorphins and forgetfulness, which is printed here in the last section, Return. With it, I have included a chapter, *Two Afternoons in the Sixties*, from the forthcoming book, to give a glimpse of where the idea is now going.

Finally, a direct request: From you who read the literature of mountaineering, I ask a favor. I have collected many written examples of visionary experience, accounts of the familiar "summit euphoria." If you run across a good one that I may have missed, please send it along to the publisher. The best of them will find their way into "The Alchemy of Action" as prime examples of the visionary experience of climbers.

In 1914 George Mallory, later to become famous for an offhand definition of why people climb, wrote an article entitled *The Mountaineer as Artist*, which appeared in the British Climbers Club Journal. In an attempt to justify his climbers feeling of superiority over other sportsmen, he asserts that the climber is an artist. He says that "a day well spent in the Alps is like some great symphony," and justifies the lack of any tangible production–for artists are generally expected to produce works of art which others may see–by saying that "artists, in this sense, are not distinguished by the power of expressing emotion, but the power of feeling that emotional experience out of which Art is made...mountaineers are all artistic... because they cultivate emotional experience for its own sake." While fully justifying the elevated regard we have for climbing as an activity, Mallory's assertion leaves no room for distinguishing the creator of a route from an admirer of it. Mountaineering can produce tangible artistic results which are then on public view. A route is an artistic statement on the side of a mountain, accessible to the view and thus the admiration or criticism of other climbers. Just as the line of a route determines its aesthetics, the manner in which it was climbed constitutes its style. A climb has the qualities of a work of art and its creator is responsible for its direction and style just as an artist is. We recognize those climbers who are especially gifted at creating forceful and aesthetic lines, and respect them for their gift.

But just as Mallory did not go far enough in ascribing artistic functions to the act of creating outstanding new climbs, so I think he uses the word "artist" too broadly when he means it to include an aesthetic response as well as an aesthetic creation. For this response, which is essentially passive and receptive rather than aggressive and creative, I would use the word visionary. Not visionary in the usual sense of idle and unrealizable dreaming,

Gordon Wiltsie photo

of building castles in the air, but rather in seeing the objects and actions of ordinary experience with greater intensity, penetrating them further, seeing their marvels and mysteries, their forms, moods, and motions. Being a visionary in this sense involves nothing supernatural or otherworldly; it amounts to bringing fresh vision to the familiar things of the world. I use the word visionary very simply, taking its origin from "vision," to mean seeing, always to great degrees of intensity, but never beyond the boundaries of the real and physically present. To take a familiar example, it would be hard to look at Van Goghs "The Starry Night" without seeing the visionary quality in the way the artist sees the world. He has not painted anything that is not in the original scene, yet others would have trouble recognizing what he has depicted, and the difference lies in the intensity of his perception, heart of the visionary experience. He is painting from a higher state of consciousness. Climbers too have their "Starry Nights." Consider the following from an account by Allen Steck, of the Hummingbird Ridge climb on Mt. Logan: "I turned for a moment and was completely lost in silent appraisal of the beautifully sensuous simplicity of windblown snow." The beauty of that moment, the form and motion of the blowing snow was such a powerful impression, was so wonderfully sufficient, that the climber was lost in it. It is said to be only a moment, yet by virtue of total absorption he is lost in it and the winds of eternity blow through it. A second example comes from the account of the seventh day's climbing on the eight-day first ascent, under

trying conditions, of El Captain's Muir Wall. Yvon Chouinard relates in the
1966 *American Alpine Journal*:

> "With the more receptive senses we now appreciated
> everything around us. Each individual crystal in the gran-
> ite stood out in bold relief. The varied shapes of the clouds
> never ceased to attract our attention. For the first time we
> noticed tiny bugs that were all over the walls, so tiny they
> were barely noticeable. While belaying, I stared at one for
> 15 minutes, watching him move and admiring his brilliant
> red color.
>
> "How could one ever be bored with so many good things
> to see and feel! This unity with our joyous surroundings,
> this ultra-penetrating perception gave us a feeling of con-
> tentment that we had not had for years."

In these passages the qualities that make up the climbers visionary
experience are apparent: the overwhelming beauty of the most ordinary objects-
clouds, granite, snow–of the climbers experience, a sense of the slowing down of
time even to the point of disappearing, and a "feeling of contentment," an oceanic
feeling of the supreme sufficiency of the present. And while delicate in substance,
these feelings are strong enough to intrude forcefully into the middle of dangerous
circumstances and remain there, temporarily superseding even apprehension and
the drive for achievement.

Chouinard's words begin to give us an idea of the origin of these
experiences as well as their character. He begins by referring to "the more
receptive senses." What made their senses more receptive? It seems integrally
connected with what they were doing, and that it was their seventh day of
uninterrupted concentration. Climbing tends to induce visionary experiences.
We should explore which characteristics of the climbing process prepare its
practitioners for these experiences.

Climbing requires intense concentration. I know of no other activity
in which I can so easily lose all the hours of an afternoon without a trace. Or
a regret. I have had storms creep up on me as if I had been asleep, yet I know
the whole time I was in the grip of an intense concentration, focused first on
a few square feet of rock, and then on a few feet more. I have gone off across
camp to boulder and returned to find the stew burned. Sometimes in the
lowlands when it is hard to work I am jealous of how easily concentration
comes in climbing. This concentration may be intense, but it is not the same
as the intensity of the visionary periods; it is a prerequisite intensity.

But the concentration is not continuous. It is often intermittent and
sporadic, sometimes cyclic and rhythmic. After facing the successive few

square feet of rock for a while, the end of the rope is reached and it is time to belay. The belay time is a break in the concentration, a gap, a small chance to relax. The climber changes from an aggressive and productive stance to a passive and receptive one, from doer to observer, and in fact from artist to visionary. The climbing day goes on through the climb-belay-climb-belay cycle by a regular series of concentrations and relaxations. It is of one of these relaxations that Chouinard speaks. When limbs go to the rock and muscles contract, then the will contracts also. But at the belay stance, tied in to a scrub oak, the muscles relax and the will also, which has been concentrating on moves, expands and takes in the world again, and the world is new and bright. It is freshly created, for it really had ceased to exist. By contrast, the disadvantage of the usual low-level activity is that it cannot shut out the world, which then never ceases being familiar and is thus ignored. To climb with intense concentration is to shut out the world, which, when it reappears, will be as a fresh experience, strange and wonderful in its newness.

These belay relaxations are not total; the climb is not over, pitches lie ahead, even the crux; days more may be needed to be through. We notice that as the cycle of intense contractions takes over, and as this cycle becomes the daily routine, even consumes the daily routine, the relaxations on belay yield more frequent or intense visionary experiences. It is no accident that Chouinard's experiences occur near the end of the climb; he had been building up to them for six days. The summit, capping off the cycling and giving a final release from the tension of contractions, should offer the climber some of his most intense moments, and a look into the literature reveals this to be so. The summit is also a release from the sensory desert of the climb; from the starkness of concentrating on configurations of rock we go to the visual richness of the summit. But there is still the descent to worry about, another contraction of will to be followed by relaxation back on the ground. Sitting on a log changing from klettershoes into boots, and looking over the Valley, we are suffused with oceanic feelings of clarity, distance, union, oneness. There is carryover from one climb to the next, from one day on the hot white walls to the next, however punctuated by wine dark evenings in Camp 4. Once a pathway has been tried it becomes more familiar and is easier to follow the second time, more so on subsequent trips. The threshold has been lowered. Practice is as useful to a climber's visionary faculty as to his crack technique. It also applies outside of climbing. In John Harlin's words, although he was speaking about will and not vision, the experience can be "borrowed and projected." It will apply in the climber's life in general, in his flat, ground, and lowland hours. But it is the climbing that has taught him to be a visionary.

Lest we get too self-important about consciously preparing ourselves for visionary activity, however, we remember that the incredible beauty of the mountains is always at hand, always ready to nudge us into awareness.

The period of these cycles varies widely. If you sometimes cycle through lucid periods from pitch to pitch or even take days to run a complete course, it may also be virtually instantaneous, as, pulling up on a hold after a moment's hesitation and doubt, you feel at once the warmth of sun through your shirt and without pausing reach on.

Nor does the alteration of consciousness have to be large. A small change can be profound. The gulf between looking without seeing and looking with real vision is at times of such a low order that we may be continually shifting back and forth in daily life. Further heightening of the visionary faculty consists of more deeply perceiving what is already there. Vision is intense seeing. Vision is seeing what is more deeply interfused, and following this process leads to a sense of ecology. It is an intuitive rather than a scientific ecology; it is John Muir's kind, starting not from generalizations for trees, rocks, air, but rather from that tree with the goiter part way up the trunk, from the rocks as Chouinard saw them, supremely sufficient and aloof, blazing away their perfect light, and from that air which blew clean and hot up off the eastern desert and carries lingering memories of snow fields on the

Dana Plateau and miles of Tuolumne treetops as it pours over the rim of the Valley on its way to the Pacific.

These visionary changes in the climber's mind have a physiological basis. The alteration of hope and fear spoken of in climbing describes an emotional state with a biochemical basis. These physiological mechanisms have been used for thousands of years by prophets and mystics, and for a few centuries by climbers. There are two complementary mechanisms operating independently: carbon dioxide level and adrenaline breakdown products, the first keyed by exertion, the second by apprehension. During the active part of the climb the body is working hard, building up its carbon dioxide level (oxygen debt) and releasing adrenaline in anticipation of difficult or dangerous moves, so that by the time the climber moves into belay at the end of the pitch he has established an oxygen debt and a supply of now unneeded adrenaline. Oxygen debt manifests itself on the cellular level as lactic acid, a cellular poison, which may possibly be the agent that has a visionary effect on the mind. Visionary activity can be induced experimentally by administering carbon dioxide, and this phenomenon begins to explain the place of singing and long-winded chanting in the medieval Church as well as the breath-control exercises of Eastern religions. Adrenaline, carried to all parts of the body through the blood stream, is an unstable compound and if unused, soon begins to break down. Some of the breakdown products of adrenaline are capable of inducing the visionary experience; in fact, they are naturally occurring body chemicals which closely resemble the psychedelic drugs, and may help someday to shed light on the action of these mind-expanding agents. So we see that the activity of the climbing, coupled with its anxiety, produces a chemical climate in the body that is conducive to visionary experience. There is one other long-range factor that may begin to figure in Chouinard's example: diet. Either simple starvation or vitamin deficiency tends to prepare the body, apparently by weakening it, for visionary experiences. Such a vitamin deficiency will result in a decreased level of nicotinic acid, a member of the B-vitamin complex and a known anti-psychedelic agent, thus nourishing the visionary experience. Chouinard comments on the low rations at several points in his account. For a further discussion of physical pathways to the visionary state, see Aldous Huxleys two essays, "The Doors of Perception" and "Heaven and Hell."

There is an interesting relationship between the climber-visionary and his counterpart in the neighboring subculture of psychedelic drug users. These drugs are becoming increasingly common and many young people will come to climbing from a visionary vantage point unique in its history. These drugs have been through a series of erroneous names, based on false models of their action: psychotomimetic for a supposed ability to produce a model psychosis, and hallucinogen, when the hallucination was thought to be the central reality of the experience. Their present name means simply "mind manifesting," which is at least neutral. These drugs are providing people with a window into the visionary experience. They come away knowing that there is a place where the objects of ordinary experience are wonderfully clear and alive. It may also be that these sensations remind them of many spontaneous or "peak experiences" and thus confirm or place a previous set of observations. But this is the end. There is no going back to the heightened reality, to the supreme sufficiency of the present moment. The window has been shut and cannot even be found without recourse to the drug.

Gordon Wiltsie photo

    I am not in the least prepared to say that drug users take up climbing in order to search for the window. It couldn't occur to them. Anyone unused to disciplined physical activity would have trouble imagining that it produced anything but sweat. But when the two cultures overlap, and a young climber begins to find parallels between the visionary result of his climbing discipline and his formerly drug-induced visionary life, he is on the threshold of control. There is now a clear path of discipline leading to the window. It consists of the sensory desert, intensity of concentrated effort, and rhythmical cycling of contraction and relaxation. This path is not unique to climbing, of course, but here we are thinking of the peculiar form that the elements of the path assume in climbing. I call it the Holy Slow Road because, although time-consuming and painful, it is an unaided way to the visionary state; by following it the climber will find himself better prepared to appreciate the visionary in himself, and by returning gradually and with eyes open to ordinary waking consciousness he now knows where the window lies, how it is unlocked, and he carries some of the experience back with him. The Holy Slow Road assures that the climber's soul, tempered by the very experiences that have made him a visionary, has been refined so that he can handle his visionary activity while still remaining balanced and active (the result of too much visionary activity without accompanying personality growth being the dropout, an essentially unproductive stance). The climbing which has prepared him to be a visionary has also prepared the climber to handle his visions. This is not, however, a momentous change. It is still as close as seeing instead of mere looking. Experiencing a permanent change in perception may take years of discipline.

A potential pitfall is seeing the "discipline of the Holy Slow Road" in the iron-willed tradition of the Protestant ethic, and that will not work. The climbs will provide all the necessary rigor of discipline without having to add to it. And as the visionary faculty comes closer to the surface, what is needed is not an effort of discipline but an effort of relaxation, a submission of self to the wonderful, supportive, and sufficient world.

I first began to consider these ideas in the summer of 1965 in Yosemite with Chris Fredericks. Sensing a similarity of experience, or else a similar approach to experience, we sat many nights talking together at the edge of the climbers camp and spent some of our days testing our words in kinesthetic sunshine. Chris had become interested in Zen Buddhism, and as he told me of this Oriental religion I was amazed that I had never before heard of such a system that fit the facts of outward reality as I saw them without any pushing or straining. We never, that I remember, mentioned the visionary experience as such, yet its substance was rarely far from our reflections. We entered into one of those fine parallel states of mind such that it is impossible now for me to say what thoughts came from which of us. We began to consider some aspects of climbing as Western equivalents of Eastern practices: the even movements of the belayer taking in slack, the regular footfall of walking through the woods, even the rhythmic movements of climbing on easy or familiar ground; all approach the function of meditation and breath-control. Both the laborious and visionary parts of climbing seemed well suited to liberating the individual from his concept of self, the one by intimidating his aspirations, the other by showing the self to be only a small part of a subtly integrated universe. We watched the visionary surface in each other with its mixture of joy and serenity, and walking down from climbs we often felt like little children in the Garden of Eden, pointing, nodding, and laughing. We explored timeless moments and wondered at the suspension of ordinary consciousness while the visionary faculty was operating. It occurred to us that there was no remembering such times of being truly happy and at peace; all that could be said of them later was that they had been and that they had been truly fine; the usual details of memory were gone. This applies also to most of our conversations. I remember only that we talked and that we came to understand things. I believe it was in these conversations that the first seeds of the climber as visionary were planted.

William Blake has spoken of the visionary experience by saying, "If the doors of perception were cleansed every thing would appear to man as it is, infinite." Stumbling upon the cleansed doors, the climber wonders how he came into that privileged visionary position vis-a-vis the universe. He finds the answer in the activity of his climbing and the chemistry of his mind, and he begins to see that he is practicing a special application of some very ancient mind-opening techniques. Chouinard's vision was no accident. It was the result of days of climbing. He was tempered by technical difficulties, pain, apprehension, dehydration, striving, the sensory desert, weariness, the gradual loss of self. It is a system. You need only copy the ingredients and commit yourself to them. They lead to the door. It is not necessary to attain to Chouinard's technical level-few can or do-only to his degree of commitment. It is not essential that one climb El Capitan to be a visionary; I never have, yet try in my climbing to push my personal limit, to do climbs that are questionable for me. Thus we all walk the feather edge, each man his own unique edge-and go on to the visionary. For all the precision with which the visionary state can be placed and described, it is still elusive. You do not one day become a visionary and ever after remain one. It is a state that one flows in and out of, gaining it through directed effort or spontaneously in a gratuitous moment. Oddly, it is not consciously worked for, but comes as the almost accidental product of effort in another direction and on a different plane. It is, at its own whim, momentary or lingering suspended in the air, suspending time in its turn, forever momentarily eternal, as, stepping out of the last rappel you turn and behold the rich green wonder of the forest.

At Home in the High Sierra

Off season on the John Muir Trail, Kristen Jacobsen descends Mt Whitney

Four Feet Over Sierra

Yosemite punctuates the crest of the Sierra just at the point where its character changes profoundly. Turning north from there toward Lake Tahoe the divide runs lower, rarely poking its head above timberline, with milder and more rolling terrain. But to the south it builds dramatically to become the High Sierra, the long, craggy crescendo of the range, and it resonates that chord all the way down past Mt. Whitney. It was into this alpine heart of the Sierra that I headed once my Yosemite apprenticeship had begun to run its course.

I already had a taste for that timberline country, starting much earlier. As a Boy Scout I explored the Evolution region, and by the time I became a camp counselor I was guiding six-day backpacking trips that included a cross-country stage over Alpine Col. I was fifteen. On one of those trips I very nearly climbed the north side of Mt. Mendel without a rope, and on another scrambled up Lamarck Col and looked, for the first time, down the steep eastern escarpment of the Sierra and past the town of Bishop into the basin-and-range country beyond. The summer that I was eighteen and ended up living in Yosemite and climbing continuously there for the first time, had actually begun in the Evolution country. From there I hiked alone, at first southward, then lingering to crampon up a few peaks, over 150 miles of the crest to get to the Valley. For most of the summer my ice axe

leaned incongruously against a hot granite boulder, but at its
end I was back up high for a tuesday morning on the Lyell
Fork.

In Yosemite I fell in with Sheridan Anderson, the alpine
cartoonist. (Look for "The Climbing Cartoons of Sheridan
Anderson," edited by Joe Kelsey, recently reprinted) We became friends, and he introduced me to both the Irish pubs of
San Francisco and the Eastern Sierra town of Bishop. Sheridan
went there to set up a sign painting shop; when I came to visit
he was trying without much success to blend into that redneck
desert town. He didn't need to for long. Sheridan found
Smoke Blanchard living there, who took us all out to the Buttermilk, and through him we met the legendary Norman
Clyde. Sheridan got me a job hoeing weeds in the July sun;
whenever I leaned on my hoe handle I got a salt-smeared view
back up to Lamarck Col on the crest. So I quit and hiked up
to the Palisades, where I met Don Jensen and at his invitation
went to work as a guide.

Mountaineering Guide Service was the first, and at that
time the only, climbing school west of the Tetons. Unless of
course you count Clyde, who had guided people up those
peaks twenty, thirty years earlier. I learned the guiding craft
there from Don Jensen and Bob Swift, and in turn I brought
in Carl Dreisbach and John Fischer. John later bought the
school—by then it was called the Palisades School of Mountaineering—and still later ran me out of the canyon for freel-
ancing. Clyde would have laughed. But I'm getting way
ahead of the story.

It was a most unusual guiding job that gave me the chance
to move to the Eastern Sierra in the fall of 1969. My challenge
was taking a brilliant but slightly autistic 17-year-old on an ex-
tended course of climbing and ski mountaineering while he
finished high school by correspondence. We moved into a
cabin high on Bishop Creek, right below Lamarck Col and in
the shadow of a succession of the Evolution peaks. I couldn't
believe my luck to be living on a corner of the Mt. Goddard
Quadrangle map, which felt like hallowed ground.

That's where I met Carl McCoy and hatched a plan for a
ski trip that would take us all the way along the crest of the
High Sierra.

> The line of our desire
> Weaves an enticing theory
> Along the Sierra crest,
> And it draws us upward.
> But how will it feel,
> Cold and slippery
> And steeped in solitude?

What can I say about the Sierra Nevada, where I have lived the
clearest hours of my life for as long as I can remember? That it laid hold of
my senses and compelled me years ago to live at its feet, in sight of its very
blue-edged crest, and that in order to be commanded by a fuller expression
of Sierra wildness I find myself on this late day of March 1970 pulling north
on skis across the Kern Plateau. Six days out of Whitney Portal, four feet over
the Sierra, bound for the spring wilderness of the high country, hoping for
Yosemite later. Yosemite, the northern terminus of the John Muir Trail which
we will alternately follow and abandon for another 200 miles through the
longest unbroken stretch of high mountain wilderness this side of Canada.
Yosemite, we dare not really dream it with packs dragging our shoulders. Six
days into the logic of snowy wilderness, fixing its image on us as the strictures
of civilization spall off.

For those of us who had
been going to the Sierra for a long
time—and all of my young life
pales beside some pilgrims—the
pressure of new visitors was starting to wear on the wildness of it.
So we began years ago to avoid the
Muir Trail in August as too
crowded. Of course we all had our
little secrets, high pocket basins
and cross country tramps where

Carl McCoy photo

we could count on personal solitude for years to come.

Yet the population pressure was there, and if one way out of it was spatial, then another might be seasonal. Last fall, the first for me in the High Sierra, had been magical when scattered leaves gave even the trail a freshness walking up into the Palisades. Aspens and willow thickets shot yellow and red along the creek bank, while above, rocky ridgelines cut to high contrast black and whites. Frozen mud crystals in the trail gave way to bitter mornings over timberline, and brittle afternoons in the gullies above, where fiercely hooked blows from my ice axe shattered the silence of steep sheets of green ice. Then to descend canyons roaring with wind to a sheltered stop high in a rock alcove above Third Lake before trucking it on back home to sleep on the edge of Bishop Creek, waking to new tunes of the creek playing on its own fresh ice cantilevered from bridge timbers. That had lasted into November.

What might spring, white and drifted and empty, be like? None but the resident snow surveyors would admit to ever being out in the Sierra spring, a good sign.

Architecturally, the Sierra runs a northwest-southeast axis, as if guarding entry to the lower dogleg of California. In cross-section it is like a long wave building slowly up from the coast side to crest before breaking off sharply into the Owens Valley, two miles below to the east. Lengthwise, the crest is like a great ripsaw set to cut one way only, toward Oregon, with gentle southern risers. As the layout became clear, I realized which way one would want to ride winter along the Sierra crest, to climb gently on sun-stabilized snow, teeter with exhaustion in a breathless high notch, and rip off a northern powder bowl. Those who say there is no powder in the Sierra haven't looked closely at the ripsaw effect; those who would ski it must travel with the grain from south to north.

> Returning to the winter mountains
> To feel the earth
> Through a lens of crystalline water.
> It lies white upon this upturned land
> And we are free to obey its cold laws.

With a climbing eye we had come to expect the steep summer granite and gullies frozen in autumn ice to live in northeast cirques. Bishop Creek, which drains several of the steep cirques, runs past the site of the Cardinal Gold Mine, which had worked one of the richest lodes in the Sierra until a reservoir built upstream flooded its thousands of feet of tunnels and producing galleries. Their warrens flooded, the miners abandoned their cabins as well, which went with the times to become the Cardinal Village fishing resort (in season), and happened this winter to be sheltering a herd of mountaineering Armadillos migrating from the broken dreams and dirty needles of the Haight-Ashbury to live in the shadow of our vision of verticality in the Sierra winter of 1970.

Cardinal Village was becoming a remarkable community. The Christmas party from the city had just gone home. John Fischer, with whom I had stumbled into ski touring on a shrivellingly cold outing to Matterhorn Peak four years before, was packing to return as fast as possible. Saint Carl showed up with his sewing machine, and Barry Knowles traded his road-racing motorcycles for chessboard and cooking sherry. Tim Harrison was bumping around the yard trying to learn to ski. I had just opened up my typewriter when a VW bus pulled up by the next cabin in the yard. The promised manuscript was shelved until the middle of March.

At Cardinal Village: Carl McCoy, Claudia Axcell, Larry Reynolds, Curt Foote, Sandy and Eben Axcell, Tim Harrison, our landlady Nadine Stratton, Joe Brennan, John Fisher, Alex Fisher, Barry Knowles, Doug Robinson. Jan. Tiura photo

Yes they would like some tea. He is Carl "Peanut" McCoy, a photographer and onetime ski racer, alternate to the Men's National Team until he had run off a downhill course at Aspen breaking his leg in five places which put an end to all that; and she is Claudia. We drank black tea in the sunroom and talked. My front room had once been a porch and was now ringed with windows facing south so that the sun, once it finally rose over the cirque wall, poured in. It quickly became the winter gathering point of this neighborhood in the making. On the north wall of this sunroom was a composite topographic map of the Sierra, starting at the floor with the southern end and stretching two thirds of the length of its highest reaches before running out onto the ceiling and giving up still well short of Yosemite. Sitting in the sunroom drinking tea you had to either look out at the mountains or up at the swirled lines representing them, tacked up there on the wall. Sometimes when coming home in the evening I would see the kerosene lamp bobbing along the floorboards, following the course of some argument about the geography around Mount Whitney. Carl and Claudia had spent the summer exploring some trailless reaches of the Middle Fork of the San Joaquin, and now he was looking for something a little mellower to do on skis. John had left his touring skis, so we started taking trips up the canyon, Carl learning to wax while I continued to flail at improving my downhill skiing.

It must have been the ever-presence of my wall map that focused our general restlessness onto skiing the Muir Trail. I think it happened right around the time when a full moon rising late over the canyon rim interrupted goodnights at the cabin door to send us running for skis to cruise the night away on a moonlight ride to North Lake and on toward Paiute Pass until thickening forest darkened our prospects. Then turn and tuck, four-foot children's skis—the current theory—clattering down the iced road to stamp and puff goodnight, goodnight as the moon rode away west over the brow of Emerson. Looking at the trail thread its way up the wall and run out on the ceiling short of Reds Meadows, and at our inch or two of progress that night, we could not comprehend the magnitude of our fledgling project, nor could we from any point along the way, nor now. Soon enough we began to transcend the trail anyway. A few more hours of poring over the map and we realized that all of our cross-country ramblings and hours of staring over the terrain from peaks had led us into some alpine parallels more exciting than the trail, and our conception of the trip evolved into not just skiing the Muir Trail but rather the finest sequence of the Sierra crest that we could imagine.

Our preparations were frantic, of course, but not unusual. Don Jensen had designed a wind-stable tent for Alaskan climbing, and a contoured pack without a frame that fitted better to one's back the tighter it was packed. It was especially good for mountaineering. We wrote for the patterns and

Claudia and I built two packs and a tent that totaled five pounds. The tent pitched with our touring poles, and the packs, now being produced commercially, were to carry sixty pounds and more, and proved the only practical way to battle the lurching weight shift of a packframe that is so perilous to equilibrium on skis.

Carl McCoy

Meanwhile, Carl was building our skis. His friend Hub Zemke had conceived of laying-up fiberglass skis on a core carved from aluminum honeycomb instead of wood. Honeycomb has amazing structural strength for its weight, so it is valued for stiffening airplane wings and helicopter rotors. Hub's ski was very lively and quick in competition, and pounds lighter than a ski had ever been before, which was its main advantage to us. Carl had helped to design the giant slalom model; now he disappeared into a basement workshop at Mammoth Mountain and came back smelling of resin with two pair of incredible, light skis. Plastic and aluminum from tip to tail, nothing organic whatever, with a fluorescent green finish finger-painted into paisley swirls: Hexcels, serial number 6 and number 9. We epoxied-on Silvretta bindings.

Then we spoke to Carl's father about wax. Dave McCoy had been a snow surveyor for seventeen years in the era before there were any ski lifts on the eastern side of the Sierra. He and Joe Miller had done their backcountry surveys—checking the water content of the snowpack to predict spring runoff—by skiing on wax and would often relax on weekends by touring up Mammoth Mountain for a good run off the cornice. That wasn't too unusual: for decades before the early fifties, when Dave McCoy put the first lift up Mammoth Mountain, anyone who skied, toured. Yes, he said, you'll need four tubes of klister and a little less paste wax. And that's exactly what we used, though in disbelief we carried at least four times that much.

What would spring be like, we wondered. The trails would be buried, and the trail signs. And so, of course, the trail pounders would be

Carl McCoy photo

gone too, and their garbage. No fire-black rocks, no Dentyne wrappers punctuating the trail at chewable intervals, no horseshit, no flies, no pop-tops glittering in the beds of the holy streams. No more wheezing questions of: "How far'z the lake?" We had slower questions to ask.

By March the sun was rising sooner and higher over the canyon wall, until it slushed and muddied the midmorning yard. Spring was coming, or was it already here? We panicked and bolted. Three food caches—hot cereal, hot cocoa, tea; cheese, crackers, sardines and chocolate; and endless variations of bulghar wheat glop with tuna fish, plus stove gas and even more spare wax—went up to Bishop Pass, Paiute Pass, and Reds Meadows. Stocking Kearsarge Pass would have taken two more days we thought, standing in the mud, so we lashed the cache to already overloaded packs.

Shortly after the Ides of March we ate a predawn breakfast of wheat germ pancakes and low-geared it up to Whitney Portal, the southern terminus of the Muir Trail. Our stove leaked gasoline vapor as the van climbed. We choked and threw it out; wood and water camping it would be. Not such a bad decision. Two months of preparational madness and suddenly we were there, pulling up from the end of the road into a muggier than spring day, running slushy traverses into the forest. Beginnings of a trip, full of relearning: learn the effort of climbing again, the rhythm of sidestepping on skis, how to cook over a fire. Re learn—yet again—to carry a load.

It was only March and we were already taking the wilderness to heart for another season. We camped on a dry patch of ground at the edge of Outpost Meadow and built a fire. That was our first real sitting-around-the-campfire-keeping-warm evening for the year, so early I hadn't thought to anticipate it. Then on to a breezy blue klister day, climbing out of timber among the fine white granite of the Whitney group, which freshened to a blowing and suddenly stormy lunch on running water benches. Larry Reynolds, who had come along to see us off, turned valleyward and in a moment was gone.

Night and exhaustion fell upon us along with a gusty graupel snowstorm in a broad but steepening chute just below Trailcrest. It was very close to winter now in a waterless, foodless, blown-snow night bivouacked on a snow ledge hastily stomped below a boulder. The tent flapped around us as a sit-up bivouac sack while we waited for the morning that brought us gale winds sweeping up the face to freeze our fingers and toes and blow us over, perilously, as we scratched for purchase with our ski edges in the steep, wind-crusted gully. Twenty yards over the ridge it was spring again with snow plumes blown off the ridge above, and stayed spring while kick turning down a steep gully and navigating through benchy country to a glacier-polished writing desk at timberline, there to sit with boots off in the afternoon sun and watch the new light of spring begin to add a little warmth and color to the flat, white, intense, high-contrast light of winter. Now it is way below freezing and not yet dark.

> Just before dawn
> Just over Mount Whitney
> A comet hanging in the eastern sky.
> We stared and stared
> But could not make it go away.

The sheer weight of preparations had compressed normal life, but once underway the detailing, the pressure to start before snow melted, all of our reasons and expectations were suddenly gone. We decompressed into wilderness and silence, spewing residual tension and noise in all directions until we approached the emptiness of our surroundings and could feel again. Absorb again. To this all of our reasons had just been civilization's excuses to itself; before us lay at least two hundred more miles of real, pulsing wilderness, even now pushing on our senses with its own program.

Now, skiing through open forest on the Kern Plateau, floating four feet over the Sierra, four feet gliding north, trail underfoot or half a mile west, or maybe east out of sight over a rise, we let any line that pleased us choose our way over open country. Passes and watersheds were obvious, and skis aren't feet anyway, eliminating another dimension of habit, prodding preconceiving minds to know more directly. Being on a trail in the mountains engenders a trail consciousness, a manner of being locked onto a dusty thread stomped out for miles ahead of you into the wilderness, until the transference succeeds and the trail *is* the wilderness, just as the layout of a road determines your perception of countryside. But we were not going anywhere on trails that spring, and we had had enough of the engineering vision and wanted mostly to escape its strangle hold on the twentieth century and on our own minds. So we got rid of our instruments one way or another: the clock and the calendar, the thermometer and compass. We did keep the maps, and at first they replaced the trails for us. But as our senses grew out into the wilderness swooping roundly in every direction from the green tips of our skis, our vision was no longer bounded by Theodore Solomons' conception (he laid out the Muir Trail) of how one should go along the backbone of the Sierra, and we began to see by watersheds and ski by the contours of the country before us.

We could see Diamond Mesa for days, its unlikely flat blown clear of snow, so we knew where Forester Pass should be. This first leg of the trip as far as Glen Pass was the only section new to both of us and we had prudently asked for advice from Doug Powell, head snow surveyor on the east side of the Sierra. He said, "You can't ski over Forester Pass," so of course we had to try. After all, he had also said, "waxing is mysterious," and in print too.

Forester Pass, at 13,200 feet, is the highest pass besides Trailcrest and has a reputation for steepness. It was nearly the last section of the Muir Trail to be completed in 1930. Until then the trail swung west to drop over Harrison Pass, a notch in this relentless ridge that divides the Kern River from the Kings drainage to the north. Finally it was straightened and forced over Forester by dynamiting switchbacks up the steep cirque headwall on its south side.

From the flat surface of the highest tarn a snow gully rose before us up that cirque and continued, by filling in a depression on the rock headwall, right up to a cornice leering over the pass, as if to punctuate where the sky began. It rose a thousand feet in one parabolic sweep that would have done credit to a fastidious geometry teacher brandishing three colors of chalk. We switchbacked into the bottom of the gully, crunching only the edges of our skis into the frozen old snow and leaning into our packs, until we could exit rightward onto a thin ribbon of white zigzagging on the rock wall—snow sitting on the trail ledge.

Finally, a mere hundred feet short of the pass, the trail vanishes under the gully. Roped climbing above or icy gullet ahead, but we were determined to stay on skis. While we stood there looking at our route across its parabolic climax, Carl spun a theory about slipping out there, recovering with his skis pointed downhill, a simple tuck and ride it out: "...probably be going 70 or

80 when I hit the lake," he concludes. I'm thinking that even *he* might have trouble pulling off that act with his heels loose, sixty pounds on his back and an unprepared course, but the thought fills a moment of doubt to the brim and Carl, elected for being the better skier, spilled over into the gully and trickled across. He got out the camera and it was my turn. Hand jamming between rock and ice, I sat down and lowered my skis down a four foot wall onto the gully surface, leaned out to plant a downhill pole, stood up and scratched and tiptoed my way across toward the lens, ever ready to immortalize disaster.

From the top we got our first glimpse of the Palisades on the northern horizon, with Mount Sill standing out bold and unmistakable in the middle. Its very distinctiveness became a lodestone for this first, and most springlike, part of the tour. Or perhaps it attracted us because it hid Bishop Pass behind its shoulder where, under a pile of rocks, lay a five-gallon mayonnaise tub with another week's food inside. This was our first glimpse of how far away it really was. It was also the day we had predicted, at summer rates, that we should be on top of Glen Pass. We could see that too, beyond the deep valley of Bubbs Creek. The wind was rising. We got on our skis, sighed on packs, and leaned north.

I slid straight into a valuable ski lesson. Carl had given me wordless clinics all winter just by letting me follow his turns and mimic his form. Now we were perched on top of a truly delicious-looking bowl, which lay deep in north-facing snow. And it had quite likely never been skied. So of course the snow turned out to be breakable crust, a foot deep. Carl traversed in, hitting his edges, testing...and then kick turned. I could hardly believe it. Here was a nationally ranked downhiller, capable of subtle edge control at adrenalizing speeds, and he wasn't even *trying* to make turns. It wasn't just my technique, then—or even the lack of it: there really is snow that no one can ski.

We were late off the pass so by the time we had kick-turned down the headwall and were rolling down benches looking for open water the light was falling around us. We were thirsty and weary and spaced, but entranced with dropping into the twilight canyon, drifting powder patches dark against the luminous wind crust. Floating down long open slopes we would be suddenly airborne over unseen bumps. Finally we were reduced to skiing one at a time in thickening darkness, feeling our way down canyon, calling out the terrain and sensing the storm closing overhead, several miles to the gurgle of open water just in the trees at full dark. We set up the tent and built a fire in the doorway.

The night was way below freezing as Carl walked off for water. At first I couldn't believe that someone would be calling me from a long way off, but the third cry penetrated. I grabbed the ice axe and found him right behind the tent, up to his knees in Bubbs Creek at the bottom of a slippery snow funnel. It flares at the top like a carburetor, but accelerating steepness shifts it to vertical long before it breaks off above Carl's waist. Then I realize that the bottom of the funnel has cracked off, fallen into the creek, and been sucked under into the swiftwater dark. In a shudder's breath I get it: he is hanging, barely, by our cooking pot and a water bottle dug into the vertical snowbank. One slip and he will be swept under. I stare for a long moment, and Carl remembers a plaintive, "What do you want me to do?" It was not obvious. Our shorty ice axe—just saving weight—sinks with a whimper into the steepening bank as I kick descending foot notches. Easy now, the solution to this is *not* to drop both of us in the creek. Carl spins off his hand holds, hurls the cookpot over my shoulder, and we lock forearms. The axe squeaks with the strain, then holds, and Carl's shoelaces quick-freeze as he pulls out of the funnel. Sitting right in front of the fire Carl's leather boots were freezing as fast as we could get them off him. "That's the closest I've ever came, man." His voice was very small. With no water collected we melted snow for dinner, and were glad enough for the rest to loaf through the stormy morning as his boots and wool knickers dried. His socks stayed so damp for the next week that they sprouted blisters.

Fine skiing off Glen Pass led to an open water lunch below Fin Dome. We dropped on down to 8500 feet at Woods Creek, lowest we'd been in over a week, where a pine needle bed felt like summer. The next morning we carried our skis for the first time, a mile up the creek bank trail toward Pinchot Pass. A lone coyote just ahead of us and going the same way eyed us over his shoulder. That morning on our third try to wax for warm, slushy snow we discovered yellow klister, which gripped so well that it stoked us, gathering all the frustrated energy from bare ground walking and scraping off failed waxes to shoot us over the pass to another full-dark camp at first water. Brother coyote was long gone ahead of us and had turned west down the Kings River.

The next day we were only good for three miles and an afternoon nap in Upper Basin, a place where you could camp for half a month and ski a different major cirque every day. We got over Mather Pass early the following morning to find a foot of settled powder in one of the most beautiful bowls we had ever seen. We swooped down, wishing we had time to climb back up for another run free of packs, and slogged across Palisade Lakes to lunch at the outlet.

Moving with a new pace and gait over remembered watersheds recasts their image, passing me back to when I most loved the Sierra by walking it.

Doug Robinson

And the light: we were getting to know the time of day in the mood of the sun slanting across a sidehill, in the quality of the light. Silver for mid afternoon, following Carl's traverse above Palisade Lakes, stretching into motion again after breaking down in midday heat and lounging naked on an open rock at the outlet. "...Bet this is a hot one in Stockton."

We still crossed two more unnamed high notches, coming to a bivouac high up under North Palisade in the starlight dark. Stonefall once in the night, off Thunderbolt. Next day, first food cache at Bishop Pass: midmorning gorge. And an early stop in Dusy Basin at the insistence of an afternoon snowstorm.

From Bishop Pass we followed the frozen ski tracks of four friends who had come in to meet us at Muir Pass, halfway through our journey. But we were nearly a week late, the fireplace in the hut was cold, and their fresher tracks slid on north toward Lamarck Col a day or two before, leaving us to our solitude.

> High cirrus, low morning sun
> Tea in the doorway:
> Muir Pass Hut

Looking after the essentials at home in the hut involved a pleasant reversal of the summer routine: chopping water and carrying wood. The wood is three miles away and over a thousand feet below, but one load lasts three days. And where there's wood, there's water.

The hut was full of associations. The log book revealed that Rick Sylvester, who would later attract attention by skiing off El Capitan with a parachute, had been there just the spring before, trying to become the second person to ski this route. He had been making good time in May after a record snowfall winter, and doing it in spite of his touring technique: he would walk up to the passes in rigid Lange boots to snap on Rossignol downhills for a swoop into the next valley, and then begin trudging again, moon-walking in one of the stiffest downhill boots ever built. Rick wrote a blistered, lonely note in the hut log that ran to several pages, then continued a few miles north before bailing out to the west side to save his feet.

Orland Bartholomew doesn't mention the view from Muir Pass, although he crossed it on the fourth of March 1929 on his way to becoming the first to ski the John Muir Trail, all alone. His sparse notes show that he didn't stop long but hurried on down toward Evolution Lake for the night; the octagonal beehive of a stone shelter wasn't built until two years later. Bartholomew loved wildlife, so his notes warmed when he saw fresh bear tracks later that spring in Yosemite. He also heard wolves (which were thought to be extinct) and even made the rare sighting of a wolverine.

Orland Bartholomew

Bartholomew was a snow surveyor working the west side of the Sierra in those years, and he put a lot of preparation into his hundred-day trip which began at Lone Pine on Christmas Day 1928. He had put in eleven food caches the previous fall. He traveled on specially made solid hickory skis, with hickory hoe handles serving as unbreakable poles. He had a small double-bitted axe for building a lean-to against storms, a "twelve-pound down robe," cast iron skillet, and a self-timer camera. Like us, "no timepiece, compass, or firearm was carried." We envied him the leisure his thorough preparation had bought him, for he lingered a week or more at several spots, and climbed a few peaks along the way. Yes, skiing the entire length of the High Sierra had been done with style the first time. Bartholomew saw the whole season, stopped where he liked, and got clean away, explaining none of it and keeping his reasons to himself. (For his story see "High Odyssey" by Eugene Rose, which is illustrated with Bart's own photos)

For the next seventy miles to its low point at Reds Meadows the trail pokes its head above timber into the alpine zone only briefly over Selden Pass and again at Silver Pass for a total of four miles. To alpine tastes that is too low and too far west, becoming irrelevant. We had already made a major detour by straightening out and raising the line where it ran along the base of the Palisades. So heading north we stayed close along the base of the crest again, and in our next forty miles we dipped barely into timber at Pine Creek Pass and again to cook in a storm at Lake Italy.

Afternoon in the tent, half hanging from the hillside in a clump of Whitebark Pine above Lake Italy. Nothing Mediterranean about the weather, which blows cold snow out of the northwest. A Pacific front, and no telling how long it will last. Hungry, since it's too miserable out to cook, and we've already eaten more than we dare of the lunches.

It's been a cold leg of the trip. Wind blew us inside most of our second day at Muir Pass; snow fell through the dusk. Then a surprise of quick turns on frozen crust down to Wanda Lake in the morning, and we skated on down the basin to blue klister at Evolution Lake and lunch on Alpine Col. Picked up the Paiute Pass food cache. A breezy night bivouacked on a rolling polished slippery slab island in the immense snow basin below Mt. Humphreys, brought a blowing day with wind swinging to the southwest. Carl's leg ached, we were out of klister and too cold to put more on, but we still made three passes and ended here at early dusk.

Since resting at Muir Pass we have felt very strong and our packs light. The snow has been firm, the country open and very high. We've made amazing time and hope to keep it up all the way into Yosemite. Two-thirds there.

> Spring retrograde into winter this afternoon
> Playing along the crest of the range,
> Contouring toward Italy Pass
> Wax gone, too cold to put more on
>
> Mount Tom over a shoulder
> And sagely green in sunlight beyond
> The Owens Valley—
> First view in almost three weeks.
>
> Heart spills over the ridge.
> Skis falter and shuffle
> Then turn north:
> Take the long way home.
>
> Pack feels heavy again
> And it's a long way down
> To Lake Italy in the twilight.
> A narrow band of the last gold
> Just on the horizon
> Under miles of cloud.

Stuck in the tent another morning, it occurred to me to wish I had an evolution book to read through this snowfall day, which showed me that I had been living for these last three weeks with my body and senses chiefly, and that my mind had been quiet save for diversionary adventures during long hot climbs. Songs, as usual, filled it, but not with thought as with sense, poetry, sensuality. Mainly I've had my senses out, learning the high country. As before, the distinction between feeling and dreaming is sharpened, outlined like a task. The night in Humphreys Basin I dreamed of endless shopping centers in Atlanta, Georgia. Wandering through, always slightly lost, with a warmth of human confusion and drama around and of me. It is functionally the same dream as five years ago in the Ionian Basin: at the crisis of solitude the mind tries once again for security by immersion in ordinary life.

The storm will not relent so one afternoon we go anyway, over Gabbot Pass. On top the cloud drops on our heads. I know from summer that there are cliffbands scattered below us everywhere; this whiteout hides treacherous dropoffs. We ski blindly into Second Recess, squinting and wiping ice out of our eyelashes. Finally, trees. We've made it. Just below timberline, we camp.

Eventually the storm lifts and we can move, but a mile down canyon Carl's binding dismounts again. Trying to set epoxy over a fire; another day gone. Our food is nearly gone too. Over Red-and-White Pass and on to the last supper in Tully Hole. But the weather has settled, and the next three days go well fueled on tea and vitamin B.

Late afternoon is the golden hour when sun falls slantingly through western smoke and haze. I felt it especially that day when we had hardly seen the sun, which suddenly turned diffused gold, pulling up from the Duck Lake drainage an hour before the light faded. We navigated carefully the next day through the long featureless forest, huge Red Fir growing on volcanic ash. We're slowing down, starving, so it's the following afternoon and snowing again before we come out to the San Joaquin. We're not sure where along the river we are, which way to turn to find our food cache at Reds Meadows. We choose upstream, and are soon shocked by two figures on the far bank. Their skis are parked and they are fishing intently in the snowstorm. We yell to ask directions, but with the wind and water they don't hear. We wave our arms, scream, but finally shrug and just ski on upstream.

Our last mayonnaise tub of a food cache is undisturbed in a tree right by the Reds Meadows Store. It is still snowing hard as we get it down, so with very little discussion we pry our way into a boarded-up cabin with the ice axe and scrounge squaw wood for the stove. Fortunately Carl knows the packer who owns it. This summertime shack is barely shelter; snow blows through the walls. But the real problem is that our stomachs have shrunk. So for two days we sit right in front of the wood stove waiting for our bellies to unbloat so we can stuff them again.

With the clearing comes more binding trouble, so we are two more days just to Agnew Meadows, which should have been an easy morning. But

Doug Robinson

when we finally get moving we truck: we are on Thousand Island Lake early one morning where I fulfill an old ambition to visit some of the islands, then over Island Pass and Donohue Pass and down to Tuolumne Meadows in one push.

> Three ducks on their way north in the new dusk
> With spring in their minds under a heavy sky
> Fly about for open water
> Up and down the Lyell Fork
>
> Suspicions of a dome
> Far down river in the fading stormlight
> Yellow sliding under piles of gray
>
> Just where the Lyell empties onto the flat
> We got off our skis and sat
> Half an hour on a patch of grassy bank
> Staring at the stream bottom
> Open water and dark pebbles vivid to whitestruck eyes
>
> And then we're off
> Sliding fast before the dark
> Clear to the Meadows

We just made it across the Meadows in a closing whiteout to the Sierra Club cabin for another two days of sitting it out, now anxiously close to Yosemite Valley. Hungry again, we wished to swoop over the Cathedral Range and down into the Valley. Instead, we broke a heavy trail in dense new snow, weather eyes over shoulders—even set up the tent for a noon false alarm—and came, poling mostly, down aside Sunrise Mountain to sleep. We had broken all four heel cables by this time. Mine went first so I got the two spares; Carl finished the trip on parachute cord. In the morning, while sidehilling the edge of a little valley and looking for Clouds Rest to show us the way and feeling hungry, we saw a large brown bear making his way upstream, breaking trail with a powerful stroke, heading purposefully toward the Meadows. He looked hungry too. In spite of that he was heading away from spring, higher into the still white wilderness. Holding our breaths in the shadows, we failed to take it as a sign.

The Valley is where I had always lived, in a sense. In the sense that it is where I had lived so intensely that intensities elsewhere somehow seemed to be of the Valley too, the emotional home. So it was a fitting coming down point for me, the only one possible really. A going home, a getting fed and warm, plus the odd chance that love lay waiting for me there, unlikely and at last.

The Silver Divide. Carl McCoy photo

I would like to say that we came down into the Valley like a mattress balanced on a bottle of wine. But it was not the year for that, the test being apparently not yet over, and after snow ran out above Little Yosemite's rim we stumbled, sloshed and dripped our way down the afternoon, fought manzanita and raised another bear who treated us to the trail behind Half Dome, and started getting brought down into the Valley.

We got there very late, begged a yogurt from the janitor at Degnans, and slept on our stomachs one last time in the church bowl behind the village waiting for dawn and the store to open.

In the morning in the meadow we soaked up sunshine and french bread with real butter while talking with Chuck Ostin. Gradually we began to notice a man loitering nearby who ignored Yosemite but strained to eavesdrop on us. Self-consciousness returned with the thought that I hadn't combed my hair in thirty six days. The giveaway, though, came when our spy was offered a friendly ride from the California Highway Patrol, which was cruising way beyond its usual jurisdiction. Hmmm...welcome back to your culture, hippies. Two months later the Valley would erupt with the "ranger riot" descending on hippies in Stoneman Meadow.

Doug Robinson

The next day we wound north through the western oak and waving grass foothills, steeping in green, manic with springtime, dancing out through the open roof of Carl's VW van and down the sage-steep eastern slope of the Sierra toward home. We were welcomed back to Mono County by two local sheriffs, red lights grinning. They bracketed us and pulled us over: "We have a report that you are a possible drunk driver." Sorry, man, nobody drunk in here—only stunned. Welcome home.

Truckin' My Blues Away

In the fall of 1969, at Chuck Pratt's camp in Yosemite, I met Yvon Chouinard, and both of our lives shifted. Right away we arranged to meet again the next weekend, on the other side of the Sierra. I introduced him to the Palisades, he showed me modern ice climbing, and we made what we believe was the first ascent—in full ice conditions—of the V-Notch gully. After that I signed-on for the ice climbing revolution Yvon had brewing, and over the next few years worked a lot at his Great Pacific Iron Works in Ventura.

This story of our first ascent of the V-Notch was written at Parchers Camp up on Bishop Creek during the winter of 1970-71. Following Norman Clyde's lead, I was caretaking the roadhead lodge four miles on skis from where the snowplow stopped. But it was a cold and lonely place and not the best skiing, though I would skid up into the wilderness most days and got pretty good at flying down the narrow track home, and pre-jumping wind drifts in twilight or moonglow. Before the winter was over I got the call to spar another round with my Vietnam-era draft board, went on from there to work at Chouinard's tin-shed shop in Ventura and never came back. Finally I just mailed back the keys to the lodge.

Looking down the V-Notch. We Came back to do its second ascent two weeks later with Tom Frost and Doug Tompkins.

Keep on Truckin'
Truckin till the break of day
Keep on truckin, mama
Truckin my blues away

—an old blues run

A little over a hundred years ago, John Muir saw the Sierra crest shining to the east from the rim of Yosemite Valley and walked off to have a closer look. Since then, a few climbers of each generation have followed his lead and slowly climbed first the peaks and then the ridges of his Range of Light. By the early 1930s, armed with a new tool, the rope, they ventured onto the faces, starting with the East Face of Mount Whitney. Now, a few more of the faces—not large by Yosemite standards, but of good rock in an alpine setting—are being climbed. Lately there has been another, more surprising, discovery: ice gullies in some of the steep and shaded north-east cirques. From the Mediterranean latitudes of his mind, broiled so long in the Yosemite sun, the California climber has begun to conceive of ice near to home.

There is little wonder that the sunny Sierra has been so long neglected as a potential ice climbing area: it has but few small glaciers and seems at times, and especially when approached from the east, the perfect desert mountain range. That such a range might contain good hard climbable ice had not occurred to California mountaineers; freshly home from weather epics in the Canadian Rockies or doing the Andean equatorial wallow, they

Doug Robinson

went straight for warm granite. The rock climbers in their turn had just plain forgotten to look—they hadn't even seen the walls of fine unclimbed granite in the high country. "The Climbers Guide to the High Sierra," by way of introducing itself, says that "there is seldom enough hard snow or ice to justify carrying crampons." I remember reading that as a young climber and then hopefully carrying my crampons anyway, hundreds of miles up and down the Range of Light. The closest thing to a sign of interest in ice climbing I saw in those years was crampon tracks in *neve* along the John Muir Trail above Tully Hole one June.

Recently, on going to the east side of the Sierra, I have seen the light at last—streams and sparkles of it reflecting out of high steep gullies during the few minutes a day in which the sun passes their heads, or a deep blue translucence radiating from shady notches. It may be that the heat which made us unsuspecting of ice also made the ice. Spring snow melts in the gullies, speeded by summer rains washing down them, until the sharp fall winds set this surface into the water ice that we found, sure enough, when it occurred to us to start looking in the right places.

October on the Palisade Glacier was a mountaineer's clear and cold dream of the high country with a night rattling wind and the highly-contrasted lights and shadows of the day printed on our minds as if to impress us again and at last before winter took the edges off. The glacier, brittle underfoot, extracted tribute from ever-cramponed feet, and what had been sumer's mere suspicion of crevasses were now widely skirted or steeped over. Across the glacier the U-Notch, midsummer highway to North Palisade, was out in full blue ice from head to toe and probably hadn't been attempted since mid-August, despite its less than 40° inclination. The V-Notch, a few hundred yards to its left, glittered at us from deep between confining granite walls. Looking almost straight into this gully we had come to climb made it very steep in the mind.

The first pitch up the back wall of the bergschrund was the steepest. I put my axe in a pile of snow to belay and Yvon led off. This was Chouinard's first trip to the Palisades and my first outing on ice this serious; we felt a long way and many degrees centigrade removed from the kerosene-lanterned camp table in Yosemite, where this plan was gotten up only a week before.

Right away, Yvon got himself strung out on to the steepest ice just below the lip and was committed before he realized he wanted protecting. I looked from a forest of crampon points suspended in the air twenty feet above to the pile of snow I had thought would be a good enough anchor, past it into the deep blue 'schrund and back to the spiny sky. Yvon was having his own problems. The ice was so hard that his attempts to lodge an axe or alpine hammer to pull up on yielded either ice cubes or sudden opaque cones under the blade. Finally, he pulled up on delicate balance and blew out a long sigh: "I haven't been gripped like that in a while."

With a belay thoughtfully anchored far enough to the side to increase my concentration, I started up into the hardest ice I have ever seen. After producing the requisite amount of fear like a ticket of admission, I pulled up over the lip. I had been holding on too hard to run the inclinometer and was glad enough to forego the reading in order to stay out of the gullet of the blue meanie snapping at my heels. I kicked out over the crest of this wave frozen in the act of breaking onto the glacier and looked over a pitch of foam up to a slightly choppy green sea leading 900 feet to the Sierra crest.

We French-stepped up a pitch of neve and started out on to the sweeping ice of the gully, zig-zagging across it to belay on rock, being after all still Californians. Soon we were running out of rope: the gully is so well-proportioned, presenting its full height in one gesture, that pitches shrink and seem to get nowhere. On the fourth pitch, I set a Charlet-Moser "coathanger" ice screw, noticing a slight feeling of stripped threads as it went in. Coming up after, Yvon pulled out the shank broken off above the threads. I hadn't felt it break, but was probably forcing it in too fast for the hardness of the ice.

Soon we were spaced out on our ice sheet surrounded by brittle green sea-smooth 50° ice, temporarily becalmed in a gully on the eastern wall of California in its flight back to the Pacific. Feeling like fish out of water on this flinty sea, we couldn't tell whether to laugh or shudder, frolic or grip. It was beginning to feel like I hadn't made a move over 5.4 in three pitches when I put my hand out to rest in the absent, familiar way of a slab climber—it skated off and I teetered momentarily, remembered myself and tried again to decide whether I should be afraid.

Chouinard had developed a technique and two tools to help us up the gully without breaking the surface of the ice with a step. Dissatisfied with the grip of hand daggers in the Right-hand Mendel couloir a few miles north of here during a boiler-plate autumn two years ago, he forged the back of a Yosemite hammer into a small-toothed pick with a sharp droop. Swung from the handle, this alpine hammer is driven into the ice with the force of the hammer head behind it. I have pulled my entire weight up vertically on a single well-placed hammer. He also designed a beautiful flat-adzed ice axe with

The V-Notch and the U-Notch

a thin, drooping pick. Both these tools were so shamelessly efficient that I thought them at least twice as good at their functions as any similar tool I had used, even ones made in Scotland.

Not content to be merely a master craftsman, or because the efficiency of his tools forced him to it, Chouinard devised a technique for more relaxed front-pointing. Since the ankles and calves of an ice climber are both attached to his Achilles Tendon, he can rest that overworked organ in one leg at a time by turning that foot out and placing it flat on the ice French style as an intermediate step between the front-point stances of the other foot. Turning out first one foot and then the other in this fashion extends the range of front-pointing. We quickly locked into this technique, using it instead of stopping whenever we needed a rest. Our stops in the middle of pitches for protection stemmed from prudence rather than impending collapse.

Higher in the gully, with our technique sorted out to the point of confidence, we began to register impressions of our strange and beautiful surroundings. Nothing that happened here could quite be described in familiar terms. The steepness was right, but it was strangely slippery. Silence was almost recognizable, but too deep. The cold air seemed deader, or was it only thin? Ice chips dropped with explosive tinkling sounds and disappeared to leave the granite walls of this sound chamber staring at each other across their bed of ice. A seagull flew over. I looked up to see vaporous cloud fragments blow out over the top of the gully and felt the mountain falling away beneath me. Our voices took on such clear, deep and resonant tones that we could not talk and had to resort to laughing. The August high country that most climbers know was nowhere in sight. If I dug deep in my pockets for the meaning of all this, I only got my hands warm, which was quite enough of a holiday for eyes and ears until my end of the rope came up again and hands forgot their numb selves for the pleasure of moving over ice again.

We ran blocks along the ridge, the very crest of the Sierra, looking west into the golden-sun, peak-spotted wilderness, and turned down a loose face toward the long-shadowed glacier. A perfect, breathless day. We moved down in a fast-paced, free but vigilant, wordless mountaineering that danced counterpoint to the careful footwork in the gully. We had spent our day scratching upon the steep surface of the Sierra Nevada with our crampon points—a foreign, embryonic feeling to a range of mountains that has felt every sort of drama on its rocks. Coming down the eastern flank of this two-hundred mile crest, which hides many remote northeast cirques yet to be looked into by ice-conscious eyes, I dream of spending a few of the falling days of each year high in Sierra gullies, truckin' my blues away.

Doug Robinson

Mountaineering Just Means Glad To Be Here

The Palisades are surprisingly little-known in the scope of American climbing. Maybe it's because they lack the obvious, in-your-face quality of the Tetons or Mt. Rainier. You can glimpse them from the highway, but only if you look up at just the right moments. Better yet, drive up into the White Mountains to the east, to a campground called, appropriately, Sierra Vista. Arrange to sleep there if at all possible (and bring water), for the view at dawn is the most striking of Sierra panoramas, with the Palisades standing up bold and unmistakable directly in front of you. It's the best vista of this special place you will find, short of committing to the long, uphill hike that guards the high alpine basins. This is the story, never before published, of how it was for a few hippies to live summer after summer in the magical Palisades, and pioneer hard new climbs in a bold new style, but only because climbing flowed naturally out of the joy of just being there.

> Mountaineering just means glad to be here
> No climbing is required.
> Simply from being in the mountains
> It will arise spontaneously of itself,
> For sheer joy in wild terrain.
> — Palisades notebooks, 1970

A Night on the Ground, a Day in the Open

First light. Roll over and go back to sleep.

Next time I crack an eye the sun has risen, though its horizon is still below this sandy perch, out the canyon mouth and over blue Nevada ranges. Above me crisp backlight etches in a wilderness of ridge lines, the *Celestial Aretes* of Temple Crag. This scene, though I studied it through all of yesterday's shifting light, is fascinating enough to wake me up.

I squirm to a sitting position without coming out of my sleeping bag, and lean into a granite backrest. Its convenience is no accident. I have carefully chosen this morning spot, in the eye of the sunrise, and with a prospect of Temple Crag and beyond toward the Palisade Glacier. Right at hand are a book and notebook, water bottle and an entire grapefruit.

Rub my eyes and look up again. The light changes aspect so fast at this end of the day that minutes illuminate new dimensions in the terrain, like the system of corners high on the *Dark Star* buttress that had been a noonday puzzle yesterday. Then I'm distracted by the last sunrise hues bleaching to full white in the snow gully that swoops down from the glacier, and I keep tracking right across to the billowing bedrock beyond. It could be cumulus frozen into stone, scattered with the highest, most windblown pines of timberline, white barks clinging to little pockets of soil. But Temple Crag is the centerpiece of this scene, and the climbing eye returns. This time to the solarized edge of the *Sun Ribbon* Arete. All 18 pitches are visible, the spines and blocky ledges and the place where its continuity is sliced by the only natural tyrolean traverse I've ever seen on a route. The *Sun Ribbon* was named for the early view from this spot.

A trout splashes the green glacier water of Third Lake

***

There was one intersection in the Palisades, inevitable in those years, that overshadowed all the rest, and that was meeting Don Jensen. Don influenced each of us more than anything but the terrain itself. Fundamentally different from the rest of us, he was clearly the driving force of our entire era.

I met him quite by accident.

It was 1966, I think, and I walked the 5000 feet up to the Palisade Glacier for the first time, by myself, set my pack down and looked around. There was no one else there. I was surprised. Coming from Yosemite, I expected there to be some kind of a Camp 4 scene at this spot that I already thought of as a renowned climbing destination. Instead, there was no one to climb with. No human thing there at all, in fact, but a weather-beaten tent platform behind the biggest rock outcrop. A little bewildered, I soloed a couple of easy peaks and began testing out the best granite backrests for studying this striking alpine vista.

On the third day, a pile of lumber appeared on the slabs half a mile below me, moving slowly upward. It proved to be Don Jensen, with the material for a high camp hut. He had the sense to be surprised that anyone else was up there. After introductions, we made a deal. I would help Don build his hut and he would go climbing with me. One morning we set out at five a.m. on one of Don's favorite traverses, over both the Starlite and main summits of North Palisade.

Dan Asay, master bootmaker, approaching high camp.

A mile across the still gray glacier the first light of dawn caught up with us at the base of the Underhill Couloir. In the summer of 1931 Robert Underhill had taught proper ropework to a few eager Sierra climbers that included Norman Clyde, Jules Eichorn and Glen Dawson. You can tell which climbs had been tantalizing them by what happened next, a remarkable string of first ascents that August. On their way to the first ascent of the *East Face* of Mount Whitney, they stopped by here to bag the last unclimbed 14,000-foot peak, Thunderbolt. (Yes, the name reflects heavy weather that chased them off after succeeding on the bouldery 5.8 summit block.) Gaining the notch where they had gone right up slabs toward Thunderbolt, we turned left and threaded among towers on the superbly blocky 5.5 ridge leading to Starlite Peak, the northwest summit of North Palisade. Don had named the most prominent towers The Archbishop and Winnie the Poohnicle for their profiles from the high camp.

Starlite's summit was a monolith too, a single crackless block called the Milk Bottle rising out of unforgivingly jagged terrain, with an unprotected 5.6 move to its stand-if-you-dare pinnacle. A bolt now protects the downclimb, though Norman Clyde had done without it 35 years before. A quick rappel off The Sabre Gash—I was beginning to see that Don not only had this terrain wired but named as well—and we were onto cold steep blocks that never catch the sun, leading steeply to North Palisade. The ridge got easier leading to the U-Notch, where we descended a thousand feet of breathlessly steep and still frozen snow couloir and rappelled over the bergschrund back onto the glacier.

What a piece of mountaineering! And following Don, it went by so fast that we were back at the high camp by ten, ready to work all afternoon on the hut. I was replaying the route in my mind while fitting boards together, when Don offered me a job guiding in the Palisades. I had stumbled into a career, and couldn't have felt luckier.

Don Jansen. Dave Hamren photo

I don't know how Don originally found his way to the Palisades, but then he had a knack for ferreting out choice destinations. He had located and then climbed the first new route on the north side of Denali (then known as Mount McKinley), another visionary Alaskan line on the West Face of Mount Huntington, and an early attempt on Mount Deborah. The shy Jensen can be glimpsed on those .expeditions, bold ventures that set new standards of alpinism, thanks to the early writings of David Roberts. A classmate of Jensen at Harvard, Roberts was forging into a literary dimension new to mountaineering, one that emphasized interpersonal conflict and featured an emotionally muted tone. Not my style, but I'm grateful to have those fragments of portrait of Don Jensen after his rudely sudden death.

Don had already done a lifetime's worth of first ascents in the Palisades, not to mention lots of bold guiding, by the time any of us arrived. I think of the *Twilight Pillar* on Clyde, which is the best-looking line in the entire South Fork. And he had guided traverses that linked for instance Clyde and Middle Palisade with a stop on Bivouac Peak, or that jaunt over Starlite and North Pal, which with clients was a long day or more. Sometimes he guided in the winter, approaching on short skis with permanently attached skins, or spent weeks at a time soloing peaks in the spring, getting ready for Alaska. One vivid story that stands out had him soloing, alone and unroped, down the V-Notch, which drops 900 feet off the crest at a daunting 50-degree steepness before pitching off emphatically into the bergschrund. There had to be no other climbers for a hundred miles up or down the Sierra the day Don did that, gingerly kicking steps down through soft snow while barely self-belaying with the shaft of his Scottish north-wall hammer, a tool that was hardly as long as a carpenter's framing hammer.

Don more than anyone was my mentor as a guide, and during the few years that we shared in the Palisades, we became friends. Don wasn't like the rest of us hanging out in the hippie camp at Third Lake; he came into the Palisades with an agenda, and kept it. He was older and more purposeful, a graduate student in mathematics at UCLA, something that suited his creative brilliance after an indifferent career at Harvard, so he always arrived after the rest of us, stayed for the summer working hard at running the climbing school and doing his new routes on weekends. Don had a sport climbers build, wiry but strong. He always seemed to be bursting out of his knickers, which left a wide gap above the tops of LePhoque boots, advanced French affairs which buttoned like spats over his instep. When his big smile occasionally relaxed, his face was left in an odd pout reminding you of where his lower lip had healed crookedly after a fall into a crevasse in Alaska. Most of the time he seemed to be tilted forward, barely containing his energy and innocent enthusiasm, forever exclaiming things like, "Gosh, that would be *really* neat!"

When Don Jensen didn't return to the canyon one year, I moved across the outlet of Third Lake to inherit his old camp. It featured a porch-slab of gorgeous granite with an unobstructed view of the Celestial Aretes. He had named them from this spot, defining an entire facet of Temple Crag for climbing, and he invited and inspired us onto their first ascents. More than anything else in the Palisades, the Celestia Aretes are Don Jensen's legacy, and stand for his era.

Take the *Venusian Blind Arete*. (Venus was just setting behind it the morning in 1969 when Don got up for the first ascent.) It's a subtle climb; you'd have to study the peak for a while to even pick it out. It starts by cutting steps up and diagonally across a frozen snow field coming out of the left of two great gullies that cut the northeast face. Sometimes we'd rope up, since half the group would be wearing running shoes across the ice. Then tiptoe

Smoke Blanchard in the Buttermilk. Galen Rowell photo

across the Traverse of Death—not as hard as it sounds, though quite exposed. It turns a prominent corner right above a three hundred foot dropoff, where we would pause to fling our ice axes as hard as we could, sailing them far out onto the snow field below (we did break a few). Two hundred feet above there we'd rope up in earnest.

From there it's just 14 pitches to the top. The route is intricate, yet it's hard to get lost. You climb the right side of a prominent 200-foot slab to gain the arete. Above, just follow the ridge; sometimes it's only 50 feet above a gully, sometimes *a lot* more. A few of the pitches are fourth class, none over 5.7. Airy ridge moves will lead almost horizontally, protected by threading the rope around blocks, only toend abruptly against the compact face of a surprisingly steep tower, which will be plenty difficult enough to hold your attention. Finishing, it hits you that in spite of appearing so nebulous from below, the *Venusian Blind* has boldly maintained a striking position right to the end.

After I moved into Jensen's old camp, no tourists ever stumbled upon the place, but living there didn't make up for losing Don. He had gone to Scotland that winter as a post-doctoral fellow in mathematics. Then one morning on his way to school he hit a patch of black ice on his bicycle and crashed headfirst into a stone wall.

It was many years before I again moved to a new campsite. Half a mile closer to Temple Crag was a sandy wash that had been Smoke Blanchard's camp. Guiding out of there spared my clients the last half hour of threading through the talus to get home to Third Lake. They were always tired by then and often in the dark, which made it the most dangerous part of a Temple Crag day. Smoke had been in the Palisade more years than anyone, and he had learned directly from Norman Clyde, who of course did more first ascents here than anyone before him—or anyone ever will again.

Doug Robinson

As we camped in Smoke Blanchard's old spot it finally dawned on me that I had been following a trail of mentorship to get there. I had come to the end of it too, since Norman Clyde had died over a decade before. And anyway I had already fallen into the mentor role myself and had begun holding annual training camps for apprentice guides, teaching them the Palisades climbs, then backing them up as they worked with real clients. Descending from Smoke's camp in 1989 I learned that Smoke

Smoke Blanchard. Photo by Jan Tiura

Blanchard had just died, thrown from the bed of a pickup truck as it ran off a Mojave highway. So much road kill among mountain guides; I can't get into a car without remembering it.

Smoke taught us tricks on his rambling, scrambling, bouldering, soloing tours. It was all a game to him anyway, and one variation in a landscape that resembled a zen garden with sand surrounding blocks of granite was not to leave a footprint. Between each elegant climb, whether 2000 feet of alpine ridge or 20 feet of no-hands boulder, he would—when the mood was on him—pass without a trace.

Smoke's attitude fit perfectly with our growing enthusiasm for clean climbing. As we developed mastery of that technology it occurred to us that there would no longer necessarily be any physical evidence—like piton scars—left on the cliffside to show that a first ascent had been made. We were faced for the first time with the choice of whether to report a new climb or merely savor it as a personal joy. Some of Smoke's beautiful routes, things he would call a "scramble" or even a "stroll" when asking you to come along, climbs like the *Aiguille du Fou* ("If Chamonix can have one, I don't see why we can't too."), or the thousand-foot *Little Pinnacle*, or the route to the first ascent of Wells Peak, are still not recorded anywhere; he had discovered and developed them alone, and took us on them for the pleasure of company.

Smoke was pleased and a little bemused to suddenly have climbing partners in Bishop. Clyde was getting too old, and Smoke had gotten used to climbing alone after living for decades happily out of touch with much of the climbing world.

We were a little too hip to take on some of Smoke's other attitudes and techniques. Too five-ten sophisticated to appreciate using, for instance, a long ice axe as a very efficient cane while soloing up and down low fifth class terrain, chatting. If pushed he would mutter something about it being "only about 3.8," which in turn provoked us to notice that his mentor Clyde had soloed routes like that up here fifty years before. The same routes we were now guiding with ropes and hardware. Smoke would stow the axe (it broke down into two sections to fit in his daypack) when the going got a little tougher and keep right on soloing with an easy confidence, still telling stories, up to about 5.7. He carried a 30-foot hank of 5/16-inch rope, nylon but ancient, and at tricky spots he would offer to belay us. Smoke called it his "string" and was fond of relating that one day the great Chuck Pratt had accepted his belay. He never told that story to his own advantage, but rather with an eye toward showing that even a renowned climber can be modest and humble.

I once offered Smoke a pair of smooth soled PA rock shoes to try. He took them to a boulder problem in the Buttermilk Rocks that he had dubbed *The Rubber Tester*. That's not in the part of the Buttermilk that you're thinking of if you have bouldered there. You were in the Peabodies boulders, but where Smoke liked to go is not far east of there, into the jumbled ribs and corridors of bedrock where, over several decades, he had fashioned an intricate scrambling course that went over a dozen summits. It was a kind of bouldering course for mountaineering with moves of up to 5.7 and occasionally exposure of a hundred feet or more (including the spot where Pratt had accepted a belay on Smoke's string). We called it Smoke's Rock Course. Even if the rope didn't come out, it took most of a day—and solid chimneying technique—to get through it. Anyway, he returned the shoes, saying politely that they cramped his toes, and went right back to that hard soloing in his old lug-soled mountain boots.

After Smoke left the Palisades and shifted to guiding more international trips, he began living parts of the year outside of Tokyo. He took up with a wonderful Japanese woman half his age, Keiko Ishikawa. Then his home in Bishop, a tiny one-room apartment perched on top of a house, took on even more of a Japanese feel. The futon bed folded away during the day, while he wrote "Walking Up and Down in the World" ("uphill, downhill, it's all the same now" he said when we bumped into each other on the Khumbu trail

Doug Robinson

in Nepal) at a stand-up typewriter with a view of the Sierra crest. A visitor would be offered green tea at a table decorated with a chart for learning kangi characters. Looking a little like Sean Connery in "Rising Sun" (which is a good part in a bad film), Smoke now balanced his anonymity on East Willow Street and his days as a poetry-reciting Buddhist truck driver with a growing reputation as an international guide, whose little scrambles began to include outings in the Port Hills of Hong Kong.

Above Smoke's camp, 2200 feet of snow gully leads in one bold sweep to the old High Camp at the edge of the Palisade Glacier, the spot where I had first met Don Jensen. During the years after that when we told clients that they would be bivouacked in the hut there, we had to quickly admit that the accommodations were really more like crawling into an Arkansas pig shanty. High Camp is breathtaking. 12,500 feet, for one thing. And after slogging the last pitch of snow, or the long alleys of slabs that finish the dry land route, you finally break into view of the North Fork summits. The most alpine cirque in the Range of Light rises above its largest glacier—a worthy place to stand and stare.

We would cache our mountain boots up there, along with crampons for going out on the glacier, commuting up and down the slabs in running shoes. That left room in the pack for occasional luxuries, like the steak I unpacked one day, imagining it sizzling on the little hibachi grill that lived under the hut. But I turned around a few minutes later just in time to see my steak clenched in the jaws of a pine marten, who bounded away over the talus and streaked up a fifth class pitch beyond.

We never managed to live at High Camp for more than a week at a time—we would just spent too much of it zipped up against the cold and the slam-dancing wind until our lips cracked and we

Clyde on the Milk Bottle in 1931. Jules Eichorn photo

craved the gentleness of timberline, with its wind-bunched trees and a few blades of grass.

But legend had it that Norman Clyde did live up here, or at least stayed for long stretches when there was a Sierra Club basecamp below. A few climbers would come up each morning to do a high peak and then return; Clyde stayed high and guided every day. I wondered how he cooked in those days before stoves, until John Fischer found a pile of wood cached in a cave in the moraine. It was a huge pile, squirreled away well over a thousand feet above the highest trees. After Clyde died we hauled it out in sight of the peaks and had a big bonfire as a memorial.

***

For a while, several seasons in the wilderness, I awoke every day in one of those granite glades with the sunrising below me. A few of us did. Then, we lived the exact opposite of the weekend mountaineer's familiar routine, the slog to altitude, score, and frazzled retreat, all bracketed by endless hours of night driving. Instead, time was our basic commodity. Contemplation was far from a midweek footnote to weekend action. Rather, it became the fabric of our days, fully immersing them. We were awash in seasons. And without really trying to, we spawned the most prolific surge of new routes since Norman Clyde had been in residence. Day by day, though, we were more immediately captivated by the kaleidoscope of light and silence—and a few boulder problems just across the trail.

Mostly we would, as Han Shan the ancient mountain madman and early Zen Master said so well, "linger, watching things themselves." That's what separated us from those weekenders rushing headlong into the mountains. We had calmed down enough by absorbing mountain rhythms that we could actually manage to do the simplest of all things, to stand and stare.

So, to invoke a phrase that has become action's best parody, there I was: reading and writing, stretching and sweating, gazing, staring and spacing out, even startling the silence with shudders of delight, with whoops of laughter, and all the while risking total sunburn, when the morning would reach its significant juncture, the point at which my legs were numb and eyes had fondled an entire horizon of terrain in sixteen shades of light, and sweat had pooled in my navel.

I stood up.

It's an odd transition. Even though I've waited for the tingling to drain out of my legs (where does it go, till next time?), I am lurching and stiff, as if freshly hatched. That, however, lasts only a few steps. Rhythm returns. Moments later I'm dancing down the slabs and over gully stones into camp, quite barefoot and carrying a stack of grapefruit peels. That's the odd part: how swift and irrevocable is that shift from stillness into activity. There is ponderous inertia before, and gathering momentum after, so slight a change as getting to my feet.

Barely stopping to grab a peanut butter sandwich and PAs, I was gone bouldering. In this ice-scoured upper canyon, all our boulders were bedrock, and there were outcrops everywhere. Come to think of it, that made our choice of Third Lake for a vagabond climbing camp about as obvious as Camp 4 is to Yosemite: in the eye of the sunrise, convenient to the best climbing and furnished with the most entertaining bouldering right at hand.

By rattling the camp garbage cans that we used to store food I brought Tim Harrison up from fishing in the lake, so he picked up a rope and came along. Choices, choices. We headed across the main trail to a 30-foot granite edge and top-roped some cracks. Inevitably we ended up hours later at a particularly daunting set of flared grooves, and expended the last of our energy. Again without success. Years later, whenever I'd hear that question, the one that would be stupidly inane except that it is always so innocent, the question of "What was the hardest climb you ever did?," I would think again of those particular grooves. They kept the answer from being Ama Dablam, or the 25-pitch *Dark Star*, or some name-brand free climb in the Valley. By the time I finally got up the thing it was the end of one of those summers, 1971 I think, and I named it in honor and in fun of the breakthrough Yosemite free climb of the time. It's called *Few Dimensions*.

We often seemed to be looking over our shoulders at Yosemite as we played the naming game. *Monday Afternoon Slab*, for instance. Standing at the head of the lake, it was a particularly beautiful one-pitch slab of fine-grained dark granite like Temple Crag. Obviously inspired, the geologists had typecast this rock Inconsolable Granodiorite, naming it for a ridge bounding the canyon to the west that was easier for them to get on top of. Tim was especially at home on the slab, poised on micro flakes. He valued difficulty and scoured the canyon for more bouldering edges without bothering very often to climb the peaks. Tim Harrison was the happiest with subsistence living of anyone I had ever met. Hitchhiking everywhere, he would arrive at our Third Lake camp with his Kelty bulging full of rolled oats and whole wheat flour, ready to stay a month.

Tim was the consummate hitchhiker, as bold over the road as on the rocks. He once showed up at my winter cabin at Tom's Place with an eight-foot teardrop trailer someone had given him; he had literally "hitch"-hiked across the Mojave with a portable bumper hitch, and continued on to Yosemite. Another time he was working the tiedowns at the Santa Maria airport for a ride toward the Valley when the cops swooped in on him. It seems they mistook his pack for a parachute and decided Tim was a hijacker. Telling the story, Tim's long blond hair shook with laughter. He could not believe his

luck just to be in the Palisades, fishing for dinner. Having escaped from industrial South Pasadena, his heart opening onto a world of Granite. Sorry, granite—I'm forever capitalizing the thought of it. Tim proved to be a really talented face climber in Tuolumne, but it was only a couple of years later that a bolt failed in Yosemite Valley and he was gone. It was probably the hardest climb of its day on the Glacier Point Apron; friends named it *Anchors Away*, and left it unfinished in Tim's honor. I was left with an uncanny sense that some of Tim's energy had passed into me; I proudly bore an enhanced lightheartedness.

Tim Harrison

The other regular at the Third Lake camp was "crazy Lester" Robertson. A former motorcycle road racer who I met in the Haight-Ashbury, Lester would hunker down in the dust by the campfire, shake his head and wax pessimistic. The beauty of the Palisades always seemed to remind him of how much mankind was destroying. He was a good climber too, and together we first did the crux pitch of the Dark Star Buttress. Daunting at 5.10c, it opened up a wall that became the biggest climb of the era. The moves on that fine dark granite were reminiscent of Middle Cathedral Rock in Yosemite, with delicate small-hold climbing on steep faces (now they would be called slabs) alternating with bold cracks.

Others who came through from Yosemite to teach at the Palisades School of Mountaineering included Chuck Pratt, Chris Fredericks, and Steve Roper. I-hate-snow Pratt was a little out of his element in the alpine zone, but he treated it with his usual ironic humor and moved on to the Tetons, which at least offered the Moose Bar at the foot of the range. Fredericks got more enthralled with the alpine arts, and we did a fine new route together on the Thumb, but he didn't stay long either. Maybe it had something to do with meager pay for carrying a 117-pound load up to the Willow Lake camp in the South Fork, which caused Smoke Blanchard to quip that "Chris Fredericks is cheaper than a mule." Steve Roper loved this alpine climbing too. He came back to the Palisades for several years, climbed widely and contributed a new route or two, but several years after he left he seemed to have amnesia for the place. We were shocked when his "Climber's Guide To The High Sierra" came out to find that he had downrated many Palisades routes (and others like the *East Face* of Mt. Whitney) to a uniform 5.4, and that the *Dark Star* was a horrendously sandbagging 5.7, and had mysteriously sprouted some aid. Guidebooks were just a living, I guess, while Roper's literary editing at "Ascent" reflected more of his passion.

Venturing out of the Palisades in July and August of 1969, Roper and I and Jim Sims took a classic road trip together, traveling an arc of glaciated peaks from Oregon clear on up to the Canadian Rockies. Actually we began by aiming even beyond there, setting out to make the second ascent of the Lotus Flower Tower, which is nearly on the Arctic Circle in the Northwest Territories. After pounding up the Alaska Highway and driving another 200 miles on a side road to the Cantung tungsten mine, we had hoped to hitch a ride on the prospecting helicopter and jump over the remaining 35 miles of grizzly- and brush-filled wilderness to get set down in Fairy Meadow.

That was the plan, but at the roadhead early in August it began to rain. Fortunately there was a hot spring nearby, so we jumped in to wait it out. The rain turned to slushy snow—even at 3000 feet, down in that northern forest of trees as thin as toothpicks. Three days later it was still coming down and we had turned to prunes. We went up to the mine and asked around. "Well..." drawled one of the locals, "winter doesn't usually start up here until—oh, maybe the first week of September. Guess it's early this year..." We drove back down to the Canadian Rockies and in the next two weeks managed to squeeze one and a half climbs into gaps in the wall of weather. Mostly we sat in pubs getting fat on cheap beer and writing forlorn postcards. Finally I bailed. Roper dropped me in the freight yards at Golden, British Columbia, to begin wending my way south toward the sun, a trip that included the surprise of a psychedelic afternoon in a North Cascades fire lookout.

It was the locals from Bishop who lingered in the Palisades, added significantly to the climbing and helped fuel the scene that started to convene as early as the beginning of May. Gordon Wiltsie and Jay Jensen were still in high school when they began hanging out in the canyon. Gordon's parents actually sent him to the climbing school one summer, a move I've often wondered if they doubted later as he befriended the transplanted hippies and became a guide, then a mountain photographer. Gordon has now been to both the North and South Poles and displayed a lot of fine work in *National Geographic.* Jay Jensen, who accompanied me on the first grade IV and V climbs to be done clean in Yosemite, gave up guiding for a real job and a real family. Busy as a contractor and working the "rolling J" ranch, he still finds time to go with Gordon as a ski model, so we get used to seeing him in photos from the Alps or Spitzbergen. And once, for a few months, Jay's face stared down from billboards wherever we went, advertising "Real" cigarettes.

Gordon Wiltsie puts down the camera to do some bouldering.

John Fischer wasn't a local at all, but another transplant like me. John had been my first climbing partner, beginning in the late fifties. When in the early sixties I walked 150 miles of Sierra crest to Yosemite to rendezvous for one climb, it was with John, and we tried again to get up the *South Face* of Rixons Pinnacle. And failed again. We had climbed off and on in the Valley with our old three-strand Goldline ropes and klunky mountain boots, but more often we were up in the high country. I remember one trip before we were out of high school. We went to Cathedral Peak with a Sierra Club party, and were very disappointed when the leader warned us away from the classic *Southeast Buttress.* Years later when I finally did the climb I realized that it would have been perfect for us that day—all we could handle but with ultimate success, and saw that what had prevented us was more the leader's ego (the buttress was tough for him) than our fledgling ability. That experience has influenced my guiding ever since. And guiding, after all, occupied the eight or ten-week heart of every Palisades summer for well over a decade. I pushed one student after another way beyond their perception of their limits, so they returned to the basecamp staggering with exhaustion, but left the canyon with a considerably expanded horizon of potential.

Climbing students who are treated well—with sensitivity toward their feelings of vulnerability, a dose of respect for their flatland lives (which are usually very interesting), and a nudge of that gentle sandbagging—often develop a fierce devotion to their guide. It happens all the time. In some ways it is not unlike the 'imprinting' that baby ducks demonstrate toward humans in psychology experiments, which isn't to take anything away from the sincerity of the attachment. I have been shuttled to mountain ranges all over the west, and treated to more than one ticket to Europe, on the strength of such relationships. And I have made a number of lifelong friends.

Later, John Fischer bought the Palisades School of Mountaineering, and things shifted. He began to act as if the students who came to the school somehow belonged to him, even in the face of their growing attachment to whoever actually guided them. It's a common enough feeling among the directors of climbing schools. For awhile I continued to be enthusiastic, recommending the school in one of the first issues of *Outside* magazine. But when I showed up in the canyon in the summer of 1978 privately guiding some of "his" former students, John attacked. The next thing I knew I had a federal warrant for guiding without a permit (true enough), and had become his prime example of the "rogue guides" who he felt were ruining the business. The clients still seemed to love it, but my relationship with my old partner John has cooled off ever since.

The trail up into the Palisades climbs singlemindedly from a sage brush roadhead, barely branching. Yet it is full of intersections. Like crossing avalanche paths, for instance. And here and there a faint trace veers off that might be an animal trail except that too many boulders are pushed aside. We follow, and discover that this was an earlier version of the canyon trail. Delighted, we come to see that the trail is fairly braided with its former selves. Time thickens. And of course there are human intersections.

Saturday morning, school's out. We emerge from camps tucked away in the rocks and turn downstream—and startle to find weekend climbers ascending. We'd exchange with them anything from a smile to a complete topo for the *Swiss Arete*. Soon we're running, flat out with only laundry on our backs and already anticipating the hot springs.

Hikers and fishermen gasping and shuffling upward, would be staring at the dust before them. We'd come pounding around a switch back, suddenly upon them, and ricochet off the embankment or tap over trailside talus without breaking stride. We're past by the time they notice. Trying to see the encounter from their point of view, I think—with only a hint of pretension--of Thoreau's feeling that "we need to see life freely pasturing where we fear to wander." Strong boys, running wild; we could get carried away with our mastery of this terrain except for one liberating fact: that only absolute attention moment by moment stands between this rush of freedom and broken ankles.

We too crave that example of life freely pasturing. We devour the flight of hawks, the legends of wild mountain men and great climbers, the humanity of poets.

I had an odd intersection coming back up the trail once too. It was early in the season, no one around yet, so when it got hot on the hike in I took off all my clothes and just kept walking. I was carrying the boom box up to camp, strapped on top of my pack with the Rolling Stones playing, pushing uphill on auto pilot, sweat dripping into the dust, when around a switch back I met a couple of fishermen coming downhill. I don't know which of us was more startled, but I just kept on truckin' uphill, and as I passed them Mick Jagger was singing *Sympathy for the Devil:* "Please allow me to introduce myself ...."

You could mark the years passing by our campsites. Not their content, which stayed the same, but their location.

We started out camping in the most obvious places, like a few steps off the trail just after it comes in view of Third Lake, in a spot that was thoroughly trampled long before any of us ever saw it. But as we got to know the canyon our camps filtered into gaps in the long dike of bedrock that dammed the lake; we lodged like so much flotsam into sandy corners out of the wind but full in the view.

Rarely did anyone else happen across those spots. But once, early in the season when I had left footprints in a snowdrift that covered the shortcut up from the trail, I was shocked to return after a two-day shopping trip to town to find my tent stripped. Gone was a healthy backpack-load of expensive ropes and climbing hardware. I was crushed. There was no way to replace all that climbing gear at the dirt-poor end of the season before the climbing

Mount Sill

school paychecks started rolling out. And this was when we had time for new routes. They had left the box of books, but taken my irreplaceable journals. The next day Tom Frost arrived, and oddly he had news. He had run into people coming down the trail carrying some familiar-looking gear—mine. I was amazed all over again to have it back, even if I did have to carry the hardware up from the roadhead twice that spring.

A few years later the High Camp hut that Don and I had built blew away on a scouring spring gale. As snow melted out through the summer, we kept finding the twisted and splintered remains clear down the gully as far as Third Lake. With respect for the new Wilderness Law it was never replaced. With the hut gone and the school shut down, remaining relics of our buoyant era are few, subtle, and even more widely scattered across the Palisades. The climbs are clean, free from bolts and pin scars, and not repeated often enough now to wear a trail across the lichen. But a knowing eye will gradually tune-in to rappel points that Don Jensen had sculpted with blows from his heavy north-wall hammer, or a rounded spot just where your rope would pass over an otherwise cord-slicing edge.

We thought, just assumed, that the Third Lake camp would reconvene every summer. But granite has fallen out of fashion. Wilderness too. Sport climbers dismiss the merely vertical as slab climbing. As it becomes socially acceptable and even flirts with mainstream America, climbing has lost some of its introspective tone, and huddles along the roadside ignoring the horizon.

A Night on the Ground, a Day in the Open

Life hurtles onward. But those sandy timberline corners in the eye of the sunrise, the upstanding blocks and blades of lichen-spattered granite, even the bright sky filled more with light than air are very patient. They await without judgment a shift in culture, a dislocation of civilization itself, or just a few bright souls who want again more than moves from their climbing.

All That Evolving

Poems from the Palisades Notebooks

Only a few of these poems have been published before. Perhaps because they are so simple—simple to the point of transparency—they seem a product of mind gone wild at the time they were written. So I was not too surprised when Mike Moore once returned a batch of them while he was the editor of *Mountain Gazette.* Since we were friends I wrote back, struggling to explain that: "I agree that the poems are not very 'strong.' I dislike emphatic writing so I prune mine until sometimes it gets too dense and a little bleached out. The poems are mostly spontaneous products of extremely simple states of mind, so are perhaps most viable in the wild context from which they arose. It seems to me that a lot of wilderness thought/feeling is simple and subtle enough to feel flat in civilized context..."

With all that evolving spread out behind us
We dance this frost fall morning away
On the sunward sides
Of granite boulders

June storm retreat from the Palisades:
Manzanita blossoms in the near wet dusk.

If you are more at home
In the mountains than anywhere
You are a mountaineer.
No climbing is required.
Being among the peaks
It will arise spontaneously
With no other motive
Or justification
Than itself.
To be a mountaineer
Is first to love the mountains
Then to climb them.
Technique
Can never replace
Devotion.

Stuck in the city again:
Too crazy to write a poem.

Stone down
boulder running
Falling light
Slab sailing
Wind building
Rock freckle darking
Cloud pushed star dying
Dark
    Light
    Random rain
    High dark South wind sailors
    Morning sleep
    Rain wake
    Heather clump back nestle
    Cool fresh face rain
    Short burst of sun warm
    In a week you will be home

Doug Robinson

Kristen Jacobsen

On the best of days
A clean animal
Running down streams of white light
Through the clear wilderness

These high mountain days
Emerging from music into dance,
Re-merging to rhythm.
Not a thought.

Bruce Robinson photo

A Night on the Ground, a Day in the Open

At Home in the High Sierra

Ice Nine

In 1977 I was catapulted abruptly into the literary fast
lane. Not that I had a breakthrough in writing style, but I defi-
nitely got a break. I had been holed up in my Rock Creek
cabin, tinkering with paragraphs in between guiding jobs, when
a letter arrived from William Randolph Hearst III, saying that
he had enjoyed my work and asking if I would write for his
new magazine, *Outside*. I went to San Francisco to check it out,
and ended up staying a year. Suddenly I was working and party-
ing alongside Tim Cahill and Rob Schultheis. The entire staff
played together as hard as they worked. Will Hearst was the
managing editor, and we did some climbing and ski touring between issues. Once we snuck into the Sespe Condor Refuge together for the treat of glimpsing what Will called "the Turkey
Vultures of the Pleistocene" soaring on the wing. Just as quietly, he helped support the desperate effort to save the birds.
Brilliant and always a bit bemused, Will read from the fron-
tiers of physics to relax.

Terry McDonell was *Outside's* first editor. Terry was the finest editor I've ever worked for, truly helping me to voice what I
was struggling to say. I went pub crawling over the hills of San
Francisco on the back of his motorcycle, and I will ever be
amazed at Terry's halfback frame coiled up into the back seat
of my Honda Civic for the 300-mile drive to the Rock Creek
cabin for weekends. Terry's gold rush novel, "California Blood-
stock," which was partly written in Rock Creek, has become a
cult classic. He turned me on to the brilliant stylists Thomas
McGuane and Jim Harrison, and I still read those two over
and over, trying to see how they go about what they do so well.
Their friend Russell Chatham, the Montana painter, sometimes
came by on his way to go fly fishing on the Russian River.
Terry went on to become the editor of *Esquire*.

I became romantically involved with Outside's energetic office manager Jodi Hoffman, a relationship that outlived the magazine's tenure in San Francisco. After running the magazine all day, Jodi would invite the staff over to her Russian Hill flat for a dinner that usually stretched into a long evening and would finally come full circle to books and notebooks littering the dining room table. Jodi presided over these literary brawls while calmly painting watercolors at the head of the table.

Back in Rock Creek I had started writing about that summer's new ice climb. Dale Bard and I were calling it *Ice Nine*, after a mythical substance Kurt Vonnegut had teased out into the world, a single crystal of which would freeze anything—a warm puddle, the Pacific... We reckoned it was the hardest of the slippery alpine climbs yet done in the Sierra. The unfinished article came in handy when *Outside* devoted its third issue to ice climbing. "Chouinard on Ice" announced the cover head, and it included some of the book I had helped Yvon to write. Jann Wenner, the founder of *Rolling Stone* who had the foresight to start *Outside* even though he knew nothing about the outdoors, had never heard of Chouinard. Jann looked at that cover and said, "What? Is he dead?"

Taken in the grand scheme of the Sierra, Mount Mendel isn't much. Seen from the John Muir Trail to the southwest, the view most people get of it, Mendel seems not so much a peak as a mere rubbly ridge leading off of Mount Darwin. You have to be a bit of a rambler to get far enough off the trail to even see the north side of Mendel, the side which, as with most Sierra peaks, is its steep, glacier cut, cirque walled side. Its interesting side.

There you will find the relatively small and underwhelming old fossil of the Mendel Glacier with the obligatory bergschrund running along its upper edge to separate it from the stationary ice sheet that feeds it from above. The ice sheet, with its covering of snow, looks at first like nothing more than a snowfield, but it goes up and up—it's huge. And it gets steeper all the way. Slowly at first, but inexorably, the angle tilts until it becomes a perfect parabolic fiend, rising to merge into a ragged band of granite cliffs that run toward the vertical to meet the jagged blue edge of the sky.

Mt. Mendel. Ice Nine and Righthand Mendel Couloir

But the sky is not the only blue punctuating the upper granite bands. There is a translucent blue ribbon running through them from the upper right edge of the great ice sheet. It is a gully, set back into the broken cliff face, and in the bed of this gully, in its cooler, deeper shade, a ribbon of steeper ice runs nearly to the crest of the ridge. It is almost a hundred feet wide and it comes down in two great smooth rolls. This is the right hand Mendel Couloir, an estimable piece of ice, its upper bulges sweeping toward 65 degrees. It is considered the classic ice climb in the Sierra. Certainly it is the longest, and it is steeper than most.

I had been making hesitations and starts toward Mendel since 1967. I had failed to rendezvous with climbing partners at its base, skied by it with friends and once even buzzed the summit in a light plane. Finally, climbing with Dale Bard in June 1976, I was going to put a crampon to it.

But surveying the climb from Lamarck Col, about a mile away, my eyes kept straying from the Mendel Couloir to a ribbon of ice on the granite, some distance to the left of the gully. In the half dozen or so times I'd stood on this spot, I'd never seen ice there before. It was a runnel so thin that it didn't live in the gully, but just hung frozen to the granite wall.

Because of our vantage, the bottom few meters of this intriguing runnel were coyly hidden from view...if they were there at all. Still, climbing plans were changing fast in a hopeful imagination.

My toes were cold again. But as I shuffled back and forth from one foot to the other, I was barely aware of them. I was too intent upon Dale's toes ten feet above me. I could see only the soles of his boots, 20 crampon

Doug Robinson

points hanging straight down toward me. I'd done it again. For the second time that day I'd ended up belaying under one of the steepest ice bulges. My scalp shuddered.

Dale was acutely conscious of his toes, poised an inch off the ice on the two remaining points of each crampon. The horizontal front points beaked gently downward to lodge less than a quarter inch into the ice; it is on these that Dale's weight was delicately suspended. Dale was thinking about his heels, too, hanging out there in the breeze. He kept them low, relaxed and steady, his calves long and loose, so they wouldn't cramp up into "sewing machine leg," which could knock his front points out of the ice. His ice hammer kept him clawed to the bulge. He was also resisting the temptation to overreach toward a too high hold, a move which could break out the brittle ice that supported his toes. He wasn't saying much as he moved up. He grabbed

his right mitten in his teeth; his short ice axe remained in a belt holster while his bare hand slid into a crack running up the wall on his right. The crack would put the ease to this ice bulge if only it weren't covered inside and out by more ice, a thin layer of ice seductively close to invisible and not thick enough to take the pick of his ax without breaking away from the rock. Bare flesh slid knowingly in the icy slot until, with rock climber's craft, it jammed enough to maintain balance. Now his attention slid over to the ice hammer in his left hand. He began rocking it up and down to free its hooked grip, buried half

Dale Bard bouldering under Mt. Whitney

an inch into the ice. Up to the left, an arm's reach over the lip of the bulge, the ice narrowed to a column eight inches wide, two inches thick, and frozen tightly to the speckled granite. He aimed there, and swung the hammer over his head, guiding the pick with measured force. Crack! Just hard enough to hold—hammer to ice, ice on the wall. Now back to the toes. One foot at a time, eight inches up the wall, smooth kick to lodge, holding him in delicate balance. His right hand shot up to an ample grip on rock. A long exhaled sigh, a graceful two step up, and Dale was quietly panting on the top of the bulge.

"That would be 5.10 if it were rock."

"What's it like above?"

"Easy for a ways, a whole pitch, then blue ice again, getting narrower and steeper, maybe 70 degrees, turning into sort of a chimney. I can't see above that."

In a rock climbers' decimal estimation, 5.10 indicates the relative degree of resistance to ascent offered by a stretch of rock, to be overcome only by a corresponding subtlety of technique. Five-ten is the beginning of the extreme grades in rock climbing, accessible only to those who will refine their mental balance while training their technique.

In his early 20s, Dale Bard is a master (a "Stone Master" by the legend on his T shirt) of the extreme grades that now push through 5.11 to scratch with fingernail holds on the definition of the unknown at 5.12. Legend has it that Dale, when asked what he thought of a mere 5.10 climb in Yosemite, replied "It was casual."

But Dale's stone mastery lives in a fleeting world where a climbing generation succumbs to natural selection every two or three years. Already, the keen younger climbers have been perfecting the forefinger pull-up in camp and walking the slack chain to hone their balance, while Dale's generation has been taking its place at the local bar to down a pint and tell a tale. The newcomers are breathing their fierce yogurt breath at his heels, and Dale is beginning to show a gentlemanly interest in old fashioned mountaineering.

Beyond 30 myself, yet still climbing—an anachronism from a bygone generation to be patronized in Yosemite's Mountain Room Bar—I was a bit taken aback to hear the ice bulge categorized with a decimal rating. My own generation had described its ice in terms of steepness and quality underfoot (its brittleness and hardness resolved into color gradings from white ice to blue and green and, finally, black ice). We refused to affix numbers to a medium that seemed to vary too much from one ascent to the next to be compared decimally. But I didn't mention this to Dale.

To the new climber it often seems that the generation then at the height of its powers has put the final capstone on the limits of creative climbing. So it had seemed to me when I arrived in Yosemite Valley in the early sixties to find a "golden age" of big wall climbing reaching its full maturity. Chuck Pratt, Tom Frost, Royal Robbins and Joe Fitschen had, in

1960, made the first continuous ascent of El Capitan, leaving the ground with everything they would need to get them over the top seven days later. Robbins was developing a technique that Warren Harding would later call "vertical freight handling"—getting the food, water and sleeping bags up the wall behind you. At the same time, Yvon Chouinard was refining the design of the alloy pitons that became the key to narrow and shallow cracks; already he was beginning to assume his role as innovative toolmaker to American mountaineering. With improved technique and technology, the fear of flaming out high on a sun eaten wall gradually subsided. In 1964, with Chouinard replacing Fitschen, the same team concluded its own era with a successful ascent of the fiercely steep and unrelenting North America Wall.

But while the big wall era was ending, wavelets of the future were already lapping at the foot of hard free climbs. Indeed, Pratt introduced the 5.10 era in 1961 with his unaided climb of the gently overhanging Crack of Doom, an event which shocked and amazed them all. "What!" asked Shakespeare, "Will the line stretch out to the crack of doom?"

Today... well, the latest on rock is likely to be an improbable combination of knuckle jams and microflake footholds 80 feet up a thin crack to the non-summit of a three inch ledge just left of blank space, gained only to rappel quickly back to the bar—a full day's work for the few who would even attempt it.

While American climbers were shifting from big walls to the free and unlikely acrobatics of the new "rock stars," something like an aside was taking place off the rock, on ice. And this quiet arrival of ice climbing had a lot to do with Yvon Chouinard, and not a little to do with Mount Mendel. Chouinard had wandered into the French Alps and returned with a keen interest in ice climbing...as an alternative to rock, as something to do in the winter. He had brought back with him the fabled "French method" of flat footed cramponing. And, always the toolmaker, he returned with a new design for an ice axe. To the eye, his new axe looked pretty much like the old one. All he had done was to curve the pick a little more sharply and add a few small teeth along its bottom. But this simple refinement made the axe stick so much more securely in the ice that it sparked a revolution in ice climbing.

The effect of the new ice axe was comparable to the introduction of the crampon for the feet, way back around the turn of the century.

Mount Mendel became a proving ground for Chouinard during this period, and it was after losing a battle with the couloir that he returned to his

Ventura forge and emerged with yet another ice climbing innovation, the Alpine Hammer.

With the new tools, it was now possible to free climb a brittle, water ice overhang, as Dale Bard and I had amazed ourselves by doing.

But Dale and I were now far to the left of the Mendel Couloir. The ice tongue had faltered, ducked around a corner and become a mere frozen rivulet on the wall before disappearing over a ten foot overhang. It had taken us nearly an hour to discover that there was ice above...that we had a climb. We had found Ice Nine.

Ice Nine — In the upper ice chimney

Two hours later, we were standing above the second overhang.

"Your lead," said Dale

I started up the ice chimney. It began wide and gentle, but as it got steeper the walls closed in until it became almost claustrophobic. There was no room to swing an axe. I tapped at the ice, trying to plant my hammer. The chimney closed in behind me. I had my back against the wall—but that helped me through the steep bit. The angle eased, revealing the summit just above.

Ice Nine had proved to be the most difficult ice climb yet done in the Sierra.

Later, Bard told Chouinard about Ice Nine, and the next summer Yvon and I made plans to climb it. I knew that in full-on drought, the Palisade Glacier and its cluster of gullies had been melting, but I hadn't had the time to hike in and check the conditions on Mendel. Then, in late August, I ran into Dale in the Tom's Place bar. "Ho, maaan," he said when he spotted me. "There's a big stripe melted out clear across the gully . . . Ice Nine is gone."

POSTSCRIPT: Publicity in *Outside* gave Ice Nine a reputation, and ever since then, whenever people can catch it in shape, it has been climbed several times a summer. If you too dream of going up there, here is a tip on timing. Commitment backed by major effort, like a 5000-foot climb over 13,000 foot Lamarck Col, are required to even get a glimpse of whether the ephemeral ice runnel is formed up. For the best chance of catching it in shape, the hot tip is to go early in the season. Don't wait for traditional ice time, but go during June or into July.

Ice Nine and the rocky trace leading over Lamarck Col to its base can handle any amount of climber traffic they attract. Remoteness and effort are potent antidotes to popularity. But since this piece was written, and as *Outside* has grown, a concern has emerged about damage to fragile environments from the hot focus of publicity, especially, it seems, in *Outside*. In 1991 the magazine had reached a circulation of 400,00, with a pass-on readership over a million. That summer they pinpointed an obscure but lovely rockbound lake in the Wind River Range as an idyllic backpacking destination. Now the Winds are further than a weekend from every population center but Salt Lake City, and the lake's new stardom was guarded by thirty miles of dirt road, a wilderness boundary, and eight miles of uphill trail. Still, the glossy allure pulled 10,000 extra visitors the following summer, according to a survey of the trailhead register by the brilliant wilderness writer C. L. Rawlins, then working for Bridger-Teton National Forest.

Meanwhile, the reputation of Ice Nine has spread. A steady stream of climbers keeps showing up, pilgrims as well as one eastern Sierra local, Dean Hobbs, who prefers solitude and anonymity but has made the one-day round trip to solo Ice Nine nearly every year. It is still considered to be the hardest alpine ice route in the Sierra, and in 1993 it was included among a hundred "Sierra Classics" Selected by Claude Fiddler and John Moynier.

But there has always been a lingering question about the climb. "Sierra Classics" put it this way: "Ice Nine had always been one of those routes shrouded by an aura of mystery. Was it a separate climb?"

I had long been uncertain myself. My doubt stemmed from another climb, the Left-hand Mendel couloir, which was somewhere on the wall nearby. Michael Cohen and Roy Bishop had climbed it first in 1967. Comparing the scant guidebook description with views of the face in varying seasons, I concluded that the Left-hand Couloir sounded like a dry chimney in the granite headwall, and not too hard. But where was it? There was a chimney-like recess right of Ice Nine, between it and the well-known Right-hand Mendel couloir, which I had always assumed to be "Mendel Left." It rose from about the top center of the sweeping snow/ice apron that gave entry to the face.

In 1993 I ran into Michael Cohen, and his recollections clinched it: Ice Nine and Mendel Left are the same line. The only difference is that he and Bishop had traversed in from the right, above where we found both crux overhangs. That lower section had been dry for them, and they bypassed it on easy rock. They did the first ascent of the cramped upper chimneys, an extraordinary piece of climbing in floppy boots with hinged crampons, and before the advent of drooped-pick ice axes. We were lucky enough to find ice all the way through, and so we were able to make the first continuous ice ascent of the most direct line.

The Pinheads Meet the Yo-Yos

Norman Clyde pointed me toward Rock Creek Canyon.
The details of that story have been told in *Wanderers of the
Range of Light,* but the essence is that I loved listening to
Clyde's opinionated yarns and along the way he announced flatly
that Rock Creek Canyon was the finest skiing on the eastern side
of the Sierra. I moved right in, and lived up there most winters
for a decade, guiding ski trips out of Rock Creek Winter Lodge.
Daily life in the canyon offered a convenient framework for this
article for the *L.A. Times Magazine,* a chance to span both downhill and backcountry skiing.

Dawn light wakes me as always up here, a hot flash of color
radiating into the loft window off the upper snowfields of Pointless Peak. The
cold seeping off the glass sends me burrowing back under the down quilt, but
just for a moment. Today I'm headed for the downhill slopes at Mammoth,
but there will be plenty of skiing just to get there from this cabin, snowed in
five miles from Rock Creek Road. Halfway down the loft ladder, my breath
goes visible. I drop straight into moon boots, grab a down jacket off its peg
and hurry to lay a fire in the wood stove. Just minutes old and still far short
of coffee, this morning already echoes many of the feelings that made ski trips
special back when I was a kid and commuting to them from the city.

I hadn't even heard of cross-country then; now it is the only life.
Living back here for a good part of the winter, the best part of the year, I'm
rewarded with direct access to the wildest season in the mountains. Most days
I turn out the cabin door to go up-canyon and ski in the lonely, high bowls
tucked under the crest of the Sierra. But today it's submit to gravity and the
allure of Mammoth Mountain, 20 miles to the north. The downhill skiers
call us pinheads after our flimsy-looking "three-pin" Nordic bindings; we joke
back about their realm being yo-yo skiing, their slopes mere practice hills for
a wilderness of mountains. But we go to Mammoth anyway, for the sheer joy

Doug Robinson. Photo by Helen Robinson

of vertical miles on perfectly groomed runs, free of avalanches. And we seem to go back nearly every week, commuting on skis to ski.

By the time coffee is ready, my leather ski boots have warmed enough on the stove door for a coat of Sno-Seal. They look a lot like the old square-toed lace-ups that I began skiing 30 years ago. The best of today's boots for skiing downhill on cross-country skis sport a little extra stiffness here and there, or perhaps a buckle over the instep. And some manu-facturers are flirting with plastic. All of which leads to jokes about the reinvention of downhill skiing. That's fair; yet the gear remains an odd mixture of traditional and high tech, leather boots and fiberglass skis.

Outside, it's still quite brisk at 10,000 feet: 20 degrees Fahrenheit. I skate across Rock Creek Lake and lock skis into the twin grooves that form the Nordic track heading down the snowed-over road. For the novice, the track is like being on rails; for the racer it's a license to speed. The hardest fall I took last winter was blowing out of these tracks on the last sweeping curve before Rock Creek Road.

Halfway down, I break my tuck, throw out a snowplow and bank over the bridge to pull up panting in front of Rock Creek Winter Lodge. The staff there enjoys being snowbound as much as their guests from the city, who ride a Sno-Cat up from the highway. They are cross-country ski bums—a new breed.

"Anyone want to go ski Mammoth?"

Marty Hornick does. Marty has worked at the lodge six winters, splitting firewood and setting ski tracks. Summers he ranges the backcountry for the Forest Service as captain of a trail crew. He is incredibly fit and is the local master of a new game that is emerging up here—a cross between Nordic racing and ski mountaineering. It is 21 miles from here to Mammoth Mountain as the crow flies. But no crow would choose that line, which crisscrosses Sierra ridges and weaves among 13,000 foot peaks. On the ground, it is easily more than 40 miles; I have spent several days skiing it and snow-camping along the way. Three years ago, Marty surprised everyone by skiing it with his friend, Rich May in 13 hours. Last spring he lowered it to 8:37, alone. Today will be easier; we'll ski two more miles to the highway and drive. But Marty's presence guarantees a challenging time of diving off the corniced summit of Mammoth on metal-edged cross country skis.

Marty Hornick

At Toms Place, Rock Creek Road comes abruptly onto the four lanes of U.S. 395, easing out into the mainstream of skiers headed for Mammoth. There's an expectant air among those robot-walking across the parking lot in plastic boots. Even the lift operators seem to share it, asking, "How's the snow?" We'll soon see.

A ride up the lift gradually reveals scenery unrivaled this side of the Alps. To the west, the Minarets form a spiky skyline. To the North, a string of volcanic cones marches into Mono Lake, slowly drying up in the winter sunshine. The view of the White Mountains to the east will come into its own in the afternoon sun. Southward from the summit, the Sierra stretches away forever, a horizon littered with peaks. It amazes me that non-skiers so rarely take advantage of this view. Forget the sun deck; buy a gondola round trip to the summit and bring a warm jacket. There isn't a vista like this from the top of Aspen or Alta or Sun Valley or Squaw. Someday this place will become the international resort that its setting and snow deserve.

"Look at them yo-yos—that's the way you do it." Marty grins, borrowing the line from Dire Straits, and tips over into Climax gully in perfect imitation of the downhill skiers. The regulars here ceased years ago to be amazed at telemarking, the traditional Norwegian ski turn revived by Americans during the '70s. As Marty winds his way rhythmically down this expert run off the top of Mammoth, anyone would think from a little distance that he was on downhill skis. His parallel technique is that smooth.

Back in the lift line, it's quickly evident that we aren't the only ones having a good time. People are warming up, shaking out; amid the stomp and shuffle, strangers occasionally lock eyes and smile, united in the Brotherhood of the Burning Thighs. We're not that different from a gang of kids playing on plastic cafeteria trays, all anxious to get back up so they can slide down again.

All of a sudden, it seems, the light is drawing sideways and the snow is icing up. When half the afternoon can disappear unnoticed, you know you've been having fun. Time to blow off the last run and go in. If you're skiing well, you don't need it anyway. Racers, skiing the best of all, are often on the snow only three or four hours of the day. Pressing into each turn for a clean carve, that's all the skiing they can take. Skis clatter down St. Anton's to the lodge. We slip out of the parking lot ahead of the traffic.

It's harder to pass on the cold margaritas and hot salsa at Las Montañas in town. At this weary end of the day, one could almost envy those with but a short trip across town into a steaming hot tub. Some days I make it down to the freeway in time to watch the light slide from gold to rose on Boundary Peak in the White Mountains off to the east. Its spectacular, serrated face runs thousands of feet right up to the highest point in Nevada and has never been skied. It would require a full and stable snowpack in the spring to even consider it, and two days of bushwhacking to get to the top. And then the avalanche conditions might turn you away. That kind of ski mountaineering would require at least as much patience and caution as sheer skiing ability. Nonetheless, it makes a persistent twilight dream on the southern road.

Back at the Rock Creek roadhead, it's dark. Slot into those rails; they know the way home. Touring wax grips nicely as the temperature drops. After half a mile we're unzipping jackets. Thighs that had complained at the lifts work out again, only now they get a stretch at the end of every stride. Soon

The legendary Elderberry Canyon, 5000 ft. down Mt. Tom

enough they have put away the two miles up to Rock Creek Winter Lodge, just in time for the second seating of dinner.

Platters of herb chicken are passed down the long wooden tables, followed by baskets of homemade rolls. Ski talk flows with the wine. One couple had skied all the way to Long Lake, not quite believing that they could make the 12-mile round trip their third day on skis. Others had taken a telemark lesson that morning and were surprised to find that they, too, could ski parallel on skinny skis. Their instructors, John Moynier and Dion Goldsworthy, had sneaked off for the afternoon into the steep woods, where they knew that powder would be lingering even 10 days after the last storm. They laugh about luring one another off cliffs in the forest—a sandbag game with the loser giving the evening slide show.

It seems like midnight as I crawl back onto the snow one last time, pacing uphill in the starlight to rattle in the cabin door and stoke up the fire.

There won't be any question of skiing like this again tomorrow, but one of the best things about such an exhausting day is that the next morning I'm really ready to sit still and write. As the stove crackles to life, I back my chair up to it and sink into the seat. Preferring not to light a lamp, I'd rather scan for a glimpse over the Sierra crest of that snowball in space, Halley's comet, pulling away for another lap around the solar system.

Climbing with Style

Technology is imposed on the land, but technique means conforming to the landscape. They work in opposite directions, one forcing a passage while the other discovers it. The goal of developing technique is to conform to the most improbable landscape by means of the greatest degree of skill and boldness supported by the least equipment.

Gordon Wiltsie photo

Doug Robinson

The Whole Natural Art of Protection

In 1967 Royal Robbins returned from climbing in Britain with a new tool and a new game. The tool was nuts, the game clean climbing. Five years later my article *The Whole Natural Art of Protection* appeared in the first real catalog of the Chouinard Equipment Company. That article is often credited with carrying off the Clean Climbing revolution. There is no doubt that it slam-dunked the endgame, but many interesting events bridged Royal's trip to Britain to that Catalog, and the highlights are worth retelling before we get to that piece.

Returning from England, Royal and his wife Liz quickly climbed *Nutcracker,* which was the first time a route had been led clean on its first ascent in Yosemite—probably in the whole country—and he wrote a short piece about it in Summit. I was hooked. I filed the threads out of a size-range of brass machine nuts and took them up to the Palisades, where I had begun guiding the summer before. High Sierra rock fractures into a perfect medium for nuts and runners, so by 1969 I had converted the rest of the guides and we were doing first ascents, first clean ascents, and most of our guided climbs without carrying hammers.

Offseason we went to Yosemite and took along our new clean tools, which by then included a few British nuts like the highly prized brass hex from Clog—the first nut any of us had seen that was so small it had to be slung on a loop of swaged aircraft cable—and a sandcast MOAC that is still on my rack. Yosemite's smooth and often flaring cracks made climbing clean a more daunting proposition, and we prudently carried hammers on most of our climbs a while longer. But confidence built until in 1971 Jay Jensen and I climbed hammerless up the East Buttress of Middle Cathedral Rock, the Valley's first clean grade IV. The next summer we pushed it further, up to a grade V on the Steck-Salathe on Sentinel Rock. The clean crux was running it out from small wires on the friction headwall. Still, no one else paid much attention, except in the Palisades and Ventura.

Ventura is a long ways from Yosemite and the high Sierra, but it was already becoming a stop on the fledgling California climbing circuit. It seems that Yvon Chouinard's true favorite sport was, and still is, surfing. So in the late sixties and early seventies the Chouinard Equipment Company, which was nearly in sight of several of California's finest surf breaks, dragged a major focus of the developing front of climbing style right out of the mountains and plopped it down among the unlikely surroundings of oil derricks and palm trees. Chouinard's surfer soul had brought a focal point of the evolution of climbing down to the beach. So naturally along came climbing's latest development, the clean revolution. Chouinard Equipment was prospering, beginning to outgrow its original tin shed, and it was pretty common to see Jim Bridwell or Dennis Hennek crawl out of an old van in the courtyard on a foggy morning, and fuel up with breakfast at the Vagabond before firing up the forge to make pitons.

On Friday afternoons the company van would unload its last batch of heat treating and we would pile in climbing gear, clip a hammock diagonally inside the back, and party and talk climbing for the long moonlight ride across the Mojave and up to the eastern Sierra. Depending on the season we might do a new ice route in Lee Vining Canyon, rock on Cardinal Pinna-

Chouinard Equipment factory. Tom Frost photos

cle, or head on up to the crest to test ice screws. Tom Frost and I tried each successive generation of our evolving design for Stopper nuts in the Buttermilk. I was pleased with our design, but almost more excited to bag the prize of naming them too. There was more intense competition to name products than first ascents in a company that was rolling out such labels as the "climaxe." Meanwhile, Yvon was pushing the Hexcentric nut shape. Later I turned an old idea of my dad's—he had done his thesis for a degree in aeronautical engineering on the strength of monocoque construction (tube shapes) for the fuse-lages of airplanes—into the design for Tube Chocks to protect the offwidth cracks that were then at the cutting edge of free climbing. Those tools were my first foray into equipment design, but far from my last.

Tom Frost on Cardinal Pinnacle

Tom Frost was a real design partner for me in those years, even more than Chouinard. "Ho Douglas, what you got?" Tom would sing out from behind his drawing board, then we would spend the afternoon crawling around on pattern paper working, for instance, on turning Don Jensen's cleverly compartmented soft pack design into the Ultima Thule. Tom was known as the silent partner of the big wall Golden Age in Yosemite, the one who produced all the hauntingly classic black & white photos from the first ascents of the Salathe and North American Walls. Fewer knew that he had been an Olympic 5-meter yacht racer and had an engineering degree from Stanford.

Chouinard was more of an intuitive designer, and it was he who had the business vision to start a company and make, for instance, the hard steel pitons that John Salathe had pioneered but wasn't about to produce. But Frost did more for the partnership than to buttress intuition with solid engineering, for his esthetic sense was as strong in chrome-moly steel as behind the lens of his Leica. Tom Frost is still the most cheerful non-Sherpa I've ever met.

The Whole Natural Art of Protection was written especially for the first real catalog put out by the Chouinard Equipment Company (since sold and renamed Black Diamond) in 1972, to spread the word about clean climbing technique, and to explore its stylistic implications.

"Vedy clean, vedy clean"
—Pablo Casals

There is a word for it, and the word is clean. Climbing with only nuts and runners for protection is clean climbing. Clean because the rock is left unaltered by the passing climber. Clean because nothing is hammered into the rock and then hammered back out, leaving the rock scarred and the next climber's experience less natural. Clean because the climber's protection leaves little trace of his ascension. Clean is climbing the rock without changing it, a step closer to organic climbing for the natural man.

In Britain, after thousands of ascents of popular routes, footholds are actually becoming polished, but the cracks that protect them are unscarred and clean. The Nutcracker in Yosemite, which was deliberately and with great satisfaction climbed clean on the first ascent, doesn't have polished holds yet, but has obviously been climbed often and irreverently; some sections of crack are corrugated into continuous piton scar for several feet. It can still be done with nuts—they even fit into some of the pin scars—but no one will ever again be able to see this beautiful piece of rock the way the first ascent party did. It didn't have to happen that way. It could still be so clean that only a runner-smooth ring at the base of trees and a few bleached patches where lichen had been worn off would be the only signs that hundreds had passed by. Yet the same hundreds who have been there and hammered their marks could still have safely climbed it because nut placements were—and are frequent, logical and sound.

In Yosemite pins have traditionally been removed in an effort to keep the climbs pure and as close as possible to their natural condition. The long term effects of this ethic are unfortunately destructive to cracks and delicate flake systems. This problem is not unique to Yosemite; it is being felt in all heavily used areas across the country. In the Shawangunks a popular route can be traced not by connecting the logical weaknesses, but by the line of pitons and piton holes up the cliff.

As climbers it is our responsibility to protect the vertical wilderness from human erosion. Clean climbing is one approach to this serious problem.

Right from the start, clean climbing demands increased awareness of the rock environment....

"Relax your mind,
Relax your mind,
You've got to relax your
mind..."
—an old blues run

The use of nuts begins with solving environmental problems, but it ends in the realm of aesthetics and style. If technical rockclimbing in places like Yosemite were still confined to the handful of residents and few hundred occasional climbers who bought and used the first Chouinard pitons, then the switch to clean climbing would be purely a matter of individual preference for the aesthetic opportunities it offered, for silent climbing, lightness, simplicity, the joys of being unobtrusive. But the increased popularity of climbing is clearly being felt in the vertical wilderness, and if we are to leave any of it in climbable form for those who follow, many changes will be necessary. Cleanliness is a good place to start.

Then there is the matter of style. When going where cleanliness has been established, the climber may leave his pitons at home and gain a dividend of lightness and freedom; but if on new ground or the not yet clean, he can treat his pins and hammer as the big wall climber does bolts and leave them at the bottom of his rucksack, considering the implications before he brings them into use.

The most important corollary of clean climbing is boldness. When cracks that will accept nuts peter out, long unprotected runouts can result, and the leader of commitment must be prepared to accept the consequences that are only too clearly defined. Personal qualities—judgment, concentration, boldness, the ordeal by fire—take precedence, as they should, over mere hardware.

Using pitons on climbs like the *Nutcracker* is degrading to the climb, its originator, and the climber. Robbins may have been thinking of that climb when he wrote, "Better that we raise our skill than lower the climb." Pitons have been a great equalizer in American climbing. By liberally using them it was possible to get in over ones head, and by more liberally using them, to get out again. But every climb is not for every climber; the ultimate climbs are not democratic. Fortunate climbs protect themselves by being unprotectable, and remain a challenge that can be solved only by boldness and commitment backed solidly by technique. Where boldness has forced a line to come clean, we should tred with respect. There, as well as with unclimbed rock, patience is the key. The clean climber stands humbly before untouched stone. Otherwise one could become guilty of destroying a line for the capable climbers of the future to satisfy his impatient ego in the present. By waiting he might become one of those future capables. Every climb has its time, which need not be today.

Besides leaving alone what one cannot climb in good style, there are some practical corollaries of boldness in free climbing. Learning to climb down is valuable for retreating from a clean and bold place that gets too airy. And having the humility to back off rather than continue in bad style—a thing well begun is not lost. The experience cannot be taken away. By such a system there can never again be "last great problems" but only "next great problems."

Carried out, these practices lead from a quantitative to a qualitative standard of climbing, affirming that the climbing experience cannot be measured in pitches per hour, that a climb cannot be reduced to maps and decimals. Rather, the value turns inward. The motion of climbing, the sharpness of the environment, the climber's reactions are still only themselves, and their dividends of joy personal and private.

Half Dome Comes Clean

By 1972, when the *The Whole Natural Art* came out, I had climbed hammerless up grade IV and V walls in Yosemite. Then along came Galen Rowell's first assignment for *National Geographic*: cover a big wall climb in

Yosemite. Galen invited Dennis Hennek and me to do the classic *Northwest Face* of Half Dome, and I said sure, as long as we could try to climb it clean. Dennis and I both knew that we were ready and the time had come for a hammerless ascent of a big wall. Galen, however, had a crucial assignment for his budding career to get in the can, so he suggested putting pins and hammer in the haul bag just in case.

Galen Rowell was a Chevy mechanic at the time, and the proprietor of a somewhat greasy dive of a shop down on San Pablo Avenue in Berkeley. Once when my Volkswagen blew up near Sacramento, Galen generously drove all the way up and towed my car back to his shop. There were limits, however, to his hospitality; I did my rebuild out back, where my foreign car couldn't offend any red-blooded customers. Every spare minute Galen slipped out of the shop into the office in back, pounding away on a well-lubricated typewriter. He wrote, for instance, about one of the many thousand-mile weekends when he would appear on my doorstep at Cardinal Village up Bishop Creek for a quick bivy on his way into the mountains.

We had done some fine routes together, including *The Smokestack*, the first modern route on the Wheeler Crest, which featured offwidth and flaring-chimney cruxes. Looking up at the thousand-foot buttress from Round Valley, it was dwarfed by the backdrop of the 7000-foot escarpment it lived on; we underestimated it so badly as to wear mountain boots for our first attempt. Galen tilted his shot of the attempt a wee bit too much, but that didn't get us up the moves either and we had to come back to take it more seriously. The climb was so good that we soon did the buttress next door, *Adams Rib*. Today there are dozens of fine routes on the Wheeler Crest, but the pace of development has stalled. It is ironic that the Owens River Gorge a few miles away draws international attention for good but short sport routes packed into a slot in the ground with no view. Every year now ten thousand climbers pull over the rim of the Gorge with the Wheeler Crest full in their faces and don't even see it. Nearly as much exposed rock as Yosemite Valley, with major lines awaiting even a first attempt, and climbing fashion has shifted so much that this vast mountainside draped with granite has become effectively invisible. But I digress.

I was thinking more about driving, about Galen behind the wheel of many a Chevy. He is a fast driver. He is like most climbers in that he knows the mountain roads well, has an adrenalized urge to get places in a hurry using them, and does it just for sport. But unlike the rest, he had that shop to rebuild and tune and tinker. The result was a succession of powerful

Robinson on the aborted first attempt on the Smokestack. Photo by Galen Rowell

mountain cars. Add a dose of testosterone, and it's easy to see that everyone who has climbed with Galen for any length of time ends up with at least one epic tale of a badly stuck vehicle. Mine took place at 10,000 feet on the Rock Creek road. The snow was getting deeper as we climbed, and Galen had been suffering the usual beginners frustrations on skis, and... Anyway, a lot of digging ensued

Dick Dorworth wrote some inspired words in *Mountain Gazette* around then about *Night Driving*, and it was he who captured the archetypal image of Galen at the wheel of a Chevy hurtling through Nevada at ninety per and all the while carrying on an animated discussion full face with someone in the back seat. One of the best things about traveling with Galen was that those conversations kept spilling over from climbing into a much broader world of ideas, and ranged from the place of aggression in the evolution of man, to how climbing fit into the life of the satanist/magician Aleister Crowly, to—whoa, stop!—there's an eagle.

Sure enough, the eagle was standing on the edge of a gravel road in eastern Nevada. Galen reigned in the Chevy and backed up until we were staring at the great bird from ten feet away. It stared back, steadily. Magnificent being, it could easily have carried off a large marmot, and wasn't the least bit intimidated by a pack of humans in a big car. When it had had enough of us, it turned and stalked off, rather stiffly, into the sage. We had been summarily dismissed.

Dennis Hennek on a Choinard Equipment production line, making "bongs". Tom Frost photo

Dennis Hennek had already made the second ascent of the *North American Wall* by the time we met. He loved the challenge of clean climbing, and one of the early places we practiced it together was weekend forays from Ventura to Tahquitz Rock. There we made the first clean ascent of the *Open Book*, which had become the first 5.9 in the Americas when Royal Robbins freed it in 1952. My prototype Tube Chocks were handy in the offwidth crux. Later Dennis got the job of tearing down the movie set of Lago, which had been built near Mono Lake for a Clint Eastwood epic, "The Good, The Bad, and the Ugly." Dennis crafted together a fine little cabin from the salvaged wood. It sat in the first line of willows up from the waters edge. From the loft you could see the sunrise over the lake, then roll over and watch 'baby cakes' and coffee underway on the wood range. One day we got completely skunked on the north pillar of Mount Goode. Almost worse than missing the climb was abandoning the name we had already picked out, *Goodie Goodie*, from a line in "The Night Climbers of Cambridge": "This climber had the interesting habit of saying 'goodie goodie' after each successful ascent." Our consolation was a superb first ascent on Cardinal Pinnacle, clean all the way, and named after a cucumber we peeled on the summit.

August 1973: The biggest aluminum steamer trunk you could imagine arrived air freight from *National Geographic*, and it was just bursting with Nikons, lenses, and many cases of film. Galen went to work sorting and packing camera gear for Half Dome while Dennis and I racked the hardware. On the climb I could only manage to shoot three rolls of film, which was a lot for me, and Dennis did about the same. Galen, of course, rarely emerged from behind some lens or other. In the end a *Geographic* editor commented that this was the smallest lot of slides they had ever picked a story from: 10,000.

The climb went "vedy" clean, including anchors constructed of nuts and runners even when there were fixed pins and bolts right in our faces. The hardest part of the protection and aid was finding alternative placements to fixed pieces that were often lodged in the best parts of the crack. The crux was clearly Dennis' lead of pitch 23, an incipient crack sprouting rurps and bashies; it would not have gone clean without prototypes of Tom Frost's wild new Crack'n Ups. In the end we did use one fixed pin, though Galen remembers it being one Dennis clipped for the pendulum in the Robbins Traverse, while I thought it was one Galen clipped for aid up in the Zig Zags.

Three pitches up the face, far enough so we figured that it would be too much trouble to go back down for them, Dennis casually mentioned to Galen that he had been rummaging through the haul bag and couldn't seem to find the pitons anywhere. Galen's only comment was that Dennis wasn't a very convincing liar.

Seven pitches up is a ledge, sloping but good sized by wall standards, where we stopped for the day. We were getting comfortable and sorting gear when Galen suddenly decided we needed a shot of bivouacking in a hammock. In a flurry he dug one out, set it up, and hopped in. I snapped a photo, and no one could tell when it came out in the *Geographic* that Galen was hanging just above a big ledge. What I didn't realize until much later was that Dennis was behind me, documenting the whole process. Apparently an old-maid photo editor kept this shot in the lineup right up to the final edit, leading to speculation that I might become the first white male nude in *National Geographic*.

A highlight of the second day was the Robbins Chimney, and right after lunch I drew the lead. Quite recently a friend overheard in Boulder, Colorado, a modern nerve-center of climbing wisdom, the opinion that "nobody climbs the Robbins Chimney, you just go around to the left." I guess that news hadn't gotten to Yosemite twenty years earlier, because I was eager for the notorious lead, though it was narrow, flaring and steepened inexorably to a runout crux. At that point I was eighty feet out with no chance of fitting any clean hardware into the flaring offwidth crack, and gulping down little waves of panic. The pitch was typical of Yosemite climbing of that era: awkwardly offwidth and completely unprotectable, with the climber making

Photo by Dennis Hennek

sweaty progress only inches at a time, his back against the wall and staring out over thousands of feet of lovely but quite empty space, all the while trying to maintain his cool and a few shreds of concentration, as carefree shouts from swimmers in the Merced River drifted upward on every meager puff of breeze.

Higher, another notorious offwidth was completely missing from the face. Psych Flake, as it had been called on the first ascent, was 80 feet tall, only eight inches thick at its base, and detached from the face along its bottom. The route followed an offwidth crack up one edge. Legend had it that the whole flake would vibrate if struck by the heel of the hand; and legend also made it out to be a spooky lead. Then one summer not long before our climb, the first party up there for the season found it missing, just completely gone. We stared at the downsloping ledge where Psych Flake had recently rested. It was still covered with some of the sand and gravel that had lubricated the great flake's passage. Fortunately, a straight-in crack in the wall behind made an easy alternate pitch. It even had a lieback edge not far inside, hinting at future exfoliation.

Thank God Ledge, with its dramatic position just under the Visor leering over the top of the face, was named for offering a timely escape from the prospect of climbing the Visor's stacked crockery. It is exfoliating too. Recent years the crack behind Thank God Ledge is twice as wide as when we tiptoed and then shamelessly crawled across. Perhaps it will become a horizontal chimney before disappearing completely.

Chuck Pratt, who was probably the first person to walk upright across Thank God Ledge, was once coiling his rope on the summit. He began to complain loudly to no one in particular or more likely addressing his monologue toward the heavens in general, commenting on the perversity of ropes, and the cheerful and seemingly willful way that they become caught under flakes, stuck in cracks at inconvenient times and distances, and generally make life miserable for the poor climber, who is minding his own business and just humbly trying to make a little vertical progress on the rocks of the world, thank you. All the while he was laying on neat coils and shaking out kinks in his meticulous fashion. Having finished both his soliloquy and a textbook mountaineers coil, and having made perhaps too convincing an argument to

Chuck Pratt. Tom Frost photo

the fates at large, he flung the coil with all his strength out over the dozens of acres of gently-rolling summit slabs. It sailed directly into a deep crack parallel to and not far back from the Northwest Face, never to be seen again. Someday, in the geological equivalent of a glacier spitting out a climber swallowed by its bergschrund centuries before, Chuck's rope will fall out of the sky into the forest that replaces the meadow that in the next hundred years will replace Mirror Lake.

Which reminds me of a geological interest sign along the Tioga Road that announces "Exfoliating Granite." That makes the process sound so immediate, that every time I see it I'm tempted to screech to a stop and watch for it to happen. On the other hand, after a few decades of seeing the walls in the Valley change, after hiking over freshly deposited talus beneath Sentinel, the Three Brothers, Glacier Point Apron, and Elephant Rock as well as Half Dome, I realize that it *is* a relatively immediate process. With all that exfoliation going on, climbing the face of Half Dome begins to resemble a game of 'flakes and ladders.'

Tom Frost photo

Tool Man

When I came to Ventura to work, Chouinard invited me to stay at his house out on the beach north of town. It wasn't much more than a shack, really, and had probably once been a Portuguese fishermen's cottage. You could see right through cracks in the walls, and hear the waves pounding forty feet away. Sometimes we would gather mussels at low tide and the whole shop would come over to eat, drink and dance to Hank Williams ("Drinkin' wine, spodie odie...") or the Rolling Stones.

Mornings, when Yvon would drive in to the shop, I took notebook and pencil and rolling tin down to sit against the seawall, stare out over the Pacific and write barefoot about ice climbing until sweat stung my eyes. I elaborated and clarified Yvon's text for "Climbing Ice", elucidated his techniques, added experience from my own guiding, and spun out the sections of context included here. I didn't realize what intense authorship I felt for these passages until one of them was printed in a Sierra Club calendar and credited to Yvon. Otherwise it was his book, really, though I doubled its length over a year's time. And the ice climbing revolution laid out in those pages was Yvon's too, perhaps more purely his than any other of the many innovations that spun out of the Chouinard Equipment Company and later Patagonia, because of one deceptively simple and profound design: he drooped the pick on the ice axe, so that when swung it would stick in the ice rather than shatter it, as all ice axes had done before. With that pick firmly lodged in good ice, the limits of ice climbing suddenly jumped to vertical and beyond. I got to join in on the revolution, learn ice technique from the master as it was evolving, and add a little literary spit and polish to the writing.

Malinda Pennoyer moved in, she and Yvon got married, and soon after that he took off on the Fun Hog expedition, surfing and skiing southward, all the way down the west coast of the Americas, which culminated on the summit of Fitzroy, the highest point of Patagonia. Which is how I happened to spend Chouinard's honeymoon with his wife.

When Chouinard came home I moved to Santa Barbara, thanks to a generous offer from Ken St. Oegger to live in the apartment over his garage in the upscale Hope Ranch district. Ken's van also plied the roadways to the Eastern Sierra, with an ever-changing crew of climbers and skiers. In between I sat at a tiny table and chair set his kids had outgrown to continue writing about ice, as well as fleshing out the ideas about running talus as a way to learn climbing. Over the next year Ken and Ruth's kindness amounted to a sort of writing scholarship, which I still appreciate.

The Ventura years became my opportunity to help influence the development of two great facets of climbing, clean protection and ice, and to do both simultaneously on the levels of equipment design and the tuning of ideas. My only regret was that some of this writing that I added to the ice book has not appeared, until now, under my name.

W e are *Homo Sapiens*, the tool users. We earn the name by developing tools to increase our leverage on the world around us, and with our increased technological leverage comes a growing sense of power. This position of advantage which protects us from wild nature we call civilization.

Our security increases as we apply more leverage, but along with it we notice a growing isolation from the earth. We crowd into cities which shut out the rhythms of the planet—daybreak, high tide, wispy cirrus high overhead yelling storm tomorrow, moonrise, Orion going south for the winter. Perceptions dull and we come to accept a blunting of feeling in the shadow of security. Drunk with power, I find that I am out of my senses. I, tool man, long for immediacy of contact to brighten my senses again, to bring me nearer the world once again; in my security I have forgotten how to dance.

So, in reaction, we set sail on the wide sea without motors in hopes of feeling the wind; we leave the Land Rover behind as we seek the desert to know the sun, searching for a remembered bright world. Paddling out again, we turn to ride the shorebreak landward, walking on waves, the smell of wildflowers meeting us on the offshore breeze. In the process we find not what our tools can do for us but what we are capable of feeling without them, of knowing directly. We learn how far our unaided effort can take us into the improbable world. Choosing to play that game in the vertical dimension of what is left of wild nature makes us climbers. Only from the extreme of comfort and leisure do we return willingly to adversity. Climbing is a symptom of post-industrial man.

The technological imperative of modern man has always been that if it can be done it should be done. There is no choosing; if it's possible it must be right. Modern man, enslaved by his technical imagination, is shoveling coal to a runaway locomotive. But technology should set him free, opening choices instead of dictating them. Declining a possible technology is the first step toward freedom from that bondage—and returning human values to control. The whole direction of climbing moves against the technological gradient. Here personal qualities like initiative, boldness, and technique are supported rather than suppressed by the tools of the trade.

As I become more sure of myself and more poised in balance on ice, I find myself stretching technique. For instance, I use only a single ice axe for clawing in steeper and more brittle situations. Rock climbing moves in this same direction as it works its way from aid to free climbing, from using pitons to the less secure but more natural protection of clean climbing. This is the technological inversion: fewer tools applied with increasing delicacy. I am rewarded for walking this edge by seeing more sharply what is around me, and feeling more deeply what comes boiling up from within. Thoreau put it that "simplification of means and elevation of ends is the goal." They can't help happening together.

Dances With Gravities

The earth, cooling and wrinkling, pushes up mountains. Gravity calls them home. These improbable minarets stand up in a sea of air that is itself changing—cycling in water that the sun stole from the sea and flinging it back to earth. When the ocean of air runs into rock wrinkles standing up into the sky, it gets wrenched from its placid flow along trade wind channels; it is raised and cooled. Inevitably it fights back, pouring torrents of wind and water—much of it crystallized—onto the rocky heights. All that water soon begins its journey downhill, and inevitably it will take some rock with it. Rockfall, waterfall, icefall, avalanche: the climber must deal with each in turn or become their victim. Knowledge is power is life.

Nowhere on the planet are the forces of change more active than in the mountains. Mountain building is often abrupt, and ever after their destruction is ceaseless. The climber thrusts himself into the midst of this metamorphosis. Rockclimbers think their world stable, their creations everlasting as they climb the surface of the outermost exfoliation shell while it is busy delaminating from the mountain. Alpinists are less illusioned; frost-wedging and thermal cracking have left their landscape more shattered, loose at hand, and hanging overhead. They have learned to tiptoe.

Change may be relentless, but it is not often random. As Einstein said, "God does not play dice with the universe." The spindrift avalanches of new snow sluffing off a steep face fall into a clockwork pattern. Today the slides in this gully are coming three minutes apart; there goes another—now quickly scuttle across. Most mountain hazards are not that precise, yet they do follow some pattern of daily or seasonal cycles. The mountaineer's best defense is timing. Climb snowfields when they are frozen into a good working surface, glissade just as the surface has thawed, and be gone by the time softness has reached deep enough for the slope to avalanche. The same frost that incrementally wedges blocks off of north faces also glues them stoutly in place during early morning hours.

Travel light and move fast; speed is safety.

Running Talus

This article was written for the second Chouinard catalog, which appeared in 1975. Since it describes such a novel way to begin learning to rock climb, it generated quite a bit of interest and was revised and reprinted several times. I have tuned up some of these ideas while teaching climbing. On several occasions I have actually edited the initial lecture all the way down to just two words before leading off slowly into the nearest boulder field. Those words were "Follow me."

"Every boulder is prepared and measured and put in its place more thoughtfully than are the stones of temples. If for a moment you are inclined to regard these taluses as mere draggling, chaotic dumps, climb to the tip of one of them, tie your mountain shoes firmly over the instep, and with braced nerves run down without any hag-

Doug Robinson

gling, puttering hesitation, boldly jump from boulder to boulder with ever increasing speed. You will then find your feet playing a tune, and quickly discover the music and poetry of rock piles—a fine lesson, and all nature's wildness will tell the same story." —John Muir

Talus running is one of the best ways to begin mountaineering, yet it is so simple that it usually gets overlooked. In our haste to begin toying with the intriguing equipment of technical climbing, we often overlook this first exposure to the medium, to rock itself.

Photo by Bruce Robinson

Simplify the learning process by going straight to the rock. Talus running—or boulder hopping—puts you in touch with a lot of rock right away, without the interference of rope and hardware. In fact, all you need is a pair of hiking boots—or better yet, your old tennis shoes. Climbing shoes are OK, as long as they're not too tight, but running shoes pad the contact too much. Hundreds of friction stances, moving by too fast for thought, will teach your body directly. The secret is to relax and let yourself learn without thinking of what you're doing.

You could come to this novel exercise from any of several directions. It's for the mountain rambler who aspires to become a mountaineer, or the rock climber growing into alpine climbing—though he won't believe this exercise can teach him anything until he tries it. It's for the novice who is full of the spirit of mountaineering, but wary of the technical entanglements of pure rock climbing. But even if you ultimately aim to climb in technically sophisticated places like Yosemite, don't overlook talus running as a beginning. The old alpinists knew what modern rock technicians have forgotten—that scrambling leads to climbing.

The minute they step onto the rock I can spot the hikers and backpackers in any climbing class. They have learned a lot about climbing just from rambling along rocky trails. They own a sense of the friction of rock, of balance and movement, that is quite unconscious, absorbed through the feet. Fortunate is the climbing school with a long trail and a short scramble leading to its teaching rocks.

Pete Sinclair, who taught climbing for years in Wyoming, has made a worthy point about learning to climb. You don't need to learn to climb at all—you already know. You only forgot when you "grew up," when you quit climbing trees and fences. Those reflexes slumber in old nerve memory banks, just waiting to be reawakened to the new medium of stone. You just need to recall what you once knew instinctively; relax a little, and it's right there.

People don't teach you to climb—the rock teaches you. You can simplify the learning process by going directly to the source.

Talus running is as close as the nearest pile of rocks, perhaps along a local streambed. Its ultimate terrain, however, is the miles of piles of talus—rocky debris and boulders—scattered at the foot of peaks in every alpine mountain range of the world, and its joy is as much in the setting as in the action.

If you are already a serious backpacker, just loving the mountains and striding across country on and off the map, you have probably come upon talus in the course of your desire and crossed it simply because it was in your path. But if you start climbing before you actually get into the mountains, your apprenticeship must nevertheless begin on the first rock between trail and peak—on the talus.

Perhaps a local streambed. Bruce Robinson photo

Doug Robinson

Climbing with Style

But beware of live moraines. They are being pushed along by moving glaciers, their rocks clink tentatively forward and rest unsteadily. They are quite unstable—better to stay off. Talus boulders, on the other hand, usually fall off of peaks with enough momentum to sort into more stable configurations below. They shift too, but less often.

Suppose that instead of choosing alpine country, you had gone for your first climbing to Yosemite Valley. The initial lesson would be quite different. The basics in either case are friction and balance, and in the Valley they are best learned, or relearned, on a slab. So you would probably truck off to the Glacier Point Apron where the climbing would be somewhat slow and exacting. It would also be rather difficult, reflecting the studied, careful, and precise way a rock climber approaches his chosen terrain. You would probably slip and come onto the protection of a friendly rope and so begin to learn not to lean into the rock but to make your feet stick by standing over them. By the end of the day you would have mastered climbing problems beyond your previous imagination.

But we are in the high mountains. The high country does not lack in slabs, and we will play on them in due time, but since our goal is mountaineering, we will make a crucial detour. We live in a world of larger scale. For years we have been covering country, large hunks of it—first on trails, later breaking out across country. Sometimes going up and down peaks, running down scree and hopping from one talus block to the next. We have grown accustomed to seeing the skyline change in proportion to our effort. We are creatures of motion, and in becoming mountaineers we have high hopes of increasing our mobility, not limiting it.

Direct aid climbing up a vertical and otherwise holdless wall, attached to one thin crack, is certainly challenging, but it stifles our animal joy in pure loping motion. It is not nearly kinesthetic enough to satisfy the sense we have come to feel of our-bodies-moving-in-the-mountains. Later we will, for a while, have to accept the limitations imposed by the exposure of a new and steeper environment—to slow down and sweat and hold the rock tight and think; to rope up and secure each other by belaying the rope; to lug the rope, coil and uncoil it, and constantly, ceaselessly, untangle it. But this, we hope, will be just a stage, for our hearts are set on more freedom in the mountains, on being free in ever wilder places. So we do not start with the steep rock and the rope, but on familiar, gently sloping ground—in a talus field.

The experienced backpacker is snickering a little here, thinking this a bit foolish. He is recalling memories of past miseries on talus, doubtless aggravated by his strapped-on, aluminum-framed equilibrium destroyer. That backpacker would benefit from personal application of the recent proliferation of lightly internal-framed, body-contoured packs.

To the new talus runner, a boulderfield will seem at first to be a sea of holes, which must be avoided by means of a deliberate technique. Just walking over the field will be a handful: need I say be careful? Literally running is, after all, the advanced course.

There are but two essentials, friction and balance—the staying power of a foot resting on the rock, and the dynamic of moving the body to the next foothold. The motion is like walking, of course, only more broken and much more studied. This combination of balance and friction is the basis of all climbing The application of these two essentials will be added to, refined, extrapolated; both will be pushed to unexpected limits, in awkward and improbable combinations But the basic requirement, friction and balance working in harmony, is always there.

Moving over the talus, we begin to see that coordinating the step from one point of balance to the next implies another quality—rhythm. A good dancer becomes a good climber; the mere weight lifter is helpless. We build up momentum. Each step becomes less of a stance, more of a brief way-station to the next step. The dynamic overcomes the static.

Momentum will keep you going past the sum of your stances, just as it holds the bicyclist on his line over the succession of pavement under his tires. You may begin by stepping into the notch formed by two blocks coming together, but by the time you actually start running, speed and confidence will accelerate you like a hydrofoil coming up on the wing, until you're running along the tops of the blocks. Or, in really big talus—car-sized-blocks—you can end up ricocheting off a sequence of facing friction slabs in a sinuous dynamic, scribing an energy arc that is always leaning forward by tilting sideways.

Upend that ricocheted balancing act and it becomes stemming—one of the most elegant of climbing maneuvers, but often the last learned. Likewise, planting a foot securely in the notch where two boulders meet anticipates jamming, the art of wedging hands and feet into cracks splitting steeper rock. Jamming technique does not come as easily as face climbing, so it helps to start getting a feel for it now.

You will occasionally miss a step, which can of course be dangerous. But instead of reverting to caution, think recovery. With good momentum, you are already halfway into the next step anyway. Hesitation can land you instead in one of the holes between the boulders.

One advantage of starting to learn climbing technique on the talus is that you won't have to try to put a lot of little pieces together later—talus running is not balance + adhesion + rhythm + looking ahead; it is one integrated motion right from the beginning. Any of its parts might be isolated as you look for their limits, but each remains part of a fluid whole, which progresses to greater speed before going on to harder problems—from talus to blocky ridges, which steepen to buttresses and then smooth out to walls. Rhythm and fast, safe alpine climbing don't grow from practicing isolated parts, but from the whole context of talus running.

Bruce Robinson photo

Having come through the preliminary talus, we find ourselves at the base of a blocky ridge, which we clamber up as if it were a sort of uphill talus. It may be at first, but soon it becomes steeper. We begin to use our hands occasionally for stabilization or pull, yet we are still moving swiftly, covering terrain. This ridge running will take us safely and quickly up and down a good many peaks, with no more added assistance than some bread and cheese for the summits. During this phase of developing skill you will notice that there are ridges and ridges. In the second case, the walls on either side are steep, so if the ridge suddenly knife-edges in front of you or if the way is barred by a blocky spire, you become exposed.

Exposure is the climber's euphemism for air beneath his feet. To continue in this circumstance may not be any more difficult, but it is more dangerous; the consequences of a fall are potentially more serious. So, discretion being the better part of safety, we have now come to the point at which technical mountaineering begins to lead beyond the scope of talus running. From here I can only recommend that while you can—and no doubt will—read about ropework, the safest way to really learn it is from a guide.

Talus running is the bouldering of the mountaineer. Just as bouldering emerged from rock climbing as a form of practice but then began to show some independent life of its own, talus running began as a necessary evil, something to be endured between the lake and the peak. It is viewed now as a nursery for the more compact rocks above; it may yet aspire to the status of an independent sport.

But the most far-reaching effects of talus running do not lead in the direction of the competition that characterizes bouldering today. Escalating from walking to loping, to a quickstep, to a gracefully dancing run, already anticipates a personal and noncompetitive kind of mountaineering. Its concentration accelerates attention closer to the present moment, where clinging to a stray thought in the instant between perception and motion can lose the climber his finely tuned edge and send him crashing. Staying on that edge, however, breeds mindfulness.

Peter Croft

Moving Over Stone

Video is a great medium for learning the moves of climbing, which is why I made "Moving Over Stone." At the end I
slipped in a few words about what can happen when the act of
climbing begins to carry you beyond those moves.

Sooner or later, climbing carries us back to wilderness. We go out
to play in the mountains, just to let the animal run. Movement.

Way in the backcountry, miles from any road, we catch sight of the
Tai Chi Master, practicing his meditation through movement on rocky
summits. The rock gymnast is out here too: Todd Skinner—one of the best.
Concentration makes Todd's climbing a meditation too.

One of the great things about climbing is that it's not just physical.
Mind is drawn in, charting moves, watching safety. And emotion. Precise
gymnastics on such a wild, vertical dance floor is a dialogue with fear, the
deepest of all emotions. Climbing can integrate body, mind and emotion.
That makes it a powerful meditation. A physical meditation.

High peaks or low boulders, rock climbing is just another way to be
alive in the mountains—an excuse, like holding a fishing pole is an excuse, to
stand on the riverbank and look around. Except that climbing adds an
emotional charge. Adrenaline surges through you. It sharpens our senses,
nudging climbers into a heightened awareness. Drink it in. Savor the new
perspective. You'll come back down changed—prophets have always known
it—from the mountain top.

Doug Robinson

Further Afield

Duane Raleigh on Master Race

Oklahoma Rock

Guiding for a living initially propelled me to Oklahoma (and Kansas and Texas) to teach beginning climbing classes, but fine people and good climbing kept me coming back. I owe my start there to Tex Bossier. While climbing Ama Dablam together in 1979, sitting up on the South Ridge looking out over the Sherpa lands of Nepal, Tex asked if I would like to take over the itinerant classes he had started back in an unlikely part of the States. I did, and Tex went on to work for Patagonia, eventually heading their Paris office.

Flatness dominated my imagination of that part of the country, so I was surprised to find quality sandstone outside Wichita, exciting limestone within the Tulsa city limits, and in southwestern Oklahoma the rocky core of the oldest granite mountain range in the country. That range, the Wichita Mountains, sported occasional outcrops of Yosemite-quality granite spread out over 50 miles. Much of it was inside a wildlife refuge populated by eagles, Texas longhorn cattle, and the largest herd of Buffalo anywhere. I would sometimes lay my sleeping bag out on a grassy knoll and wake up with tonnage of wild Bison grazing around me at dawn.

But the best part was getting to know the people. The shop owners were some of the most active backpackers I had ever met, in spite of the long, long drive to the mountains. And each week there was a crowd of new faces, mostly middle-aged flatlanders eager to step out of their horizontal lives into the exotic world of rock climbing. Also a little apprehensive. Each week I had to admire all over again their courage and curiosity.

But it was when a few of my new acquaintances proved to be far from beginners, when they began climbing circles around me on their local outcrops, that I began to see this story, which eventually emerged in *Outside*.

Duane Raleigh is the best climber in Oklahoma, which means, oddly enough, that he is world class. He was telling me where his desire to climb, which had catapulted him out of the flatlands and into a leading role in Yosemite, had come from.

"Way back in 1965," he said, "I was in kindergarten. I was watching TV, a movie called 'The Mountain' with Spencer Tracy and Robert Wagner, where a plane crashes high in the mountains on Mont Blanc. When I saw that I thought, 'Wow, mountain climbing. Looks pretty neat!'

"I had to walk to kindergarten every day. It was about a mile, and on the way I passed by a 30-foot cliff—flint or limestone, I think—and every time I passed it, I thought of the movie. One day I got sweaty palms and started climbing it. I got gripped out about halfway, but still managed to scramble up the thing. I was impressed, though. I thought, 'Yeah, I'm a mountain climber now."

By the late '70s and early '80s, something extraordinary had happened in Oklahoma: Duane Raleigh and a band of world-class climbers had arisen out of the heart of flatness.

I had lived in Yosemite during the golden age of big-wall climbing in the '60s and had seen a climbing renaissance firsthand. The golden age had been triggered by a few intense individuals who had somehow found one another. Their pooled energy had quickly assumed a life of its own and surged forward to define the future. But who would have guessed such intensity would converge in Oklahoma?

If they had lived elsewhere, nearer one of the big centers, the Oklahoma climbers would have moved early on to Yosemite, or Eldorado Canyon outside Boulder, or New York's Shawangunks, or North Conway, New Hampshire. They would have been pulled into the mainstream, and they would have absorbed its standards and limitations. Instead, out on the arid flatlands, they had to invent their own climbing boom practically from scratch. The urge to ascend had risen in a dozen hearts scattered across Oklahoma. Gradually, by congregating on the rocky outcrops—the limestone in Tulsa and the granite, believe it or not, all over the southwestern corner of the state—they found one another. There wasn't the oppressive competition of the big centers, but a friendlier sort of pushing that teased the best out of each. They became a band of brothers, discovering the excitement of a new medium.

I met them when I inherited a series of rock climbing classes in 1979. Then they were boys just graduating from high school, who would go on to study petroleum engineering or architecture at the University of Oklahoma. They'd scale anything, from the school library to the rock in some farmers wheatfield. "It s not any kind of macho," said one, Mark Herndon, an intense kid whose taste in literature and music might peg him as being from

Jon Frank. Marion Hutchison photo

Berkeley rather than Norman, Oklahoma. "There are a lot more efficient ways of looking like a big shot. Climbing is just an oasis of fun in the desert of making a living." Then his voice rose, as if to grab me by the lapels: "I've been to the Valley, Yosemite, but the face climbing at Quartz Mountain in Oklahoma is much better." Quartz Mountain, I later found out, was the rock in the farmers wheatfield.

The first climber I met in Oklahoma was Jon Frank. In 1979, he was an honor student in an Oklahoma City high school, well scrubbed and deeply religious. His growing frame could barely contain his enthusiasm for climbing, which at times spilled over into a maniacal laugh. He had signed up for the "advanced" section of my climbing course, which meant, in this case, everyone who had already climbed a few times and knew how to tie onto the rope. Since it was my first trip, Jon led me down to the Wichita Mountains, where he suggested the Narrows, a favorite spot. "Do you mind if I lead Crazy Alice?" he asked, and proceeded to set the rope for the class. Then he pointed me toward Flying Nun. I went up, but I couldn't lead it and came back down. "Hmm . . . " said Jon, and went up and led it himself. Then he took me to Leapfrog and led the first pitch before turning it over to me. But I couldn't make the mantle on the second pitch, so I traversed around it. Finally, I wrote Jon a check refunding his tuition and labeled it "guides fee." Clearly, I thought, these Oklahoma climbers were a different breed.

By the time I got there, Oklahoma already had an incipient scene. Jon and his beanpole partner, Jimmy Ratzlaff, had a favorite site in the Wichitas with a climb that kept stumping them. One day Jon came upon a lone climber soloing one of his and Jimmy s classics: His name was Duane Raleigh.

There was another group of active climbers centered in Tulsa, and I met them later that same year. The rock in Tulsa was in Chandler Park, close to town. Running along the edge of the park by the Arkansas River are limestone passageways, a literal maze with walls 15 to 25 feet high. Sam Audrain had been a teenage skateboarding whiz until he got distracted by the Chandler limestone. He and less flamboyant locals like Terry Andrews and Marion Hutchison, who had learned to rappel in the Boy Scouts, took to wandering those corridors. A staccato burst of energy applied to the smooth stone might land them on top of one of the blocks or back in the dust on the floor of the maze. After a while, their fingertips grew hard and they came home less dusty. Their style appealed to me as much as their friendliness and humility, and I found myself pushing harder on the rocks than I had in years.

Kristen Jacobsen in Chandler Park

I wasn't the only one to be impressed. Jon and Jimmy came up to Tulsa to meet these climbers, and right away they took to Terry Andrews, clearly the leading climber in that group. "He has the strongest fingers I've ever seen," said Jon. A thin kid with an infectious smile Terry could cling to minute ripples on the stone. You had to squint up close to find them afterward.

Occasionally, the climbers would be observed by other Oklahomans. Two women from Oklahoma City, I heard, were working on an overhanging sandstone wall below a trail at a place called Robbers Cave. A man's face appeared above them, stared for a long moment, then beckoned behind him. "Look, Martha, mountain climbers! I seen 'em on TV, but I ain't never seen em in person."

Before they met one another, the Oklahoma climbers had simply improvised. They each had started out, it seemed, with a partner who soon quit. As junior high students, they'd been baffled and ultimately challenged by outcrops of crumbly rock, or maybe it was really just dirt, outside their towns. Duane Raleigh had done his first real climbing on some red dirt cliffs 20 miles out of Weatherford. "We'd go out there every day after school," he recalled, "and nail our way up these things with a piece of old, green, moldy rope this guy stole off a boat out at the lake. We'd use leather belts with metal buckles, tie shoestring around the nails, and tie the rope through it."

The first time Duane saw a climbing catalog, he thought, "What is all this stuff?" As a 14-year-old, he said, "We didn't even know what climbing gear was. Saw pitons—those looked like nails that would be handy for driving into the dirt. Saw carabiners, too. We had to order more carabiners when we found out what they were for."

They might have been short on rocks and equipment and technique, but they didn't lack motivation. I taught classes all through the Midwest, but nothing could compare to the ones in Oklahoma City. The intensity was there from the start. By the fall of '80, my second year, the beginners from the year before were helping me teach. Boys like Karl Bird and Steve Gilliam had teamed up the first year and worked out every weekend on the rocks. Rick Thomas had been a beginning student in Tulsa, but a summer in Colorado had made him bold. With another climber and a bare minimum of equipment, he had free-climbed up the middle of the Diamond on Longs Peak, Colorado's largest and most notorious alpine wall, making delicate 5.10 moves over lots of very thin air and pushing through to the summit.

Enthusiasm ran so high that I didn't wait a year, but shuttered my cabin in the Sierra and came back to Oklahoma in June of '81. I hadn't reckoned the Midwestern summer—with temperatures in the 100's and

Karl Bird and Steve Gilliam

humidity to match—and I lay in a soaking sweat all night in the tent, emerging to flying bugs, occasional centipedes cruising the rocks, and even a rattlesnake 15 feet up a crack and acting territorial. It was all tolerable but the humidity: In weather like that you could practically get sweaty palms while holding a beer. My young friends hardly noticed. We were climbing, and they were just itching to show off the jewel of Oklahoma climbing, Quartz Mountain. The rock in the wheatfield.

It was a three-hour drive to the best rock in Oklahoma. We left Oklahoma City before dawn, and the heat of the day was already hanging in the air. We stopped at a rural cafe for breakfast; the waitress looked at this group of strong kids and said, "You boys hayin'?"

We found Quartz Mountain—called Baldy Peak on the topo map—in the middle of a flatlands farm: one orange dome rising out of a field of winter wheat that looked as if it got lost on the way to Yosemite. Its 300-foot face was that good, smooth and flawless. There was a fence around the field, posted with NO TRESPASSING signs, but we went over the stile next to it. Duane and the boys said no problem, they had an agreement with the owner of the land, Farmer Johnson.

If the Wichita Mountains are like "islands of rock in a prairie sea," as one geologist put it, then Quartz is at the far western end of the archipelago. The granite is actually a little rougher than Yosemite, more like you'd find it at Joshua Tree, so it yields friction climbing to a disconcertingly high angle. Jon Frank and Jimmy Ratzlaff took me on one classic line after another: *S-Wall, Last of the Good Guys, Amazon Woman.* They ascended steep, blank, crackless rock, the only anchorage to the stone provided by an occasional bolt sunk into a drilled hole. These two-pitch climbs on barely 300 feet of rock were more than just superb lines that would be considered classics even in Yosemite. As I climbed more, another quality began to emerge: boldness.

The temperature had ascended to 107 degrees by mid-afternoon. On the south-facing rock it was even hotter, so we ducked out to the lake for a swim, returning at dusk to attempt *The Big Bite.*

Fifteen feet above the belay station at mid-height there is a bolt, then nothing, no protection at all as the 5.10 friction soars upward and finally curves out of sight over the top of the dome. "Beware of the big bite consequences should you fail," warned the brand-new Oklahoma guidebook, *Southern Exposure*. A fall from near the top could crater into the ledge down there where the climb began. Bold indeed.

The rock at Quartz had been a pleasant surprise, but the climbs were downright unbelievable, bold to a standard seldom seen elsewhere. They bespoke committed vision backed solidly by technique—the boys had learned a lot since the days of leather belts and moldy ropes—and seemingly unshakable mind control. Scanning the guidebook, I could see many such routes designated by an "xx" after the rating. The definition was chilling: "xx means a ground fall is very possible."

The guidebook was something else, a beautifully literate little document, full of intriguing route names and light-hearted directions—"Do a disco step left into a red water streak," it said at one point. Duane had written it, and how he had done it was part of the Oklahoma climbers' growing cache of legends.

All the boys were students, except for Duane. Though just as capable and smart, Duane worked part time as a roofer so he could pour his considerable energy into climbing: He climbed solo or found partners among those who cut classes and climbed on weekends. Rick Thomas was so eager after his early climbing experiences that he took a semester off and spent a spring climbing with Duane. They were poor, so on the way to Quartz they bought a sack of potatoes and decided they wouldn't stop climbing until the potatoes were gone. They did hardly anything but first ascents for weeks, three or four new routes a day. Then Duane recalled a blank wall back in the Narrows, and they tackled that. Two feet below the top of a climb he intended to call Dr. Kildare, Duane fell, going all the way to the ground and breaking his leg.

So in the hospital, with "unwanted assistance from Doctor Kildare," Duane began compiling the guidebook *Southern Exposure*. But it was finished before the leg. With five weeks left to go on the meter, at the height of the summer heat, Duane took a hacksaw to his cast. His foot was still so swollen that he had to borrow a larger climbing shoe, but the next day he limped into the Narrows and finished leading the first ascent of *Doctor Kildare*.

In the winters, Duane Raleigh, Mark Herndon, Jon Frank, Jimmy Ratzlaff, and the others were always camped at Quartz. In the summers they began branching out. In 1980, Jon Frank was the first Oklahoma climber to go to Yosemite Valley. The climbers' campground there is dotted with granite boulders that function as a combination gymnasium and social center: a place to limber up after the long drive west, possibly find a climbing partner, and insert yourself in the pecking order. The locals were amused to see Oklahoma plates pull into their parking lot, and when Jon opened his mouth the amusement turned to laughter.

"Gol-ly!" said Jon. "Look at those boulders!"

But Jon Frank had been on granite boulders back at Quartz, and as soon as he put a hand to these it was familiar territory all the way. He eventually got to within one or two moves of the top of *Midnight Lightning*, the most notorious—and visible—boulder problem in Yosemite and one that still has only half a dozen ascents. The snickers subsided.

Mark Henderson on the OSU Library.
Duane Raleigh photo

Back home, Jon raved about the Valley with such infectious enthusiasm that the next summer he had no trouble talking Jimmy and Duane into going back with him. In a few days, they were ready to start up El Capitan. Since it was May, Duane took only cotton painter's pants, a T-shirt, and a down jacket to sleep in. At their first bivouac on El Cap Tower it started to rain. In the morning the other three parties that were on the route rappelled by them in retreat. Duane led upward in the freezing rain. They had to climb into the next night to reach the ledge known as Camp 5. By then it was snowing. "Those other guys had waterproof parkas and wool underwear," Duane recalled. "My down jacket was soaked; wearing it just made me colder, so I packed it away. Then I was out in the snowstorm in just a wet T-shirt and frozen pants. Lightning was crashing around. I thought I was going to die."

(Just last fall, two Japanese climbers did freeze to death in a snowstorm right above there.)

That was enough to give Duane a taste for the Big Wall, and over the next few years he worked his way through increasingly harder routes. Mark Herndon became his steady partner and recalled arriving back in the Valley to call home after doing *Mescalito*.

"Mom, we climbed El Cap."

"Again? You climbed it again?"

"Yeah, it was great. Mescalito—a hard route."

"That's nice.... Your brother won the golf tournament again."

After soloing one of the hardest of all 40 El Cap routes, *Zenyatta Mendata*, in near record time in 1982, Duane felt ready for a first ascent of his own. He had been eyeing a section of the face of Half Dome that was particularly blank, consistently overhanging, and strikingly white. He was already thinking of calling it *Arctic Sea* when he asked Houston BASE jumper Tom Cosgriff to come along. The climbing got hard immediately, but the real problem didn't start until after the ledge. They came to it on the tenth day, a two-by-three-foot platform. It was the only ledge on the whole route; they named it Ice Station Zebra and stayed for three nights. Then the pitch above, The Linear Accelerator, broke the last of their drills and they had to retreat to the ledge.

So they sat on the ledge and drank a case of beer. Well, not a whole case. They had already drunk a can or two here and there, out of the case they had loaded into their haul bag at the base of the wall last week. But they drank enough to realize that a broken drill will, after all, do what the oilfield roughnecks back home refer to as "make hole." Six days later, with a total of only 16 bolts (amazingly few bolts for so blank a wall), they topped out. So far, Arctic Sea has had only one repeat.

Getting back to Oklahoma was an adventure, too. In Reno one year, Mark Herndon ended up sleeping under a bridge with the winos while waiting for a ticket home. And one of his buddies was waylaid in Colorado's Eldorado Canyon one afternoon by a beautiful trustfunder who invited him to her cabin for the evening and then added, "...bring your rope."

But they had left their mark on Yosemite, the climbers' arena. This past spring, Rick McUsic and three of Oklahoma's younger climbers—the next generation—pulled into the climbers' parking lot. Seeing the Oklahoma plates, a few of the normally jaded locals held back respectfully for a few moments, then rushed over to greet the newcomers, eager for news of Duane and the boys. The news was that Duane and Mark were not coming to the Valley that summer. They were going to the Alps.

"You wouldn't believe the Alps!" The voice on the phone was breathless, insistent. I blinked awake. It was two in the morning in California, nearly dawn in Oklahoma, and I'd seen the Alps for myself. Twice. "I've been sitting here thinking about it and just had to talk to someone," said Mark Herndon. The flow of postcards from Mark and Duane had been teasing me all summer. They had started out innocently enough: "We're in Chamonix now. Way cool ... French babes everywhere."

But nothing in their experience had readied Mark and Duane for this. Neither Quartz nor the hot, dry walls of Yosemite were preparation enough for the rivers of ice pouring off Mont Blanc nearly to the city limits, for the ice running up the shaded gullies and plastered across granite faces, and for the deadly storms that swept regularly over the crest. It was tempting just to hang out at the topless swimming pool. Mark described a huddled bivouac in a big electrical storm: "Sparks flew and St. Elmo's fire whooped it up. This alpinism is frightening. I'm learning how to stay alive here—be cautious." His voice trembled as he talked about scuttling across 50-degree ice gullies between volleys of stonefall, and then getting hit in the arm anyway for a ballooning bruise that lasted three weeks. "Nothing a little booze wouldn't cover," Mark reported, but his thoughts were already turning homeward.

Duane and a fresh partner went back up, to the queen of the alpine ice walls, Les Droites. The ice was thin, so they climbed a direct route of steep rock. Dual soloing, they made progress swiftly, and two hours above the glacier they passed a Spanish party that had been climbing for three days. Sixty rope-lengths and not 24 hours later, they were already on their way down the backside toward Chamonix. There in the street were the Spaniards, who had rappelled off in the meantime. The Spaniards kept a respectful distance.

September 7: "It's been raining ever since Mark left the 3rd. . . so desperate to do something that we are going up today weather be damned. It should be SPORTY. I should be back sometime in October or November unless some ice chunk offs me. Then, well, see you in the next world and DON'T BE LATE...."

My friends in California are amused every time I leave the High Sierra to go climbing in the kingdom of flatness, but the truth is, I've found myself climbing in Oklahoma a lot lately. Last winter I took yet another trip, planning to go on to new rock in Arkansas with Duane and the boys. But by the time I got to Norman, snow blanketed the state and there were ice storms in Arkansas. In the end we got only a one day break in the storm cycle and opted for the familiar slabs of Quartz Mountain, south-facing and dry.

The trip had the festive air of a homecoming. Duane soloed *Jet Stream*, a 5.10 route that most of us are afraid to lead with a rope. But he had done it many times, and that day he was just using it as a convenient approach to *Master Race*, his 5.12 test piece that follows a line of extremely thin holds under a prominent ceiling.

Then Duane belayed Jon on *Master Race*, urging him on with quiet confidence and humor. As a result, we were treated to a second ascent that day. And Jon pronounced Master Race to be harder than half a dozen notorious 5.12s, like *Separate Reality* in Yosemite and *Open Cockpit* in the Shawangunks.

It was that spirit of cooperation, that downright Midwestern good-heartedness and generosity of spirit, I realized, that had fused this collection of climbers from solitary flatlanders into a band of brothers.

Last fall at Quartz the dark side of the bold standard of Oklahoma climbing surfaced abruptly. One of the up-and-coming climbers was leading high above his protection on *Glass* when he pulled a handhold off. He fell, ripping out his top two protection points as the rope came taut, and slammed into a ledge 40 feet-below. When I got to him there was bone jutting out of the side of his ankle. But he was lucky. No arteries were torn, so all we had to do was keep him comfortable until the Army medical helicopter arrived from Fort Sill. The flight medic spun lazily on a steel cable as he lowered out of the sky toward our ledge, and he arrived wide-eyed: "Eighty-three days left in the Army and I had to pull this detail," he said, gripping the back of the ledge.

"Didn't they train you for this?"
"I was trained in SCUBA rescue."

His patient was the first to laugh. After the stretcher was winched up into the chopper, we descended. There was Ted Johnson, the 69-year-old cattle rancher who owned Quartz Mountain, in his blue overalls. Uh-oh, I thought, there goes our climbing area. But Johnson was more interested in keying out a plant he had in hand: "Looks like sumac to me, but it has too many berries." He didn't seem concerned about the rescue at all. Finally, he got around to the boys.

"That's a good bunch of kids," he confided.

"Good climbers, too," I replied. By now I had been trying to keep up with them for several years, across Oklahoma and out in California. "They're world class."

Johnson wasn't surprised. He had been reading up on the subtleties of climbing ethics and style. "This climbing is a great sport," he said. Then he revised his opinion. "It's a grand sport."

Later I saw him talking to Brent Choate, one of the next generation, a punker in Vuarnets and bleached blond hair. You could hardly imagine a more unlikely pair, but in fact, different as they looked, they sounded just alike—unmistakably Midwestern. The punk matched the old farmer's easygoing and understated speech, met his steady gaze. And of course they were talking about a mutual interest.

Things are beginning to change in the lives of the Oklahoma climbers these days, and the little renaissance that arose so rapidly here is starting to fade. Terry Andrews and Marion Hutchison have become petroleum geologists, and Mark Herndon will follow them soon. Typically, they have shunned the big companies to prospect independently, scrambling together deals and dreaming of the big strike that will send them all on an exotic expedition. Jon Frank continues to climb in Yosemite and has been inspired by his girlfriend to train seriously for triathlons. Jimmy Ratzlaff teaches Sunday school and spent a summer as a chaplain in Yosemite Valley. Karl Bird has been guiding in the Sierra for the last two seasons. Steve Gilliam has started a guide service in Oklahoma City. Rick Thomas is a certified nordic ski instructor living in Mammoth. Sam Audrain is racing mountain bikes in Tulsa. Rick McUsic is sending 5.13 limestone and building pipe organs in Texas. Terry Andrews was the first of the group to get married; the rest of the boys showed up in three-piece suits and cried at the wedding.

Duane Raleigh has mellowed out since returning from the Alps. He hardly climbed for a while—the boys thought it might have something to do with a new girlfriend. But then he charged up again in the Wichita Mountains, and this past May, when he got married, he and his bride honeymooned at the base of Quartz Mountain in Farmer Johnson's field.

Rick McUsic leads Quartz Mtn. Classic S-Wall

Soaring over the Sierra Crest

Hang Gliding:
The Olympics of Lift

Back in the winter of 1974 I was living up Rock Creek Canyon, a couple of miles above the first of many attempts to get a ski touring lodge going there. Don Partridge was the head of Rock Creek Nordic, and since he didn't have much business there was plenty of time to sit around the big stove in the dining hall and talk about his other passion—hang gliding. So I watched the fledgling sport grow up, and Don become the meet director of some local meets that, thanks to excellent terrain and weather, became the ultimate international events.

When this piece was written in 1981 it looked like hang gliding would really take off. Don and Tom Kreyche were running the contests out of their own funds and good will, just holding on until, they were sure, someone like a Budweiser would show up eager to swoop in with sponsorship. It never happened. Then Don was killed in Texas. He was barnstorming around the country trying to whip up interest in ultralights, which are a cross between a hang glider and a power mower. They are now broadly considered to be unstable. One pilot said that flying them was like "just constantly waiting for the other shoe to drop." Don ran into a tree while trying to find the landing zone in a sudden fog, and the whole Owens Valley contest scene died with him. There are still aerobatic contests, in Telluride I think, and lone pilots going for distance an a good day here or in Utah or New Mexico, but never since have whole gaggles of pilots raced along the White Mountain scarp, thermalled up into the lower reaches of the jet lanes, and chased each other half way to Utah.

California's White Mountains shimmered in the distance at the end of the baking Nevada highway. It was no place for a hitchhiker, but there he stood, a young kid with a white bundle under his arm. We stopped and picked him up, wondering why anyone would be wandering around in the desert in the middle of the day. He sat in the back seat, wide-eyed and mute. "Stoned," I thought, "or nuts."

In fact he was neither. His bundle turned out to be a parachute, and it contained an altimeter and a variometer, a device that audibly indicates elevation gain and loss. He was a novice hang glider pilot who had come up from the coast to try out the long glide from the west side of the Whites to the swimming holes down along the Owens River. Instead he had run into a thermal, and in no time he was climbing at more than a thousand feet a minute.

The updraft and prevailing westerlies had blown him over the 14,000-foot summit of White Mountain Peak, and he continued climbing helplessly until he reached 17,500 feet. But what worried him more than the elevation, the turbulence and cold, or his inability to put the kite into a dive, was the onset of tunnel vision. He had no oxygen with him.

He became so scared that he climbed onto the control bar of the glider, which eventually brought the kite down. He had left it in a ditch beside the highway.

We drove over Montgomery Pass in silence. "You know," he said finally, "I never flew more than ten minutes before. Today I was up there three and a half hours."

It was our turn to be stunned into silence. If a novice could get blown clear across the greatest of the Great Basin ranges, where might experience and intention be soaring? Or was it all just crazy? Maybe the pilots had it right in their cheery break-a-leg sendoff to each other, "Sport death!"

That was two years ago, and at the time I was, needless to say, impressed. Last summer, though, I discovered that his flight would be considered small potatoes today. And the White Mountains, it turns out, are the most renowned range in the world for distance hang gliding, a place where eight-hour flights and hundred-mile glides are quite common. It is here that the best pilots in the world come to compete in the Olympics of hang gliding, the Owens Valley Classic.

Like many people, I had felt that ripple of excitement a decade earlier, when people began jumping off of sand dunes and floating down to the beach on kite wings of lashed bamboo covered with plastic. A couple of years after that I inadvertently had a grandstand seat to see a kite flying a man. I was climbing the *Royal Arches* in Yosemite, and had gotten halfway from the Valley to the rim. Suddenly there was an odd slapping noise, like nothing I'd ever heard in the mountains. Instinct shot my attention upward, searching for rockfall. None. Then I saw it: a hundred feet above, and about the same distance from the cliff face was a hang glider, the trailing edge of its sail snapping in the breeze. It cruised gently on by, following the contours of the wall.

That winter I tried it myself. Three steps off a local sand hill into a headwind lifted me into the air. I had a moment of surprise at how easily it had happened; the next instant I realized that I had to fly the thing. I started overcorrecting the control bar, pitching the nose up and down. So I wobbled away my ten second flight, coming down gently on the sand. The next week, on a less perfect day, my friend who owned the kite collected a concussion, a broken wrist, broken collarbone and a bent kite. We went back to climbing.

But this summer I went back again, as a spectator anyway, to watch the Owens Valley Cross Country Classic. I found much more than expected. This meet, which is barely known locally, turns out to be the Olympics of Lift.

At the Gunter Canyon Launch site on the sixth day of competition all eyes are on Don Partridge. Don, the meet director, is about to call the day's task, which he has kept secret until now. Well, *almost* all eyes are on Don. Larry Tudor, who is leading the field two thirds of the way through the eight day competition, is asleep, sprawled across the front seat of one of the trucks that have brought us all up here.

Launching off of Gunther

"Today we're going to Coaldale Junction." says Don, and a whoop rises from among the clustered pilots. The race course is a dogleg, running north along the Whites before veering east to pick up the obscure road junction 62 miles from launch.

At 8200 feet, the Gunther launch site sits on the western flank of the White Mountains , about a third of the way from the Owens Valley to White Mountain Peak, two miles straight above. Looking out across the valley, the eastern wall of the Sierra Nevada rises just as sharply 15 miles away. They don't call it America's deepest valley for nothing. This is probably where my young friend, the hitchhiker of two years ago, took to the air. He was most of the way to Coaldale when I picked him up. Today seventy pilots are going to race there. And to make matters more interesting, they're not allowed to just get blown over the top of White Mountain, the direct way on the prevailing westerlies. No, they have a prescribed turn point at Benton, 27 miles north of launch. They must land with a photo in their cameras looking straight down on Benton, then go on to find Coaldale Junction, barley marked by its gas pumps, bar and cafe, lost in miles of sage.

"The window will open at 1:15, one hour from now, " concluded Don. Pilots can take off any time after that and will be timed from when their feet leave the ground at Gunther until they fly over the recovery truck parked at Coaldale. Long tubes of furled gliders are pulled off the trucks and spread out along the switchbacks to set up. Larry Tudor sat up and rubbed his eyes.

Gliders were being set up unhurriedly in a dozen languages. There were Italian and Austrian contingents, and the French were followed by several beautiful girls, one of whom turned out to be a hot pilot. A cluster of British accents resolved themselves into pilots from New Zealand, Australia and South Africa, as well as the British team. The thirteen year old Brazilian ace who, according to the pre-meet rumors would be trouncing everyone in sight, failed to materialize. One Brazilian, however, did finish fourteenth. Rounding out the field was a prince—or a playboy, depending on who you talked to—from Monaco.

The pilots were in their twenties, with long hair and beards, wearing tans and cutoffs. When we stopped at the artesian for water on our way to the launch site, most of them had stripped and jumped in. Conspicuously absent this year was George Worthington. George had been a Navy jet pilot, then a championship sailplane pilot, setting distance records starting from the Owens Valley, before taking up hang gliding. He became the first man to pilot a hang glider over a hundred miles in 1977, and two years later he won the first Owens Valley Cross Country Classic. George was only temporarily out, recovering from a back operation, and was promising to be back at the starting line next summer.

To an uninitiated eye the gliders looked nearly identical. They had evolved from the diamond-shaped Rogallo pattern of a dozen years ago into beautiful hawk-wing shapes. (Hang gliding actually goes much further back. The Wright brothers flew hang gliders for years before adding a motor, and even they weren't the first.) Underneath, the basic skeleton is still a kite: a long stick lashed across a short one, draped with fabric and hung out to fly. A four-foot-high king post rises above the crossing, and a triangular control bar drops below the keel. They are both guyed in every direction by steel cables to stiffen the aluminum skeleton.

The sail is shaped by inserting battens, much like those on a sailboat but sporting an aerodynamic curve. Finally, straight battens go into a second dacron skin that forms the bottom of the wing. That was the big innovation last year, the first viable double-surface wing, introduced at the Classic by Ultralight Products (UP for short). The pilots called it a quantum leap in performance, so this year most of the gliders have gone to double surfaces, like an airplane wing. Meanwhile, UP has designed the Owens Valley Racer. Introduced at this meet, it sports mylar wings, much smoother than fabric for slipping through the sky toward ever higher speeds.

Then there was the pod. All God's quickest kiddies got to have streamlining, and with the wing cleaned up, UP turned its attention to the pilot, still dragging through the air, and gave him a plastic capsule to zip into after launch, smoothing his passage. Mylar wings were a big hit, but the pod...

Their gliders assembled and rechecked, the pilots settled into the shade under their wings. The timekeeper yelled, "the window is open," and no one stirred. They were waiting for it to build.

The Pod

July sun rises steeply into a flawless sky and bakes the southern exposure of this desert mountain range. Light reflects off ridges into dark rock canyons, concentrating heat as well as any solar furnace. The cauldrons boil off bubbles of hot air that break loose from the ground and rise like droplets of grease exploding off a hot griddle. By midafternoon the sun is straight overhead, and the bubbles have turned into columns of air rising at up to 2,000 feet a minute. Prevailing winds from the west tear loose chunks of these columns of lift and blow them east up the hill. The pilots on the ridge watch these cells blow over, some for two minutes at a time, and climb into their harnesses.

A few steps into the wind lifts them into the sky, where they turn toward the center of the thermal and begin to corkscrew upward. Twisting to point their feet toward the center of the spiral can turn the kite practically on a wingtip. That maneuver has been the envy of sailplane pilots working the same lift as they watch hang gliders climb past them, efficiently working the strong center of a thermal. They aren't the only ones to be amazed. Don Partridge once found himself sharing a thermal with an eagle. They rose in parallel, each watching the other across the unfolding spiral.

By midafternoon the cells are pulsing by and several pilots take off at a time, forming gaggles. By the time we lose sight of them, most of the kites are two thousand feet above the terrain, climbing rapidly toward White Mountain. Tactical maneuvering continues along the crest of the range. It is faster to leave the thermal early and glide north toward Benton, but that leaves less elevation to spare for finding further lift. Following behind is an advantage, watching the pilots ahead to find lift or avoid sink.

Just one hour and forty two minutes after his launch, Rich Pfeiffer, who has won the Classic the last two years, crosses above the truck at Coaldale. He averaged a remarkable 38 miles an hour straight-line speed. Considering the time out for circling in thermals, he must have been going well over fifty when he was pointed downrange. Sixty-nine seconds later Steve Moyes cruised in. An Australian with twelve years of hang gliding experience, Steve has won scores of international meets. Chris Arai was third, followed by Larry Tudor. Fourth was the lowest he had placed all week.

Larry was still tired from the remarkable flying two days earlier when he had soared from Gunther halfway to Idaho. Tom Kreyche had taken over direction of the meet that day and called a day of open distance flying. Tom saw a weak weather front coming through; even better, it was *not* overdeveloping, as it had the week before when thunderheads sent lightning branching around a gaggle, shocking pilots off their control bars while missing kites by mere winglengths, and sent them diving for the ground. Tom sensed a potential distance record day, called it, and jumped off Gunther to act as a "wind dummy," scouting thermals for the contestants.

Soon they were out over Nevada. The wind shifted around to the southwest, sending them northeast along the Shoshone Range and into new territory. "At the north end of the Shoshone Range I was with Pfeiffer," recalled Tom. "He got low, turned right and landed. I kept on north, and just before going down I caught a thousand-foot-a-minute thermal and in a few minutes was back up at cloud base. For the next thirty miles I flew through a hail shower with a nice little circular rainbow parked off my wingtip. I could see Tudor out ahead of me."

Even an airplane pilot with a good map can easily get lost in Nevada's basin and range country. Tudor and Kreyche had nothing but the maps in their heads, and had never been this far before. When they crossed Highway 50, both guessed wrong. Tom ended up five miles north of Austin looking for the road to Battle Mountain. Not finding it hidden across the next range, and fearing to land out in unknown desert with night coming on he landed, 157 miles from Gunther.

Larry Tudor thought he was a hundred miles further north crossing Interstate 80 into roadless desert. He also turned, following US 50 as it veered southeast from Austin. He was actually backtracking, reducing his overall distance until he landed, 165 straight-line miles from Gunther, and just three miles short of the unofficial distance record set last spring in New Mexico.

It wasn't missing the record so narrowly that bothered him and Tom, however. When they landed around six o'clock, both thermals and wind had still been strong. "We could have flown until ten o'clock," moaned Tom. They knew that the mythical two hundred mile day had been within reach. They didn't get back to Bishop until four in the morning, so Don Partridge called a rest for the following day.

On the last day of competition Partridge called a task which put heavy emphasis on strategy. At 46 miles it was the shortest task all week, but it started south, straight into a healthy headwind to the Bishop airport, before turning downwind to Janie's Ranch, which is in the other direction, north of Benton. Pilots who took off at midafternoon spent hours beating upwind to the airport, taking as long as four hours to Janies. Pfeiffer and Tudor waited for the evening glass off, when slackening winds would allow faster flying to the airport, but diminishing thermals would also increase the risk of landing short of Janies on the downwind leg, losing everything. Finally feeling the pressure, Pfeiffer took off. Tudor followed immediately from higher up the switchback, soaring above and behind Pfeiffer in the blind spot created b his wing. They flew identical UP Owens Valley Racers, except that Pfeiffer was in the streamlining pod while Tudor disdained it as shutting off his senses from the sky. An hour and forty minutes later they flew into Janies. Larry Tudor took the day, and thus the meet, by four seconds.

Thermaling under cumulus cloud over the Owens Valley

Tudor's winning strategy runs against the grain of technology. A sense of purity compels Larry Tudor to fly without a radio, oxygen, or the recording barograph that can keep track of the vertical profile of a flight. More crucial to him is keeping his nose in the wind. He insists that nothing insulate him from from the air he's flying in. Like the pod would. This artist of the airwaves wants to stay in intimate touch with the nuances of his environment, his senses out feeling their way into the subtle cues of the sky, sensing wind, smelling thermals, feeling lift.

A cool desert evening and a keg of beer marked the award ceremonies. Accepting third place, Steve Moyes said, "I'd be happy to fly in these mountains anytime." Rich Pfeiffer in second place looked to the future: "We have a long way to go. We just don't know what we can do." The Don Partridge said, "Well, the meet has a winner, but the winner's not here—he's still out flying."

It was nearly dark when Larry Tudor showed up. A slight and softspoken pilot from Salt Lake City who spends most days soaring along the front of the Wasatch Range, Tudor accepted his etched glass trophy, $1500 from the president of UP, and a gift certificate from the meet's first sponsor, good for $150 in trade under the revolving red beacon that marks Janie's Ranch, just over the Nevada border.

That evening's talk turned to the future potential of this fledgling sport. Last year the meets (the Classic is the heavy among four held consecutively here) produced no hundred-mile flights. This year there were thirty one. One pilot, who was so low he had his feet out of the harness to land, caught a thermal and gained 13,200 feet in eighteen minutes, ending up at 19,200 feet. The week after the meet Chris Arai topped out at 22,000 feet, probably a record. Don Partridge's reaction on the radio had been, "what's nine times six?"

Obviously, the limits of the sport, now that it has entered the Owens Valley era, are still to be defined. Pilots who cut their teeth on coastal-ridge lift and then mastered thermals in the high mountains are just beginning to discuss the potential of something called high-altitude wave lift. The waves are ripples in the lower levels of the jet stream, formed when it passes over major ranges like the Sierra and the Rockies. Lift in the wave is smooth and powerful, and it has sent sailplanes up to 46,000 feet. However, tapping that force in a conventional hang glider would hardly be possible because of air turbulence, high wind speed, and extreme temperatures. "It's possible that we'll make use of the wave in the future," says Tom Kreyche, "but we'll probably be flying something that's closer to a sailplane."

Nevertheless, Kreyche's idea of an ultimate flight would be only slightly less astounding than surfing the Sierra wave. After he breaks the 200-mile barrier he wants to go "sky camping," riding thermals from range to range during the day and stopping for the night on strategically situated ridge tops. He figures it would take him about four days to go from the Owens Valley clear across the Great Basin to Salt Lake City. For aerobat Eric

Raymond, the ultimate might consist of three consecutive loops. He has already done two, a stunt that required a 90-mile-an-hour dive to initiate.

But daily life for the hang glider pilots of the Owens Valley is already remarkable enough. Take Jeff Burnett's close encounter. He was riding a thermal up to cloud base one afternoon when an F-15 dropped out of the cloud, circled him, then came back for another look. The plane passed so close that Jeff could see the pilot giving him the thumb's-up signal.

Paul Allen

Haute Skiing

Skiing the Haute Route through the Alps began with an invitation from Paul Allen, my best client. Paul had showed up as a student at the Palisade School of Mountaineering, taking up climbing in his fifties. He was a mining engineer who loved wilderness, a corporate VP who was nowhere more at home than sitting in the dirt by a campfire telling stories. Occasionally his two worlds clashed. One day he walked out of a board of directors meeting in Vancouver (it was a Canadian mining company) and changed into boots and knickers before meeting me to climb the north face of Mt. Baker. But in the elevator he ran into two of his fellow board members. They rode down in silence, but as Paul was striding away across the lobby with his backpack slung over a shoulder, he overheard one of his fellow board members say to the other, "There goes the world's oldest hippie."

Paul has skied in the Antarctic, made a strong bid to climb Mt. Vinson there, and mounted an expedition to Spitzbergen that was photographed for *National Geographic*. In his seventies, he could still climb 5000 feet in a day and lead 5.8 friction in Adidas running shoes. We took more than one trip overseas, but mostly we criscrossed the West, skiing week-long stretches along the Sierra crest and backpacking in to climb remote peaks. Once we pulled onto the summit of Mt. Whitney after coming up the precipitous east face. We expected the crowd on top, but not the black scoutmaster cutting up a watermelon for his troop (this is true—who would dare to make up a story like it?). The scoutmaster's eyes grew wide as he gestured over the edge, "You come up from down there?" Paul allowed that we had. The scoutmaster's reply, which was destined to be repeated in boardrooms and over lunch at the California Club, has passed into legend: "You is two bodacious dudes!"

What started out as an opportunity to try the most famous ski mountaineering trip in the world, ended up offering the clearest vantage point I had yet found for appreciating something that, after growing up with it, I had taken completely for granted—the sheer wildness of the of wilderness in the American West.

The hutkeeper woke us at four. I groped in the dark for coordinates: upstairs dormitory, mountain ski hut, foreign language. After pushing back the coarse blanket, I realized that I was still dressed to ski. I slid over the end of the long communal bunk, found windproof pants, slippers and rucksack, and padded downstairs. Pitchers of coffee and cocoa steamed on plank tables in the lantern light. Heaps of rolls and jam made continental breakfast.

The food and the jostling of sleepy French guests made the "hut" seem and sound more like a small, crowded continental hotel, which was about the size of it. The difference was that we were high in the Alps, midweek along the Haute Route, ski touring from Chamonix, France, to Zermatt, Switzerland.

An Alpine hut on the Haute Route.

We Americans stepped out onto the snow at first light, not sure whether it was more unusual to be putting skis on so early or to have warm feet. The route before us amounted to a slot in the snow, two skis wide and eight inches deep, cutting across a crevassed plateau before climbing 3,000 feet to the Pigne d'Arolla. At over 13,000 feet, that would be the high point of our week along the most famous, and most popular, ski tour in the world.

It had snowed during the night. Skiers who had gotten up even earlier were already a string of dots winding across the plateau, finding the route by Braille under the drifts. A ragged line of about 70 ski mountaineers climbed rhythmically into the dawn, alpine skis gripping the steep uphills by virtue of climbing skins temporarily glued to their bases. Made of nylon plush with a strong nap facing rearward, the skins allow skis to slide forward easily, then dig in and grip. In spite of that alpine tradition, I sported a different idea, then current in California, and climbed with cross country wax on my skis. Sometimes it worked well, sometimes not.

One afternoon, when I arrived particularly late on the col, a French guide, who was waiting for his group on the high notch, volunteered his opinion, which my American friends, also climbing on skins, were happy to translate: "At last, the King of Wax arrives."

But that morning, on fresh snow, my blue wax was a dream. Inspired by the prospect of skiing powder, I worked my way to the head of the line. Only my wax wouldn't climb that steeply as the grade increased, so in my wake were switchbacks that crossed and then double-crossed the narrow path of alpine tradition. The Europeans were not amused.

Starting little more than a century ago, the long Scandinavian tradition of ski touring—a graceful glide across rolling distances—had been transformed to an alpine sport. Ski mountaineering allowed its creators to gain control over the windblown snow clinging to steep mountainsides.

Then these alpine skiers built ski lifts and carried the evolution ofdownhill control a step farther, but at the expense of any ability to climb. The mutation was so successful, though, that "alpine" skiing is now the main form of the sport.

With nothing but blue sky over me, I was happy for an hour in my cocoon of effort. As I neared the top, the powder was about a foot deep and I began to taste those first tracks. Then there was a noise, which didn't register with my wilderness sensibilities until the helicopter appeared, spiraling onto the summit just above me. It disgorged a clot of skiers in bright powder suits. They were rigged for downhill only, not equipped to be out in the alpine zone for more than the 20 minutes it would take them to ski down to the hut, and some of them were way too fat to ever climb to such a place on their own.

It was my turn to be offended. A Californian growing up in the Sierra, I took wilderness for granted. Yosemite was the way the world should be, and the backcountry of Sequoia-Kings was even better.

I had reveled in a vast, uncivilized landscape, happy to pay for its solitude by carrying what I needed on my back, and taking responsibility for my own progress and safety. Only once in 30 years of backcountry travel have I been glad to see a helicopter, swooping in to save the life of my friend Peter Nemes, whose skull had been shattered by a falling rock.

My days in the Alps helped me to realize how spoiled Americans are by so much true wilderness. Crowded by civilization, the Alps were transformed practically overnight from the realm of medieval dragons to the reality of cog railways, grand alpine hotels, ski lifts, cable cars and—far into the backcountry—huts.

We were luckier. The idea of wilderness, a uniquely American concept, arose before the continent could be completely paved over. We set aside vast tracts of virgin wilderness, and are still at it, working now to save the Mojave and Great Basin deserts, which are as fragile as they are beautiful.

Doug Robinson

Ski mountaineering—the step between ski touring and pure down-hill—was slower to develop here. It wasn't until 1975 that the finest ski tour across the Sierra was completed, following brilliant pioneering work by Otto Steiner in the 1930s. The Sierra High Route rises out of the desert east of this

"Snowy Range" and runs west, crisscrossing the high divide that separates Sequoia from Kings Canyon National Park. It was given its name in honor of its resemblance to the alpine Haute Route.

Both are about 50 miles long, and each takes a week to traverse classic high-mountain terrain, punctuated by grand vistas and fine, sometimes exacting, skiing. The most notable difference is that seeing 70 skiers in a single day is nothing exceptional on the Haute Route. Maybe a hundred skiers do the Sierra High Route in an entire season.

Tracks and company along the Haute-Route

Consider a typical day on the Sierra High Route, midway through my first crossing. The sun was welcome, rising over Mount Whitney. The temperature had fallen to two degrees below zero during the night—cold for spring in the Sierra—but we were cozy in down sleeping bags perched on half-inch foam pads in a four-person tent. We zipped open the door, aimed eastward the night before, and the bright new day flooded in on us as we fired up the stove for coffee.

This windless morning high above timberline was so pleasant that we dragged our foam pads out in front of the tent and lingered an extra hour after breakfast, soaking up sun and savoring the prospect of hundreds of square miles of mountains made wilder by the winter's snow.

We packed our camp into loads of about 35 pounds apiece, which we carried over a shoulder of Milestone Mountain. My Gallic critic would have felt smug, noticing that we had been converted to climbing on skins. On second glance, he would have become disgusted all over again to see the skins on cross country rather than alpine skis.

At 13,300 feet, Milestone Col was, literally, the high point of the tour. The slopes were so steep that we teetered on our skis, edging hard for purchase.

From there, the ski run down Milestone Bowl, which had been drawing us for days, proved difficult. The bowl offered a rich orchestration of skiing challenges. Breakable wind crust alternated with deeper pillows of dense snow. This real wilderness snow made the groomed runs at the downhill lifts pale by comparison. We got in a few telemarks, a few linked face plants. At the bottom we were panting, dripping, and laughing.

It wasn't until my third crossing that I finally found what a downhill skier would call good snow in Milestone Bowl. But perfect turns are far from the best part of wilderness skiing, whose roots and gratifications are found in traveling across country, visiting places and seasons so wild they are accessible in no other way.

Paul Allen summed it up. Paul is a remarkable mountaineer, having skied the Sierra High Route with me just last spring to celebrate turning 71. He was with me on that Haute Route ski tour through the Alps, too; and he has trekked and climbed all over the world, including the backcountry of Nepal and China. From that perspective Paul called the Sierra High Route the best trip he had ever done, and pinpointed the crucial factor as wilderness: no chair lifts, no helicopters, and no huts.

Huts, then, don't belong in the wilderness, which is such a perishable commodity that it seems best protected by difficulty of access. But I feel just as strongly that huts should be allowed around the edges of the backcountry.

Over the decades, Europeans have discovered something we are just learning about huts and backcountry skiing: Hut skiing is fun. In the right places, we should have more huts. Stepping out each morning, you leave the housekeeping behind and just go, free to ski without camp dragging at your shoulders. Backcountry slopes can be enough challenge all by themselves.

Along the margins of true wilderness, we're still figuring out how much opportunity we have for hut skiing. For example, winter expands wilderness for half a year just by closing roads. This seasonal wilderness is an ideal zone in which huts could flourish, providing halfway houses between civilization and truly rigorous wilderness.

When friends of mine started a mountain lodge, they took advantage of the snowbound Sierra. In summer, their lodge was three miles below the road's end; in winter it is isolated, seven miles and 2,000 feet above the nearest cleared highway. The owners plowed car access, but stopped two miles short

Inside a cozy Yurt on the edge of the Sawtooth Wilderness, Idaho, Tory Robinson facilitates a meeting of Ski Guides: Allan Bard (foreground), Jeff Rhoades and Kristen Jacobsen.

of the lodge. Rock Creek Winter Lodge was deliberately snowed in, creating an adventurous atmosphere.

Many novice skiers have done their first tentative shuffling at such a place, happy to have skied groomed tracks as far as the summer roadhead. Beyond lies the wilderness for those who want to meet its challenge.

Winter also provides Yellowstone's Old Faithful Inn and Yosemite's Tuolumne Meadows with temporary isolation. At Yellowstone, the concessioner's snowcoaches make scheduled trips in from West Yellowstone; and one can use the inn as a grand "hut," taking advantage of isolation without having to work for it.

Each winter, Yosemite creates a de-facto wilderness by excluding motorized traffic from Tioga Road, one of the main access routes through the park. Skiers coming up from Yosemite Valley ply the road and a connecting shortcut down the Snow Creek Falls Trail. The route has drama: it leads out of the woods and onto the rim directly across from Half Dome before dropping back into the Valley. And, in the evening, there are huts.

The small building that serves as a Tuolumne Meadows ranger station in the summer converts to a hut in winter, with bunks and wood stove for the convenience of passing skiers. The place is jammed during Easter. Just down the road, the Yosemite Mountaineering School's summer headquarters becomes a winter hut for guided ski trips.

The opening of another hut just east of Tioga Pass has increased the options. A converted lodge, Tioga Pass Resort is the last link in a chain, making possible the first trans-Sierra ski-hut route. A string of Yurt huts also have been proposed for Yellowstone, to run south from Old Faithful, offering a week's touring that would end in Teton Park.

The hut idea is exciting if it can offer access to winter without compromising wilderness. For those who would find a cramped tent or igloo forbidding or even impossible, huts allow a taste of winter's ephemeral beauty.

A wheelchair-bound kid, staying at the Old Faithful Inn, might watch a moose plowing through fresh snow in Yellowstone. A midwestern track skier with no inclination toward snow camping could ski across the Sierra.

Huts are for those who want to explore all the possibilities of skiing without a backload of pots, stoves, and tents, who want to learn how to climb on skis, skate the flats, and gain some crucial respect for mountain weather and the subtlety of avalanches before plunging into the bright wilderness beyond.

Warbonnet Peak

Hidden Wilderness:
the Wind Rivers

Here is small sketch of a granite range so fine that only Sierra chauvinism can sustain the joke of calling it "the second finest mountain range in the world." Take a declared lover of the Sierra, drop him into the heart of the Wind Rivers and remove the blindfold. It would take hours of wandering through the strangely familiar loveliness of this landscape to realize that he was not in the Sierra. The clues, finally, would be more wildflowers, greener meadows and fiercer thunderstorms.

First word of Wyoming's Wind River Range came to me around a climbers' campfire in 1966. It was midsummer in Yosemite and the heat was taking its toll: by midafternoon the granite walls were too hot to touch and our hands were too sweaty to grip the rock. There was nothing to do but swim in the Merced River and then return to the campground where even the dust seemed exhausted.

One night, after granite gossip, after the stretch of peaceful silence that always sends the weary to bed and tightens the circle of the already dreaming, a friend said, "I wonder if the snow's melted out of the Winds yet?" By then we knew it was time to head for the high country, and the Wind Rivers sounded so good that four of us pooled gas money and went to see for ourselves.

The Wind River Range keeps itself hidden. For most tourists driving on U.S. 187 between Rock Springs and Jackson, its soaring mountains appear as merely a spiny skyline off to the east; only a practiced eye can pick out Gannett Peak, at 13,804 feet the highest point in Wyoming, from the dozens of other ice-eaten towers in the distance. When visitors stop for gas in Pinedale, a town of dirt side streets set in rolling sage country, they tend to dismiss the racks of picture post cards of the Winds and continue on toward the more publicized grandeur of Yellowstone and the Grand Tetons, just a hundred miles to the north.

Heading into the Winds, 1966

Unlike the Winds, the Tetons are obvious. How could you miss them, rising 7000 feet straight above Jackson Hole, spires looming over glaciers towering over grassland? The notoriety of the Tetons, and of the town of Jackson—a kind of urban-cowboy Disneyland—have done a great favor for the Wind Rivers by siphoning off attention. I felt like a true pioneer as I pulled out of the caravan of cars headed north and turned the old Corvair off the highway near Pinedale onto an obscure gravel road running east through the sage. Here and there, isolated ranches appeared along creek-bottom meadows. Over a hill beyond one ranch, seven young eagles played in the air currents, and further on 30 antelope stood in a knot by the side of the road.

Gravel soon gave way to rutted mud, and the dirt track climbed into a wetter landscape of meadows and aspen before finally reaching the trailhead some 50 miles off the highway. There was still little sign of mountains as we started hiking up a trail winding through pine forests, past an old bull moose standing knee-deep in the creek. It was five more miles before the woods started breaking up to reveal the spectacular high country.

When you finally find them, the Wind Rivers are a revelation. Here is a mountain wilderness easily three times the area of the Tetons, with granite for climbing as fine as Yosemite and as many wild flowers as the North Cascades. Each day that week we walked past clear lakes held in basins of solid rock as we followed the sun's first light up through delicate tundra gardens to climb on angular white granite. In the afternoons we skied down snowfields on our boot soles on our way back to camp. By nightfall there would be so many trout pulled from the lakes and streams that, tired of frying them, we'd mix up a kettle of fish chowder for dinner. There were also those elements that separate the high-mountain experience from a Sunday after-noon picnic in a city park: millions of mosquitoes, the scariest lightning storms of my life, and four inches of fresh snow in the middle of August.

Many climbers feel that these half-hidden, seemingly secret mountains should be left lost behind the ranges. I have felt that way myself, only judiciously passing on the word of this special granite wilderness. So why advertise it now? The answer lies with a man who made a life out of knowing the Wind River Range—and publicizing it.

Many a stretch of rough country seems to have a guardian like Finis Mitchell. He was just a boy when his family arrived in a mule-drawn wagon in 1906 at the western slope of the Wind Rivers. Since then he has wandered over the entire range, stocked fish in most of its drainages, climbed the peaks, and taken the photos that seemed so out of place on those post card racks in Pinedale. His captions describing the beauty of the Winds at first seem overblown, the enthusiastic words of a true believer. Yet they bespeak Mitchell's firm belief that the salvation of this place lies in the public's knowledge of it, and in a growing awareness of how to tread gently in a fragile wilderness.

Walking out to Big Sandy Opening last summer I finally met Finis Mitchell. He was coming up the trail in worn blue coveralls, looking more like a Nebraska farmer than a hard-as-nails mountain man. "I want to live to be a hundred," he told me, "so I can kiss all the pretty girls who congratulate me. I want to show young people that it pays to take as good care of their bodies as they do their cars...and I want to see what people have done to these mountains. Enjoy the mountains, and take care of them so your children can enjoy them." With that he walked off into the Wind Rivers, saying once more over his shoulder, "Take care of the mountains."

Helen and Russ Robinson backpacking the Winds.

Doug Robinson

Photo by Steve Curtis

Go Climb a Desert

A few of the pieces here—and this is one—were written for a much more general audience. This short once-over about rock climbing as another roadside attraction was published in the Sunday *Los Angeles Times Magazine*, partly because I viewed Joshua Tree as a unique opportunity for anyone in greater L. A. to get a close up view of the mystery of climbing, and partly because ongoing enthusiasm for the habitat of this chunk of desert kept drawing me back and I felt like sharing the secret.

The rock in front of me is smooth and too steep to climb. Not vertical, but steep enough. No holds at hand, I squint across blank stone, bright in desert sunshine. Decidedly out of reach is a thumb-sized bump, and two feet beyond that is digital nirvana—a one-inch ledge. My left foot stretches sideways to nuzzle into a shallow notch. A puff of gymnastic chalk, used by a previous climber to dry sweaty palms and improve grip, brings my attention to a wrinkle in the granite maybe as thick as a nickel. I press the pads of two fingers gratefully onto it. Exhale, focus concentration, and pull hard.

Suddenly I'm falling. The strain that had been holding me against the stone catapults me into space. A rope stops my fall almost as soon as it begins. Securely knotted to my waist, it is clipped to a bolt driven into the granite and runs down the face to my 100-pound belayer. She catches my fall with a single hand and saves my life for the fifth time in as many minutes. We both laugh.

The rope stretched momentarily like a rubber band, yo-yoing me to a stop. Woven especially for climbing (165 feet costs $150), it's good for dozens of these inconsequential falls—as well as the one real screamer it may never get.

The climbers standing along the base of the cliff hardly notice. To them a five-foot drop onto the rope is like hitting a wrong note while practicing the saxophone. The movements of rock climbers have become subtle enough that delicate weight shifts must now be executed from full power-grip hangs, and few can master such an intricate sequence on the first try. So the climbers, if they notice at all, are more interested in critiquing techniques: Since the foot popped again, shift the body angle outward.

Beyond the climbers hover clusters of tourists. They notice the fall. These people didn't come to the desert to see climbing; to them we're just a roadside attraction. On the tip of many a tongue is the disclaimer, "You wouldn't catch me up there."

Probably not. The fear of falling is deeply ingrained, one of only a handful of feelings that psychology is willing to call "instinct." Even climbers are not immune. "Fight gravity" says a T-shirt popular in the camp. And climbs get names like "Fear of Flying" and "Aerial Anticipation."

Maybe we've just misunderstood George Mallory all these years. The British conqueror of Mt. Everest cut short a reporter who was asking yet again, "Why climb?" by replying, "Because it is there." Maybe "it" isn't the mountain at all but the void, forever snapping at the heels of the climber, escaping upward.

At any rate, I balance back onto the rock and again address the crux passage. Leaning out one or two more degrees intensifies the strain on my fingertips, but it allows me to stick my foot onto its smear hold. I slap the higher nubbin a moment before the foot skips, teeter and, holding, scramble up onto the one-inch ledge. My belayer yells congratulations, and the little knot of tourists behind her breaks into applause. My concentration slackens, and in a rush I feel the winter sunshine on my bare back.

After all that, I am 25 feet above the desert floor. I clip my rope through another bolt. The difficulty eases slightly, almost imperceptibly, but enough to allow fluid ascension. In two minutes I pull over the top of the 80-foot climb. Stella follows with disquieting ease, and we scramble down the backside of this granite bump into the Mojave.

Bruce Robinson photo

This is Joshua Tree. Like many other climbers, from casual weekenders to dedicated fanatics stretching the limits of the sport, I spend several weeks each winter at this National Park east of Palm Springs, honing the skills that go into modern rock climbing. An odd blend of raw power applied with finesse, as well as year-round training, have become essential elements in mastering the hardest climbs. The height of some of the most notorious ones is less than 100 feet. While Yosemite's El Capitan is better known and by no means passe, the demanding new climbs are the little outcrops at its base and elsewhere around the country. A number of the world's hardest climbs are in Joshua Tree, and this modest collection of granite has become a winter training mecca. During the climbing season one sees license plates from a dozen icebox states on the cars parked below the rocks and hears rope chatter in French, German and Japanese.

For the curious, Joshua Tree turns out to be one of the best places to see rock climbing, check out the moves and explore the mystery of "how the rope gets up there." Joshua Tree is actually much better for watching than Yosemite, for example, where the action on El Capitan is veiled at binocular distance, and the short climbs that would be good viewing are hidden behind trees in obscure parts of the valley. At Joshua Tree many climbs are right out in the open along the road.

But don't be lured onto the rock by the climbers' easy grace, their deceptively casual manner and occasional solo adventures; like good athletes anywhere, they make what they do look easy. Recently I came upon a teen-ager, from a South Bay church group, crumpled on a ledge. While scrambling, he slipped and fell 25 feet. He was lucky: Other than suffering some abrasions, he seemed only to have broken his wrist. But the rangers and I had to strap him to a backboard for a rough carry to the waiting ambulance, and the experience ruined the day for a lot of people. As all climbers know, gravity is unforgiving, and ever so democratic.

Out to Launch

A trade show in Las Vegas is a strange place for the birth of an expedition. Or maybe not. The outdoor equipment industry used to show its new products in the back halls of the Ski Industries of America's glitzy show there, and people you usually saw at timberline camps shuffled together in the aisles, schemed up bold ideas set on far-off mountain ranges, then canvassed the convention center for equipment sponsors before adjourning to a big ski company's hospitality suite for free drinks.

That is exactly how this trip began in the spring of 1980.

I am backing down the north ridge of Mt. Rainier on the front points of my crampons, alone and unroped. This is the steepest section, six hundred feet below the summit where the angle is 50 degrees plus. As I sink my ice axe into the windpacked crust I can see five thousand feet between my legs to the Carbon Glacier.

A faint hiss brings my attention up to powder snow sliding over the horizon of ice above. Backlit golden, the snow rolls over the toes of my climbing boots like a miniature ground blizzard, leaving a taste of vertigo in my mouth. Now the powder is coming in rhythmic waves, too small to be an avalanche. Soon I can see a figure behind them, pumping turns as he comes into view, skis flashing in the air between the edge sets that are scraping off this cascading powder. Chris Landry is *skiing* the north ridge of Mt. Rainier.

I've been waiting a long time to see this. Waiting since midnight breakfast in the tent and starting up the Liberty Ridge by headlamp. I've been waiting since we left the eastern entrance of Mt. Rainier National Park ten days ago, skiing on a snowed-in road at only 3500 feet in early May. I wondered eleven-thousand feet up the mountain, and huddled in the tent during a three-day storm after that. In fact I've been wondering ever since hearing about Sylvan Saudan, the Frenchman who started this business of skiing down ice climbs, in the Alps during the fifties. What would extreme skiing be like? I wasn't sure I wanted to find out.

It is not wild or out of control. Well, not out of control anyway. As Chris came closer I could see him plant both poles in the hard crust and pull his skis as much as a foot off the snow in a jump turn. For a split second the skis are aimed straight down the ice face. He brings them around to land with his edges sliding eight or ten feet to brake before launching into the next turn. Launching is about what it's like, too. Jumping a foot off the snow means dropping further than that to get back in contact; at this angle the terrain is closer to vertical than horizontal. Watching just one well-controlled turn at a time, Chris doesn't seem that close to the edge. His lanky frame coils and uncoils through the turns in a way that looks relaxed. But considering the view over his ski tips at mid-turn—staring down a vertical mile of steep snow and ice—brings it all rushing back into perspective.

Taken just as an ice climb, the Liberty Ridge commands considerable respect. After its first ascent in 1936, it wasn't climbed again until 1952. Today climbers with several seasons experience are drawn here to try one of the longest and most alpine ice routes in the country. Many turn back. If the five thousand foot trailless walk up to its base or crossing the frighteningly crevassed Carbon Glacier doesn't get to them, then maybe the altitude, a sudden storm or burning calves will. Those who do make it will often have bivouaced on an ice shelf midway up the vertical mile of ridge, and they will usually descend by the normal route on the easy south side of the mountain, the one that those Sunday supplement and airline magazine writers are always bragging about having "conquered."

To succeed on the Liberty is an accomplishment far beyond the usual Northwest climber's ambition of scaling all six of the major volcanoes in the Cascades—or five now that St. Helens is out of the running, for the Liberty is considered one of the fifty classic climbs of North America. A book by that name written by Steve Roper and Allen Steck, two of the country's top alpinists, has ranked the Liberty Ridge with such class acts as Half Dome and the North Face of the Grand Teton. Climb

Chris Landry

and descend the Liberty in a day, maybe, but the locals were not prepared to hear that it had been skied. A reporter from the Seattle P-I phoned Dee Molenaar, author of the definitive history, "The Challenge of Rainier," to confirm that Landry's descent was indeed a first. Molenaar sputtered, "He did what?"

Ski mountaineering edges into the realm of extreme skiing, according to Chris, at about 45°. Clinging to the smooth windboard at that angle, a surface burnished by the nearly ceaseless high altitude winds until it resembles fine-grained ice, means having an edge and holding it. The edges on Chris's Rossignol FP's have been carefully filed sharp, then rounded slightly at the tips and tails with emery cloth. Too sharp would be as bad as dull, making the edges grabby and liable to chatter and bounce the skis. Chris has carried that pair of skis on his back the whole trip, carefully taped together with a paper spacer, only taking them out the morning of the descent. For holding that edge, Chris's Dynafit boots are clamped on with Marker M5s, tightened all the way down to "Race." Losing an edge out ther would be...well, that brings up Chris's other definition of extreme skiing. "Extreme skiing begins," he says, "at the point where if you fall, you die."

It's a weird dance we do that afternoon, sort of a minuet for crampons and skis. A minuet in ragtime. Chris skis down a dozen turns showing his control by pulling to a stop anywhere he likes. I fold up the camera, back down to a vantage point below him and set it up again. We yo-yo on down the face. As a band of cliffs approaches below, Chris crosses to the west side of the ridge, into a narrow chute filled alternately with crust and crud. Leaping over rocks at the bottom takes him onto the lower face. It is still two thousand feet down to the glacier, but the angle has eased off, the snow is soft now, Chris is carving up the crud and I am running alongside, the way you do on a sand dune, trying not to get ahead of myself .

Chris called the Liberty Ridge a "Classic" extreme descent, and came back to the Sierra looking for more. He found it here in the right-hand Mendel couloir at over 55 degrees.

Chris's descent of the Liberty Ridge was the climax of what actually turned out to be something of an expedition. Eleven days on the mountain. Twenty thousand feet of climbing and descending. Leaving the roadhead with over two-hundred pounds of gear—Chris's two pairs of downhill skis for example, and two pairs of boots apiece, and we were carrying full ice climbing gear as well as ski stuff. By the time we got to the Liberty, we had already climbed the mountain once, and I had bagged the first ski descent of Rainier on nordic skis. Not to mention traversing three glaciers and a blizzard to get around to the north side.

Our first visit to the summit had been a perfect day, with air so clear we could see from Mt. Baker up by the Canadian border all the way down the Cascades to Mt. Jefferson, halfway through Oregon. But that wasn't what grabbed our attention. We happened to come over the rim right next to a steaming patch of bare ground, the only part of the half-mile of crater that wasn't choked with ice. It *was* steam, with a whiff of sulphur mixed in, showing that this volcano wasn't dead yet, either. But soon we were distracted by a cloud of ash belching soundlessly from the next cone south and rising in a few moments three-thousand feet above the mountaintop. We sat and watched as two more ash plumes chugged skyward. Mount Saint Helens was warming up. It was the sixth of May.

The accumulated ash on Saint Helens completely hid the northern glaciers which I had climbed the August before. All the way down that day I had wished for my skis. Now it's too late. Or is it?

"What if we went up there? You know, skirt the roadblock at dusk, climb in the dark, ski off the summit at first light, cutting tracks through the ash—can you imagine how it would look? White figure eights on a field of grey. It would be worth ruining a pair of skis for."

"Yeah, right. Sounds like a 'last ski descent' to me." It was typical, sitting on one mountain dreaming about another.

Chris stood up, stretched and stepped onto his downhill skis. We have five-thousand vertical feet to go back down to our sleeping bags. My cross crountry skis look thin and delicate by comparison, though 'cross country' hardly describes these sleek, fiberglass skis with a steel edge, plastic base and semi-downhill flex pattern.

Refusing to take either-or for an answer, skiers in the American West have been pushing into the void between cross country and downhill for a decade now, going nearly everywhere there's snow on these light and agile nordic mountaineering skis. Now it seems only a logical extension to find myself clipping into pin bindings—the first time anyone has done so—on top of the most glaciated peak in the continental United States. My only hesitation was these brand new Rossignol prototypes which had arrived just before the trip—I had yet to make a downhill turn on them.

Contemplations of fire faded into dealing with ice as we went clattering off the summit on a surface roughly the texture of frozen Gila monster hide. Fortunately, at the first increase in angle the ice gave way to windboard. Skiing over it was as good as running on the hard sand between water's edge and the loose, dry beach. I cut a quick series of slalom-sharp parallel turns, warming-up and playing. The new skis felt fast and sure.

Dropping over another edge put us on the main face of the Emmons Glacier. It is huge. A mile-wide in places and dropping all the way from the 14,410 foot summit down to melt away into rain forest ten-thousand feet below, the Emmons is the biggest glacier on Rainier. And the next three thousand feet is its steepest section, with the angle hovering around 35°, about as steep as the expert headwall at most downhill resorts. I slide over the snow bridge spanning a large crevasse and out onto the main face.

Unfortunately, high altitude wind doesn't always make that nice smooth windboard Chris carved up on the Liberty. Sometimes it gets weird and instead of being a carpenter's dream, the same windblasted powder forms into sastrugi. Rarely seen except at high altitudes, sastrugi resembles random stacks of sharp-edged platters strewn around on the surface of the snow. Skiing it is about like trying to hold an edge while traversing a steep slate roof. Only here some of the slates are six and eight inches thick. Climbing up, I had scouted the alleys of smoother windcrust leading down through the sastrugi and between crevasses.

Even where the crust is smooth it is still very steep. Coaxing myself into a turn, I come flying out, holding onto my balance on chattering skis sliding forty or fifty feet until I slow down enough to try again. That's skiing parallel; telemarking wouldn't stand a chance on the this surface. In fact, steep icy crust is the biggest blind spot in the world-view of those telemark fanatics. You know the type: "There is no turn but the split stride turn, and Telemark is its name."

Suddenly I'm falling. Caught an edge on that damn sastrugi, and I'm sliding out of control toward a crevasse. Chris is too terrified, watching me slide by, to take a photo. Time slows down but I don't, bouncing and slamming into the sastrugi. Finally I get my edges under me, and that, combined with dragging the tips of both poles in a self-arrest pulls me to a stop three-hundred feet below. I am sitting there shaking when Chris snaps to a stop next to me. Even his downhill skis grate on this surface. "Who-ooeee!" says Chris. "Man. Pointing those things down into the fall line takes some kind of...Let me see your skis." He fishes an old piece of emery cloth out of a pocket. "Yep. Too sharp. Brand new skis. You're coming out of the turns balanced all right, but your edges are grabbing on you." He worked over the edges, dulling especially the tips and tails while I calmed down. "That should help," he said, handing back a ski. It helped a lot.

Below, the sastrugi is rock-hard and six-to-eight inches high. The kind of frozen snow cat tracks found at a downhill resort would be easy skiing next to this, and the smooth alleys have given out. I run a long traverse to the south, holding on with my ankles for half a mile, thighs burning.

Photo by Chris Landry

All that sightseeing on top has made us an hour late for a great corn snow run down the last 1500 feet, which had frozen ahead of me as the sun left it. On the other hand, we're maybe two months early to find most of the run in that condition. I believe I'll try midsummer next time and see if I can't catch the Emmons in lazy eight corn snow all the way down. Of course, then the crevasses would be open wide...

We clattered down over the last of the ice, cut up a hundred yards of corn, just enough to show us what we had been missing, and fell into camp.

We ate little, slept hard and woke in a snowstorm. Below here the Emmons is too broken by crevasses for good skiing, so, climbing stiffly over a prow of rock, we put skis back on at the top of the Inter Glacier. It wasn't just snowing, we were in the cloud. Three inches of fresh powder merged with the sky. But the terrain was inviting and we skied with abandon. I would cut a dozen turns, skiing rag-doll loose to absorb changes in the terrain that I couldn't see. This was a perfect frolic after yesterday's tense edging. Then pull up, coast to a stop and relax, only to fall over on my face. With no frame of reference you could still be coasting along an even arc thinking you had already stopped, and get thrown. We shredded two thousand feet and all too quickly were back at the red sled cached by a rock.

It would be great to keep skiing on down through Glacier Basin from here, another couple thousand feet of good snow before the route gets tangled in the woods. Instead, we went on our way around the mountain, straining to see crevasses in a storm which wouldn't lift until we were right under the Liberty Ridge.

Back home, I keep thinking about that hot spot on top of Rainier. It is not alone. Recent years I've also been on top of Hood, Baker, Adams and Shasta, not to mention St. Helens itself. They all have hot spots on top; at times the reek of sulphur has been enough to send us running off the summit. St. Helens wasn't even as active as Mt. Hood a year ago.

Soon after I left, Mt. St. Helens blew, and a week later earthquakes started rocking my Eastern Sierra home, thousands of them in the first two weeks alone. Avalanches and rockslides were actually scaring us off from the best backcountry spring skiing in ten years.

For the big quake on the third day I was sitting on the ground in my front yard and could see a literal groundswell rolling toward me. A friend who was climbing Mt. Humphreys that day, got avalanched out of the north gully. He picked himself out of the debris and started back up, only to have an aftershock knock him down for a second slide. At Hot Creek, near Mammoth, where skiers love to soak, one of the springs turned briefly into a forty-foot geyser, and a dozen new springs popped up. In the twelve years I've been going there, the place has transformed from a single spring into a miniature Yellowstone. A week later, it's getting blase. Friends are gathered for cocktails at Andrea Mead Lawrence's house in Mammoth when a medium-sized quake rolls through. Nobody drops a canape, asiding their estimates instead: "3.4" "4.2" "3.7" We are getting pretty good at it. The quote of the year comes out about then in the *Los Angeles Times*. An unidentified scientist from Cal Tech claims that our earthquake activity has "nothing to do with Mt. St. Helens." I'm not so sure. Seems like the same junction of plates to me, pieces of crust bumping and grinding as they float around on the surface of our whirling little drop of liquid steel. Perhaps ours is the generation that will live the proof of Velikovsky's cataclysmic theories of geology. I kind of hope so. It beats getting nuked.

Second Ascent of Ama Dablam

Little was written at the time about this beautiful climb, maybe because it led to a typically overstated 17-minutes of film aired on a Sunday afternoon on ABC Sports. Oh well, the film paid for our trip. Now that the South Ridge has become a trade route and is regularly guided, several expeditions at a time climb over each other and vie for the rather scarce campsites. Many are still turned back by weather, unrelenting difficulty and the high, thin air.

Ama Dablam has been called "the Matterhorn of the Himalayas" and "the most beautiful mountain in the world." It *is* a great looking peak, an improbable fang of ice-coated granite, but perhaps the superlatives stem more from the accident of its rising right next to the trekker trail to Everest base camp. It does not come into view until pilgrims have finally stumbled over the crest of a 13,000-foot ridge. Most of the eyes that then catch the first view of it are more oxygen-starved than they have ever been.

Ama Dablam was first climbed almost as an afterthought by an expedition doing research on the physiology of adapting to high altitude, and the ascent nearly landed Sir Edmund Hilary in jail. It was the winter of 1962 when the mostly-American scientists, with Hilary as a kind of figurehead leader, set two camps high up the Mingbo Valley which lies immediately south of the peak. The Green Hut was at 17,000 feet, and the prefabricated Silver Hut perched at 19,000 feet. They shuttled between the two camps all winter, riding stationary bicycles while breathing into laboratory tubing. By spring they had confirmed what some mining villages high in the Peruvian Andes had long made them suspect: that 18,000 feet is the limit of human adaptation. Above there you may go on feeling that you are adapting, but your body is in fact steadily deteriorating. You are falling apart.

The physiologists had drawn the line, and it may be just a coincidence that at the 18,000 foot level half of the earth's atmosphere is below you. Reinhold Messner—with his flair for drama—later put some spin on the research by nameing the realm above there the Death Zone.

But the high altitude physiologists winding up their brilliant work that spring also happened to be climbers. So, after camping at the foot of this literally breathtaking peak all winter, they crossed their newly-surveyed line and made the first ascent of Ama Dablam. And photographed it for *National Geographic.*

The King of Nepal was furious. He had not given permission to climb this sacred peak. He had not collected his customary peak fee. Hilary was summoned to Kathmandu, called on the carpet, and narrowly escaped being thrown in jail. And Ama Dablam was off limits for the next 18 years.

Somehow, Tom Frost had the foresight to send in an expedition application just in time so that when the King decided to open up Ama Dablam, ours was on the top of the stack. Which is how in 1979 I ended up making the second ascent with the likes of Frost, Jeff Lowe, Greg Lowe, David Brashears and Martin Boysen. We studied the old *Geographic* for clues to getting up the South Ridge, and paid for the trip by making the film for ABC Sports.

It took us a month and a mile of fixed ropes to get ourselves and the cameras from a basecamp at 15,000 feet to the 22,495-foot summit. I ended up going on the second summit push with John Wasson, who was on the trip mostly to bring his world-class kayaking skills in front of the same cameras on the Arun River gorge following the climb. Instead of passing the time in basecamp, John went to the summit with me.

So we tagged the summit and then made it all the way back down out of the 'Death Zone.' But looking back on our summit day, I realize that I did some pretty stupid things up in that thin air, things that gave me less margin of safety than I will usually accept. Like spending at least an hour that morning in the tent, with fumble-fingers at zero degrees, sewing the Buddhist prayer flags I had been given onto a line so they could be waved from the summit. Like looking at an ample pile of snow anchors in the Camp III tent and then choosing to protect our summit bid with one snow fluke (good thinking) and, passing by several other flukes, I took a snow picket for our second anchor, a lame device that ample experience had shown me to be difficult and untrustworthy. Descending through whitout and snow-swirling wind all after-noon at a relentless 50° angle, I had to belay with that stupid picket.

Flying prayer flags in the summit whiteout.

I have often wondered since returning about any linger-ing effects of the altitude, of stumbling upward into the 'Death Zone.' Speculation runs around campfires: Has Roskelly undergone a personality shift? What about that Italian K2 expe-dition? Did the high divorce rate afterward stem from altitude or just the loneliness of months away? And what about the two members who supposedly went crazy? It's all speculation, which of course makes the whole subject ripe for the slander mills.

I do know that I had the second hardest time acclimatizing of anyone on the trip. And my friend who had a worse time was the only one who didn't summit. I know that from sheer exhaustion I had to turn down a great offer from Jeff Lowe to accompany him on the new route up the South Face that he ended up soloing a few days later.

I know that stuff I wrote in my notebook at Camp I and Camp II, stuff that excited me at the time, turned out back in the lowlands to be rather confused drivel.

I know that I couldn't seem to recover physically after coming down. I mean, there I was—in the Khumbu, in killer shape, with all my gear, and with my friend, Dr. David Schlim waiting at the Pheriche Hospital of the Himalayan Rescue Association—all ready to go climbing. I did walk the easy day from our base camp up to the hospital, but all I could muster the energy to do was sit in the sun in the doorway drinking tea and asking a few questions about the re-pressurizing treatment for acute mountain sickness that David was trying out. I stayed a couple of days before gathering the energy to abandon my ski gear at the hospital and drift irresolutely toward the lowlands.

Are there lingering effects? There is a perfect Catch 22 built into the whole question of permanent mental damage from altitude: if you get stupider, how ya gonna know?

We had an incredibly successful expedition. Not just that we made the second ascent of what people tend to call the most beautiful mountain they have ever seen. Not that we brought back the footage for a successful documentary. Not that we put ten people on the summit, cleared our trash off the mountain and escaped without injury. But that we got through the notorious stresses of fairly hard climbing at mind-numbing altitudes without so much as a raised voice, and all came home friends.

Return

Summiting Mount Whitney with Mount Russell behind. Photo by Kristen Jacobsen

Doug Robinson

Fool For Stone

After growing up on trips to the Sierra, moving there and living at timberline climbing camps during the summer and snowed-in up canyons during the winter, after taking off again and again to climb here, guide there, teach climbing halfway across the country and do an expedition halfway around the world, I come home. Not to rest and repack, but increasingly to stay. This is the place.

My buddy the guiding genius Allan Bard has it figured by latitudes and precipitation levels and prevailing wind patterns and proximity to the mediating maritime influence of the coast just what it is that narrows down the roster of mountain ranges that could possibly rival the unique pre-eminence of the Sierra. He has it down to just three other ranges in the world: the Southern Alps of New Zealand, a stretch of the southern Andes a ways north of the wind tunnel of Patagonia, and to be honest I forget which is the last.

Well, I can only say that I've spent some time in the Southern Alps of New Zealand, and while the peaks are plenty exciting and I loved sitting in the Welcome Flat hot springs under the Southern Cross, my Sierra-bred sensibilities noticed that the weather is terrible and the rock crumbly. Such bad rock that to venture out on it I was glad to have a shaky ice-axe belay in soft snow. One of the local guides, Marty Baer, explaining a 5000-foot rock slide that took 80 feet off the summit of

Mt. Cook, commented laconically that, "These mountains weren't built to last." A nice place to visit. But thanks anyway, I'll take the short pants and sunny granite and the long, lingering spring corn skiing of the Sierra.

So, return to the Sierra. Since this collection begins in Yosemite, it fits to begin this return by going right back there, as the first stop on a turning-forty odyssey that reflects on a continuing obsession with climbing, looks at what was then, in 1985, the state of that art, and leads to a moment when, abruptly, I very nearly ended by paying the ultimate price. Next, a closer look at the evolution of Yosemite climbing, as seen through the eyes of its most famous big wall, El Capitan.

By then it's spring, and time to return again to backcountry skiing, to two favorite Sierra ski tours, the High Route and a slice of the Sierra crest.

Finally, I return to my preoccupation with the visionary state of mind, an experience that first came up when I lived in Yosemite, that arises so readily from climbing, and that will be the subject of my half-finished next book, "The Alchemy of Action."

"By your late thirties the ground has begun to grow hard. It grows harder and harder until the day that it admits you." — Thomas McGuane, "Nobody's Angel"

Climbing. It seems so simple and direct when you're out there, surging upward with a lungful of bright air. Simple alright, it simply took over my life. Starting way back. My high school yearbook allowed that while I aimed to be a biochemist, I'd more likely end up a climbing bum. Suddenly I'm past forty. My first wife went on to become a professor of Oncology. I went back to the mountains. Now I'm married to a ski mountaineering fanatic who works as a management consultant. Kristen teaches leadership skills, and when the metaphor is climbing I guide alongside. The rest of my work and play still flows out of the mountains too: I design gear, I write about rock and snow. It keeps me climbing.

So the obsession isn't slacking off. If anything, it keeps on getting stronger. This ain't no midlife crisis, you know—more like a full-blown religious mania. My broken back has mended so I can touch stone again, as Dale Bard so beautifully described climbing, making it sound a little like the saving grace it truly is. I'm amazed that a back broken clean in half can be so seamlessly healed that I barely notice it. My left wrist, strained until it nearly snapped in the same screaming grounder, didn't come back so fast, though. For over a year it would tweak on me at odd moments, suddenly loosening my grip.

The boldness has practically vanished from my climbing, which is OK actually, since my mind hasn't healed as fast as my back. The other day I led, again, up a 5.9 crack in the Buttermilk rocks near my Sierra cabin. When I first tied on to a rope at thirteen, 5.9 defined the limit of human performance, straining the outside of the envelope. An hour before the fall I led that crack casually with no protection, trailing the useless rope behind to belay my student. But this time I sewed it up, by anchoring my rope six times, solid.

At odd moments now, not even while climbing, I literally shudder from the image of that forty-foot drop onto the rocks. My mind blanked out to avoid dealing with it as it was happening; now the scene keeps bubbling insistently to the surface. But there's no thought of quitting. Wasn't even that morning after, when the question began reaching me from out there beyond the oxygen mask and I.V. tubes and sister morphine. Since I had escaped starting over as a quad, it was back to this ascending passion.

Of course the plan for celebrating my fortieth year on earth, 27th on the rocks, went awry from the start. What are plans for? The idea began as a kind of homecoming, back to Yosemite in the fall of 1985. Guiding had kept me in shape, and I knew my technique was still improving. It would be fun to return to the crucible, take up old ambitions and maybe catch a fleeting glimpse of the rising standards. I had no illusions of overtaking the advancing edge of history, of course, which had long since vanished over the horizon of youth.

Instead, midlife digressions like making a living propelled me across the country, and shifted my focus to teaching climbing. But it's never strictly one or the other, paycheck or pilgrimage. I had friends to see and even a mentorship to fulfill, in Oklahoma where I'd taught so long that students had turned into apprentice guides. And then there were the return matches with some particularly gnarly stretches of stone, the ones that kept rising in my dreams. Along the way that trip began to nudge my climbing in a pointedly modern direction. And in the end it led, as obsessions will, to that December twilight.

First, Yosemite. Shortly after my birthday I drove into the Valley one morning with Vern and Margaret Clevenger. Vern was the shaggy kid who showed up in Yosemite at fifteen following Galen Rowell around like a clumsy puppy, then found his feet to become the edge-master of Tuolumne Meadows, where face climbing had already reached a high, thin art. It's hard to believe that Vern commutes to New York now, selling his fine-art photography—so much brilliance under the misfit—and that his resume characterized him as a "recreational" 5.12 climber. That's all the more hilarious because it's so true. "5.12 isn't even close to the forefront these days," Vern says. So Vern teamed up with Claude Fiddler that day to get even more honed so they could climb the Salathe Wall of El Cap a couple of weeks later in a record 17 hours.

I went to the Nabisco wall to climb cracks with Margaret, and it was a far cry from what we used to call "girl climbing" back when we were chauvinists. I led, but only because we were crack climbing, a style that felt a little foreign to Margaret after face climbing in Tuolumne where she has begun edging into 5.11. But she scampered up easily enough, stabbing two fingers into a pocket in the rock, twisting to lock them, and cranking it effortlessly. I mean, this woman was buffed: months of Nautilus had put definition into her shoulders that a lot of male climbers would covet. So in no time we were on top of *Waverly Wafer*. Could this really be 5.10c—a grade I couldn't even touch when I lived in the Valley? Vern and Claude fired up it on top rope "just for exercise." Which put us on a ledge in the middle of Nabisco Wall staring up *Butterballs*.

Out of curiosity I started toying with that infamous crack as it shot up smooth, vertical rock, as stark as a 3/4-inch gap between two buildings. Claude, perhaps afraid that I was about to reach beyond my training, set off to lead it. It was a glimpse into the workings of a very fruitful partnership as I watched Vern urge Claude, one finger-lock at a time, up the relentless pitch, and soon he was on top. Vern followed smoothly and took out the protection. Then I surprised myself by following too, with only one fall. Me, off the sofa and onto a notorious seventies test piece? Can this really be 5.11c?

That turned out to be the only day I'd spend in the Valley all autumn. So much for the dream of returning, with modern training, to the gulch of my teen dreams. For that year anyway. Life catches up with you before the adolescence wears off.

One day—really. I had spent my whole eighteenth summer here in the sixties for under a hundred dollars, climbing every day in hiking boots because I didn't own rock shoes. I didn't have a car or want a drivers license—I had hiked over 150 miles of Sierra crest just to get there in fact. And I couldn't feel luckier than to hold the rope for the likes of Chuck Pratt and flail along behind his bold new 5.10 leads. Now the backseat of my car is littered with the latest prototype rock shoes, and I don't have time to stay.

So: back to work—back to crisscrossing America. First to Wyoming to run water samples out of the already snowbound Wind River Range for a national acid rain study (yes, there's pollution, even in the high tarns there, probably traceable to a coal-fired power plant all the way down in Arizona). When I went to climb in Wyoming 20 years before, it was the big trip of the summer. This time it's the second in six weeks; on the road. On to Kansas to teach basic rock. Along the way I dropped by Quartz Mountain, Oklahoma.

Arriving was a little like a dream. After watching snow ribbons ghost-dance over frozen lakes at timberline; after sleeping in the car during another blizzard near Laramie, the dirt road to Quartz Mountain was lined with green grass and what? Autumn wildflowers? Friends ran toward my car. "Got any bolt drills?" asked Duane Raleigh and Rick McUsic. I dug through the back seat, and minutes later was sunning on a ledge while Duane hammered the crux protection. Then he danced on up the rest of his first ascent and dubbed it *The Charlie Manson Look-alike Contest.* Rick fired right up too. Twenty minutes later I was flamed. Numerous tries had finally gotten me up the first two moves, but I kept falling off the third. This was more like the consternation of 5.11. Charlie jokes were flying—I guess the resemblance failed me.

I resolved to train a little, and started doing fingertip pullups on doorjambs. Back in the sixties it was considered uncool, unsporting to work out for climbing. You climbed, and you hung out drinking beer and talking about it; at most we practiced a little on boulders. Nowadays the Yosemite climbers camp looks like a gymnastics arena and the sixties attitude is considered quaint, Victorian. And the standards have skyrocketed.

We drove to the University of Oklahoma at Norman and went climbing on the buildings. I couldn't get any more of those contorted and beefy problems than last year; still only two out of two dozen. The cafeteria crack they call *Butterballs* confounded me again, just weeks after climbing its namesake in the Valley. My last session of building climbing ended when I nearly threw my shoulder out while trying to shinny up the slightly acute corner formed between two brick walls. But *nobody* could do that one.

The Kansas class—33 newcomers avid for stone out of Wichita—just squeaked through between rain squalls. We wiped mud off our shoes on the way to the rock. Sunday evening I drove under tropical skies to Tulsa, hoping for a good day in Chandler Park. The climbs there are only 15 feet long, but

*Gary Sellers at Rock City,
Kansas*

at the time it was the finest limestone in the country. Unknown kids were firing off moves that the brightest stars in Yosemite couldn't have touched fifteen years before.

My trip was starting to feel like a modern climbing odyssey, visiting little rock outcrops across the country that were fast gaining national reputations.

In the sixties there were so few climbers that we felt like a band of crazy, misunderstood outlaws. We congregated naturally in a few strongholds like Yosemite. Of course we climbed on local outcrops when we couldn't get to the Valley, but familiarity made it hard to take seriously a sandstone bump in the neighborhood. I don't know quite how that changed. Climbing suddenly doubled in popularity in the early seventies, and again in the mid-eighties, but double of nothing is hardly a crowd. Then too, free climbing came to the forefront. With that any 70-foot rock face could be potential cutting-edge material. It just had to be fiendishly difficult; location in a famous climbing center suddenly didn't matter.

Since the sixties, the Valley had been slipping gradually from a paradise of stone into a police state. The telling sign for me came midwinter and 20 miles into the Yosemite backcountry when a nordic patrol ranger skied by wearing a can of MACE on his belt. The famous climbs are still there, of course, stations on an obligatory pilgrimage. And our old campground is no more of a slum than it used to be, really, just a more crowded one with the riot police in higher profile. But the walls of the Valley feel somehow less like Philosopher's Stone.

So in the eighties we hit the road. Vedauwoo, Wyoming, showed up on the cover of *Climbing* Magazine, and you began hearing stories about Quartz Mountain, Oklahoma, of all places. And if you went there, the campfire talk ran to Red Rock Point, Arkansas, and Stone Mountain, North Carolina. The little problems down the road that had frustrated the best efforts of locals who assumed they were "just training for the Valley" began to get the respect they deserved.

John Bachar

Rock & Road: Stone Mountain, revisited. Red Rock Point, rained out. At length I found myself headed west again, driving along the Gulf coast eating oysters ("It died going down"— McGuane), drinking beer and— temporarily—not even thinking about climbing.

It was late fall by the time I got to Joshua Tree. There was skiing already in the Sierra and snow even out there in the Mojave desert. For once I didn't care. I had proto- types of the hot new Fire rock shoes and a horizon of granite.

JT is the biggest little climbing area in the country, and an interna- tional winter training mecca. The climbs are only one or two pitches long, but there are thousands more of them in each new guidebook, on granite bumps strewn for miles across the desert. Many of the best climbs—at the Virgin Isles and in the Wonderland of Rocks—require an approach walk across the clean, bright desert, which adds a feeling of wilderness.

John Bachar showed up. Surfer-blond with a nearly shy smile and black karate pants, he jumped out of a new 4x4 riding a jazz riff from the Last Poets. The regulars treat John with a studied indifference. But donning my journalist's guise I can tag along with the world's reigning soloist, watch him climb and ask blunt questions. John started out on a 5.10b thin-hands crack without warming up, then worked his way onto 5.11 problems.

He looked so casual that you knew it had to be deceptive, moving up the rock with a fluid grace that showed as much agility as strength. His flow was broken by just the slightest hesitation on the harder moves while he affirmed a locker grip on the smaller holds. "Think of your fingers as steel hooks," he once said.

"The other day this 19-year-old kid comes up to me and asks for advice on soloing." John rolls his eyes, and I can feel the dilemma of responsibility. Genius is always responsible, but not always so aware of it. John minds his own business, just climbing the way he likes, and stays out of trouble only because his judgment is as highly developed as his strength and skill. "What could I say? I talked to him about training."

"Call me Indiana," the kid said. The next day he fell off of *Pinched Rib*, then rated only 5.8 but notorious for a tricky sequence, went twenty feet to the deck and broke his leg.

Bachar strolled over to Sports Challenge Rock and started up *Leave It To Beaver*. At 5.12 it is one of the most notorious climbs in the monument. The previous guidebook pointed out that it had been top-roped—by Bachar first—but never led with a rope, let alone soloed. The wall overhangs steadily for 50 or 60 feet, and though the holds look generous they are so rounded that hands slope off them as if you were trying to grip a basketball. Bachar points his right toe under a ceiling for balance and levers his body out nearly horizontal to reach far left and up for the next sloper. In less than a minute it was over. He made it look like a 5.7.

John Bachar soloing

I ended the day with a work-out, to put power behind the steel hooks. The *Gunsmoke Traverse* runs a hundred feet horizontally, right above the ground. But it overhangs enough to leave the forearms smoking. I got half way along it to an awkward swing-and-reach move before my fingers turned to butter. Bachar went back and forth six times, once climbing over a guy going the other way. Then he did a few pull-ups with a 50-pound weight hanging from his waist for pure power, and followed them with dozens of sets of fingertip pull-ups on a 3/4 inch edge for endurance. Everyone else had wandered back to camp by the time he was done.

I got home to late December and cold stone, but went out anyway, in long underwear, to climb in my home area the Buttermilk. There, of course, the season came to a crashing halt.

* * *

In the spring, while healing, I went to a great jam session. Larry Long was back from Minnesota, playing with Fiddlin' Pete for the first time in years. Tunes like "Sven the Mexican" took us back ten years to dancing in Sierra roadhouses, and we got a little sloppy thinking about it. I ended up talking to Pete's wife Katherine about riding ambulance as an EMT. "Haven't run into anything yet that I couldn't handle by the numbers. But I do get scared sometimes...." She paused. "You scared me," she said at last, "walking into the Emergency Room with no blood pressure. I kept taking it, and it kept coming up 60/0, then 50/0. I didn't see how you could stand up. We were all a little worried." Listening to her brought the terror rushing back again, the raw fear of teetering helplessly on the ragged edge of annihilation, with seconds to live and the strength draining from my arms. In the months since I had encapsulated that feeling and put it aside.

McGuane: "A sane man thinking of death, however casually, should immediately visit a girl whether in quest of information, affinities, or carnal gratification." I was out the door, running. I knew where I was headed.

So then, this: forgetting the rope led me onto the rocks that day. John Cooley was back, a bright and eager nineteen-year-old client; now he's an associate in the hottest law firm in San Diego and still climbing. We had planned to climb ice again, but unloading axes and crampons at June Lake, I realized that the rope was still hanging by the stove at home where I'd put it to dry. So we drove back down, grabbed the rope, and went out to the Buttermilk; might as well salvage the day by rock climbing. We did a progression of cracks. At home in my specialty, I led effortlessly up to 5.9, sometimes going 30 feet without protection, feeling poised.

At dusk, as we started back toward the car, I saw a crack I had never noticed before. I took the rope off my shoulder and started soloing up without it, just exploring. The rock overhung quite steeply for 30 feet to a lip, where the angle dropped back to vertical. The climbing was easy, though, and soon I was stemmed comfortably in two big pockets at the lip, resting and looking ahead. A minute or two more for this digression and we'd be on our way down to beer, I thought. But the crack thinned ahead, and its edges rounded. I craned my head back and forth, like a lizard doing pushups, to get perspective. Looks like better holds above the thin section, hard to tell. But I am already 30 feet off the deck, which is solid rock that slopes away from the bottom of the wall. It would be easy to climb back down. I almost do, three times. Five minutes pass. I spend them looking up and down. Finally I just go on.

Two thin-hand jams lead me to the better holds I'd seen. But they aren't. They're flared. Worse, the rock under my feet has grown rotten. My feet keep scraping crystals off. Nowhere to stand. The moves ahead look dicey. And strenuous. Reversing thin-hand jams is touchy, too much of a risk with that drop. It's all on my arms. And now they're too tired to risk the move upward. I'm trapped. The fear comes in a sickening wave. I try to keep it from washing me off the rock. My arms are flaming out. I shake out one hand at a time, but I can let go of the rock for only a few seconds. John can tell I'm in trouble. "Can you get above me and drop the rope?" He races up 5.9, on the back of the pinnacle. The end of the rope is dangling in my face. But I can't do anything with it. Can't let go to tie on. And by now there's no way that my wasted hands could cling to rope. Neither of us thinks of tying a loop in the end of the rope—I could have hung with my arm through a loop even with no grip left. As it is, I'm fucked. I will fall. I could easily die. I am vastly afraid.

The last thing I remember before blacking out is the sight of my hands three inches off the rock. I must have grabbed the rope, because afterwards there's an ugly scar in my palm, but I don't remember doing it. John told me later that I screamed all the way down. He quit climbing for months, he said, because that scream and the sound of my impact on the rocks kept rising incessantly in his dreams.

I came to three seconds after I hit. I was wrapped around a sage bush 20 feet out from the base of the wall. I was numb from shoulder blades to mid-thigh. There was blood all over the back of my knickers; I would lose two pints in the 40 minutes it took to get to the hospital. I thought my left hip was probably shattered. I could hear John running down the hill behind me. All I could think of was that my skull was intact and my legs still worked, and that this poor kid would think I was dead, so I started yelling over and over, "I'm all right. I'M ALL RIGHT!"

John threw his jacket over me and ran to bring his car closer. When he got there he realized the car key was in the jacket he'd given me, so he broke a window to get in. He tried to coast it, but the steering lock prevented that. It was five minutes before I tried to move, and then I crawled a hundred yards on my right side, and did controlled slides down a couple of sand-covered slabs. That's where John found me when he came back for the car key. After he left again the crawling got old, and I tried to stand up. My left leg accepted weight, so the hip wasn't broken. I teetered there seeing stars, but shuffled out to the parking area just as John arrived with the car. Sitting on broken glass on the way to the hospital seemed a trivial inconvenience.

Thank you again, John Cooley.

"Sit down here," said the receptionist behind the typewriter, "and give me your insurance information."

"I think I'd better just go straight in to the doctor."

* * *

That spring even the stone seemed to be blooming as winter retreated into the alpine zone. Down at 7,000 feet in the gentleness of Ponderosa forest I was camped on top of Dome Rock. The morning mountain sunlight was more finely textured than music. By an hour after dawn I could sit naked on my sleeping pad with a Chinese chaos of ridges arrayed down the Kern River canyon, and in front of me notebook, grapefruit, and McGuane for style. I brewed coffee, read and laughed, did stretches, worked on this story—and finally went climbing.

Right off the bat I was soloing again: only 5.6, but also leading quite harder than that in the peculiar guide's style that trails a rope, a dead line arcing down through space uncompromised by protection, often not even belayed. Then, without warning, I'd get gripped, locked up by waves of vertigo washing in over perfectly climbable terrain. One day I would fire off an 80-foot runout on 5.7 friction on the superb upper slabs of the secret classic *White Punks On Dope*. But then the next morning I'd be balking shamelessly on 5.8—friction again, and only eight feet above a solid bolt on *The Arch Bitch-Up*. I'd rattle and sweat, back down, try it over to the right. Up and down, indecision and dread, unable to take even the slightest risk of a short, controlled fall onto bomber pro. Finally, after maybe half an hour of that I gave up, cursing myself, and went around by the chimney—securely enfolded in stone.

Even with a rope, and on perfectly climbable terrain, the fear can take hold, evaporating my poise, leaving me shaking. Then I must collect again the scattered bits of attention, reweave them into a sharp focus. But it has always been like that, more or less. Less before, more now—the dread. Always that primordial fear of falling, varying only in degree. Now, after the fall, bits and snatches of its image arise from imagination—since memory ran away before the drop—of how it must have been, in midair, helpless to the suck of gravity, waiting on the rocks. It sickens. The resolve is visceral never again to push over the brink of the not-I.

Still, I climb as hard as I can, knotted to a stout rope now, enjoying the gymnastics balance of power applied to stone, breeze rippling over its surface, vistas of the ultraviolet zone.

The Needles in the spring. Even the stones seemed to bloom. Photo by Bruce Robinson

* * *

The rope is there to bridge gaps in judgment, the trickiest part of climbing to learn. With all those years of experience I still underestimated critical moves in the Buttermilk rocks. Crack climbing too—my specialty. The trouble is, I do that alarmingly often. If I can't read the stone accurately from this parallax view after more than three decades, then I just have to quit staking my life on it.

As soloing becomes glamorous it is the youngest climbers who take it up. They are strong; they've learned some technique. Mostly they are armed with that reckless bravery that makes teen-agers the best soldiers. And they are starting to die: a young woman at Joshua Tree; a 5.10 climber dropping off of 5.7 at Devils Tower; a couple of unexplained bodies found in Eldorado Canyon outside of Boulder.

"People don't realize just how *good* Bachar is," says Yvon Chouinard, "how much in control he is on those climbs." Not just skill either, the man has attitude control. "Do you ever back down?" I asked Bachar years before, when his fame was hatching. "Oh yes," he said quickly, "all the time. I think 'I'll just climb up and look at the crux, then come back down.' Sometimes it looks OK and I keep going. But down climbing is the protection of the soloist."

* * *

Finally I had to go back, to try it again. I couldn't tell anymore what my mind had done to that stretch of stone. Had I exaggerated its difficulty? I took a rope, of course, and Mark Herndon, out from Oklahoma, came along to belay.

We set about a dozen anchors at the top. Even ten feet back from the edge the vertigo was fierce; that void has pull. I rattled clumsily up to the lip of the overhang belayed firmly from above, and installed myself in a pocket where I could shake my arms out. I pulled up to the next move a couple of times, halfhearted and shaking. It was plenty difficult, even ten feet below where I'd fallen. But I couldn't make myself really try it.

A year after the fall, to the hour, I found myself visiting a friend in the Bishop hospital. And the vertigo caught up with me even there. When I glanced at the clock my legs buckled, and I had to kneel quickly to avoid fainting.

That was the second time that year. Six months before I had been with another climbing friend, Peter Nemes, hospitalized with a head injury, when he began hallucinating falling. Absorbing his terror, I went down then too, and nearly out, instantly drenched in a soaking sweat.

* * *

In the spring Dale "touch stone" Bard moved back to Bishop. Dale had earned a reputation in Yosemite—if not beyond—as peer and partner of John Bachar and Ron Kauk, so when he moved in he brought along an array of sophisticated workout equipment. Like the crack machine. Basically just a couple of 2x10 pine boards bolted together with an adjustable hand slot in between, Dale's is suspended horizontally six feet above the lawn. For me, it's 5.11 just to hoist myself into the upside-down position and hold. Dale swings into a parody of slothfulness and does laps. He stops to chalk up, one hand at a time, and switches directions with a swing move as neat as any swimmer turning against the wall, all the while holding a measured conversation. He comes down only to change tapes: hard rock.

Dale had only been here a few weeks when he started the tower. Two sheets of plywood stacked vertically make it 16 feet high, and it overhangs up to four feet on three sides—the fourth is a pegboard. Highway department epoxy bonds flat pieces of slate at random. This climber's playground goes together in frenzied bursts. I look up from the computer to a living road-runner cartoon, and smile: we are only five minutes away from real stone. The climbing is not desperate; the idea is to do laps. Each corner is a crack

machine, also overhanging, and they are set to the most difficult widths: 3/4",
1", 1 1/8", and 1 1/4". I have made four or five moves up the easiest, the
finger-lock 3/4". Dale calls it 5.11b. In the hardest, the 12b one inch, I am
finally able to lift off the ground. Dale, laps. Typical description of a recent
day: "A thousand feet of overhanging cracks, then I went bouldering."

* * *

So nothing turns out as expected. Fool. I set out for an epic return to
Yosemite. I half intended to sneer at the effete direction climbing has gone, in
sleek lycra tights, with its commitment softened by instant protection, and its
vision blurred by reflection in chromed workout machinery. The training and
the new technology are so logical, yet feel so at odds with the bohemian air of
the game I trundled into decades ago. Then it was a lifestyle, a Zen; now it is
perilously close to sport.

But I can't even begin to criticize without coming up hard against
my ever-growing respect for the new climbs. And then there's the respect I see
coming from the new climbers, for the ageless holy act of flowing upward
over stone. The last word belongs to the next generation, always. Dale Bard:
"It's the movement. It's just a dance on the wildest dance floor."

The dance goes on. And I—I keep struggling to rejoin it, to commit
and be fully engaged up there on the sharp end of the rope. I'm still confined,
crippled more by ghosts than confounded by granite. When Chouinard was
young he fell 160 feet—roped—down an overhanging wall in the Tetons. He
says it took three years to get his head back. By now I've put in ten. It has
goten a lot better, but.... I guess it just takes longer after the ground has begun
to harden.

El Capitan over Jay Jensen's shoulder from Middle Cathedral Rock

El Capitan:
Grand Sieges, Fast Attacks

This is the story of a failure to climb El Capitan (but hey, it was February). Even without a summit, it provided an opportunity in 1978 to look back over its history and the culture of Yosemite climbing.

El Capitan was there, sure, but I never wanted to climb it. Driving into Yosemite Valley, I could hardly miss that granite presence rising some three thousand feet above the floor, driving home a humbling sense of geological time. And the fact that I usually saw it about midnight on Friday nights—moonlight illuminating the face like some kind of monolithic drive-in movie screen—only added to my hesitation to go for the top.

But it wasn't just fear that informed my reluctance. No, there were aesthetic concerns, matters of style. As if it weren't hard enough just to get up those smooth, glacier-polished walls by any means at all, climbers like to make it even harder for themselves by tinkering with the rules, deciding what techniques they will allow. Just to keep it from turning easy, routine and dull—to keep the interest up. I'm one of the worst offenders, purely a "free" climber. Most people think that means no rope. Not true. It just means no help from the rope or the hardware. Just a mind-body trying to be upwardly mobile, hands and feet and cortex gripping the rock. The rope trails behind you, useless on climb after climb...until the day you fall. That day, of course, the rope repays you for all your patient hauling, coiling, and untangling.

Anyway, El Capitan in those days was the opposite sort of climbing— all "aid." Ironmongery holding you and the rope to the wall. Slow and tedious, it was too much rock engineering for me. Steve Roper called it "essentially safe and boring." El Capitan was too steep and smooth for free climbing, but there were plenty of other Yosemite cliffs where I could still be free and uneasy.

II. The First Ascent
Warren Harding went up the face of El Cap in 1958. It took him 12 days in the end, but all in all he had spent 45 days on the wall over an 18-month period. He really wanted it, that first ascent.

Back then, most of the climbers hanging out in the Valley were beatniks—bums who had probably studied physics someplace but had decided that it would be much more fun to hang out in a certain boulder-strewn camp in Yosemite, talk philosophy, and drink a little wine. It fit their hyperactive personalities better than sitting around reading poetry. Camp 4 was a dusty hole shunned by tourists, which gave the climbers the run of the place. It was near the Curry cafeteria, where the price of leftovers was right if you were quick enough, and the fireplace lounge was handy for sitting out storms. A pretty easy lowride, really, for the few who had gathered there in the early days of big wall climbing. The scene eventually suggested to one of the locals what has come to be known as Beck's Law: "At either end of the social scale there lies a leisure class."

The best thing about Camp 4 was those boulders. Standing around one of the rocks, a few climbers would take turns at an evening ritual that looked like contortions but turned out to be difficult free climbing, clinging to nubbins and rugosities on its smooth face. It was an education in climbing potential just to watch. These guys were committed, sometimes working all summer to get their moves together for a single ten-foot boulder. I moved right in, instantly at home. Climbing was the only thing that made sense of our lives, and we ended up nearly happy living like mountain hobos in this paradise of stone.

But Harding was different. He had a Corvette; and, while the leisure class was truffling in its boulder pile, he was holding down a job, making love to women in skirts (socialites), and driving in on weekends to work on his climb. Yet at heart he was like everyone else in Yosemite; he just couldn't stay away from that compelling something that makes rock climbing as satisfying to climbers as it is mysterious to everyone else.

The circumstances that drove Harding up the wall actually started several years earlier. In 1955 he had teamed up with Royal Robbins to attempt the face of Half Dome. A wall not on the scale of El Cap, but bigger than anything that had yet been climbed in the valley, it was the ideal target for the two most capable and ambitious climbers in Yosemite. Harding and Robbins had started out friends, working their way 450 feet up the Dome together before turning back. But in 1957 Harding returned with another team only to find Robbins and his boys already on the wall and smelling of success. Warren, seeing what was about to happen, did the correct thing. He hiked up the back of Half Dome to meet Royal on top. After all it had been a magnificent effort. Half Dome became the first climb in the world to rate the rock climber's Grade VI, the ultimate in length and difficulty.

Formalities concluded, Warren hiked down, went to the other end of the Valley, and started climbing El Cap. It was all he could do. Nearly a thousand feet higher than the Dome, El Cap faced straight into the sweltering sun and was even more intimidatingly steep and smooth. It was obviously the next great challenge.

Harding had no illusions about racing up the wall, and, sure enough, the early climbing was picky and intricate. At the end of the first weekend he left his ropes tethered a few hundred feet off the ground, jumped into his Corvette, and split. The next weekend's efforts got him a little higher, but he had scarcely reached the toe of the great buttress. Warren had his work cut out for him.

Harding could not have known then just what a project this would become. As the months dragged on, he would lose his best partner, Mark Powell, to a broken ankle. He would be forced to invent "stoveleg pitons" to fit a particularly wide crack (though it is not true that he sawed the legs off his mother's stove for the purpose). Later, Bill "Dolt" Feuerer would jury-rig a bicycle-wheeled "Dolt Cart" for them to hoist up supplies, only to find that the haul rope itself was so heavy that a payload couldn't be pulled. And, up toward the summit, he would come onto a ledge to find that his sleeping bag had been gnawed to shreds by rats that scuttled up and down big cracks in the face.

Finally, even the National Park Service turned out to be an obstacle. Tourists had been congregating in El Cap meadow to watch the show, and they, in turn, caused drivers on the road to slow down for a look. Accidents and congestion fouled the main artery into the park, and the rangers gave Harding an ultimatum: finish the climb by Thanksgiving or quit. "I have never understood," said Warren, "how this was to have been enforced."

By November 1958, 18 months after starting the climb, Harding had his fixed ropes 2,000 feet up the Nose of El Cap, two-thirds of the way to the top. Another winter was about to delay him until spring. He had already borrowed half the ropes in California to fix up the face, rumor was building that Royal Robbins would use Harding's own fixed ropes to beat him again, and of course there was the National Park Service breathing down his neck. It was time to make a move. So, with three companions, he made one last trip up the fixed lines carrying a final supply of food and water. Harding broke loose from his umbilical cord to the ground and worked his way up into the summit dihedrals.

It was a bold step to take. No one—the rangers, his friends, not even Royal Robbins—had ever made a rescue from so steep and remote a place, so of course one could not be counted on. But Royal had been up against the same possibility on Half Dome, and boldness has always been an admired quality among climbers.

Twelve days later at dusk Warren had a problem. He had reached the end of the summit dihedrals, long vertical cracks with walls that open like a book, but not the summit itself. He knew he was close, but blocking the way was a bulging, blank, overhanging wall. There was nothing he could do but reach again for the bolt drill, which had already made a hundred holes for construction bolts to get him across blank sections in the route. Harding started drilling, pounding on the back of the drill with his hammer while twisting it slowly in the rock with the other hand. A strong man in fresh condition with a big hammer can drill a 1/4-inch bolt hole the necessary 1 1/2 inches into flat granite in ten minutes. But Warren was standing high in his nylon sling ladders, stretching to full reach up the gently overhanging wall to drill, and he had already been climbing all day and it was getting dark.... What followed is typical of Harding's fanatical gutsiness; he drilled bolt holes all night, 28 in all, and pulled up onto the summit at dawn.

III. Robbins' Continuous Climb

Royal "Mozart" Robbins had of course been watching Harding's progress with interest. I call him "Mozart" because of his then-infamous writing style. (Royal has since written with brilliant honesty about climbs like "Tis-sa-ack") In those years the purple of his prose was just a shade away from the sunsets he had such a passion for describing. So, when he finished an article about a fine new route on Sentinel rock with a description of the sunset as "better than Mozart," the climb became known as the "Mozart Wall." Layton Kor later made another climb right next to the Mozart Wall. More of a happy-go-lucky type than a brooding intellectual, Kor was known for climbing with a transistor radio in his shirt pocket. When he too reached the top at sunset, he couldn't resist commenting that "it wasn't even as good as Fats Domino."

If ever there was a climber determined to be the best, Royal was the one. There is a story, likely apocryphal—and Royal certainly denies it—that nonetheless has a certain ring that makes it, in Ken Kesey's words, "true even if it didn't happen:" Around the fire one drunken evening in the Tetons, someone proposed a pushup contest. One by one the climbers went down, but when it came around to Royal's turn he had vanished into the night. Early the next morning Richie Goldstone saw something moving up and down in the underbrush. Thinking he had surprised a couple he turned away, then reconsidered and returned for another look. There was Robbins, counting pushups in the woods; sure enough, that evening at the campfire he casually proposed a rematch.

Watching Harding up there on the Nose, Royal had been brooding about style. He had climbed Half Dome in classic alpine style, leaving the ground with everything he would need for the five-day ascent. Conspicuously absent were the fixed ropes that, stretching as a lifeline to the ground, had secured Harding's siege-style ascent of the Nose. "We wished to avoid such methods if possible," Robbins said later, "to keep the element of adventure high." Royal couldn't help thinking that *he* could do the Nose in alpine style—especially since Harding had drilled all the bolt holes.

"Flaming out" was the big fear of trying a continuous ascent. Inching yourself and baggage up a big wall—a process that Harding characterized as "an exercise in vertical freight handling"—is grueling work. In summer sun the wall bakes until it shimmers; yet the heaviest part of the load is water. A balancing act ensues between the least you can drink and the most you can haul, while the bag does its best to wedge in cracks, catch under ceilings, and snag on every tiny flake on the wall. A quart and a half each, per day, is considered the minimum; compromising in either direction weighs heavily. The vertical desert is more than just a metaphor; after running out of water short of the summit, several climbers have passed out in their slings.

Four men would be a good-sized team Royal thought, two to do the clinging and hanging, leaving ropes for the others to follow, hauling and tangling. Each day they would trade off. And that's exactly what he did, along with Tom Frost, Chuck Pratt, and Joe Fitchen, seven hot days in the fall of 1960.

Their first continuous ascent was a breakthrough into a prolific era. Over the next few years this same nucleus of hard-core climbing bums did practically all of the climbing on El Cap. Their routes went up left and right of the Nose, while across the Valley Harding was bending over backwards to climb a wall that overhung, gently but steadily, for 1,100 feet—the Leaning Tower. The golden age of big wall climbing had arrived.

IV. The Rise of Free Climbing

The first time I saw Jim "Stonemaster" Bridwell, he was just a kid, a gangly 14 with big ears; but already he was showing his strength at Castle Rock, a sandstone bump in the coast range between San Jose and Santa Cruz. Jim was practicing direct aid moves for the wide cracks that he would soon be seeing on El Cap.

But there were no more reputations to be made by repeating the Nose, and Bridwell, like the rest of the big wall climbers, led a double life. On the big walls he was an aid climber. The rest of the time he polished his free climbing on shorter routes, and soon he was the best in the valley, making bold new first ascents that the rest of us hesitated to follow.

In 1968, ten years after the first ascent, Bridwell confused his two lives in a way that set the evolution of stylish wall climbing off in a new direction; he started free climbing on the walls. Beginning on the Nose with the now-famous Stoveleg Cracks, he climbed free for several hundred feet by using a technique called jamming, wedging his fists and feet into the crack for support. The free climbing of the stovelegs was a main event that season. The best climbers repeated it, ascending the Stovelegs to Dolt Tower, a third of the way up the face, and rappelling home for dinner. That was done often; there were more good climbers than ever.

The word was leaking out about that fine, hard Yosemite granite, and through the sixties the crowd in the climbers' camp swelled steadily as Coloradans and Canadians, then British, Australians, and European climbers arrived and began working their way up the big walls. More climbers, new problems, and inevitably hang-ups high on El Cap. The rangers didn't want to get into the scary business of dangling rescues and vertical first aid, so they hired Bridwell and the best of the wall climbers to take care of it. The climbing bums found themselves languishing in a free campground, compliments of the government, drawing hazardous-duty pay for doing what they knew best.

Then the first waves of hippies began rolling into Yosemite, and the climbers were displaced from the bottom of the Valley's social ladder. Worse, as more people than ever got into it, we weren't considered so crazy any more. The slight respectability made us squirm. It did not bode well for our peace and quiet. Now that it was slipping away, we realized that we enjoyed feeling like lunatics and outlaws.

Naturally, dope made its way into the valley too. But being stoned merely confirmed the sense of heightened perception that we had felt all along. That was really what kept driving many of us back to the edge long after our old schoolmates had become insurance agents in Mill Valley. The rush of adrenaline has an afterglow that is addictive.

Ending a great era is not easy. Often it takes an act of violence. Such an end came abruptly to the golden age of the big walls, the aid climbing era, on a February day in 1970 when Royal Robbins took out his cold chisel and began chopping off the bolts behind him as he ascended Harding's latest El Cap route, the Wall of the Morning Light. He was trying to erase the climb, its style offended him so much.

Harding had been run down by a truck the year before, leaving him with a shattered leg. He could barely limp his way from the bar up to the base of the wall. His partner Dean "Wizard" Caldwell, limped too, with ligaments badly torn from stumbling over a tree stump on his way to the outhouse in camp. They styled themselves "The March of Dimes Climbing Team," and they spent 27 days on the wall, the longest anyone had ever dangled from a a rock wall—a full moon cycle. In a typical Harding epic, they had mastered the long, blank wall with lots of drilling, lasting it out only because storms refilled their water bottles. But the storms caused them other problems below. The rangers who had threatened to ground Harding during his first ascent of El Cap now were thinking of rescuing him for his own good. Warren leaned out the door of his waterproof "Bat Tent" and dropped a note: "A rescue is unwanted, unwarranted, and will not be accepted." He imagined:

> "rescuers landing on Timothy Tower to find an 'exhausted' climbing team enjoying a fine mini-feast of Salami, cheese, bread, and an entire bottle of Cabernet Sauvignon, all in a beautiful moonlit setting. Dialogue:
>
> 'Good evening! What can we do for you?'
>
> 'We've come to rescue you!'
>
> Really? Come now, get hold of yourselves—have some wine..."

Meanwhile, the press had discovered that there was something dramatic happening way up on the biggest cliff in Yosemite. "It must have been a slow week for news" was Harding's laconic assessment, but he was trapped on the front page anyway, a real cliff-hanger. To hear the evening news you'd think it was the first time a stone wall had ever been scaled. Eventually they drew more press than the first Americans up Everest (including this note from the society pages of the San Francisco Chronicle: "Mountain climbing daredevils hold great attraction for young women").

When Harding stepped over the rim this time, his feet painfully swollen from a month of standing in slings, he was met by helicopters, reporters and TV crews. It was more than Royal could take. Sure, he knew they had climbed alpine style. What bothered him was all those bolts; half of the route seemed excessive. He could hardly wait to get up there and start eradicating the climb. But soon after he began, Royal stopped erasing the route, overcome with respect for the difficulty of the climbing. Word of the erasure soon reached Harding at a sporting goods trade show in Chicago. He said, "I don't give a rat's ass what Royal did with the route, or what he thought he accomplished by whatever it was he did. I guess my only interest in the matter would be the possibility of some clinical insights into the rather murky channels of R.R.'s mind...a veritable alpine Elmer Gantry."

At six o'clock on a June morning in 1975 Bridwell pulled up out of the Stovelegs again onto Dolt Tower. The climbers just waking up on the ledge were surprised to see Jim and his two companions, John Long and Billy Westbay, climbing so early and so fast. But their surprise turned to amazement as it dawned on them that these three had no haul bag. Here they were a third of the way up El Capitan with only their hardware and bell-bottoms. And then they were gone, working their way on up. That wouldn't be the last party those three would surprise and pass that day. It was the height of the season, and climbing had grown more popular than ever. "Go Climb a Rock" t-shirts advertised souvenir

Doug Pulling up out of the Stoveleg Crags. - Gordon Wiltsie.

classes at the Curry Company's climbing school, and outsized photos in the "hard man/hard rock" tradition decorated the Mountain Room Grill, where the waiters affected knickers. At the base of the Nose you stood a good chance of having to wait in line to get on the climb. But there had been no line at four that morning when those three left the ground and climbed swiftly into the moonlight. They were very fit from climbing all spring, and each of them had been up the Nose at least once before. Seventeen and a half hours later they walked into the Mountain Room Bar to celebrate the first one-day ascent of El Cap.

As if that weren't enough, they had also climbed the route 70 percent free. Free climbing was on the make, edging out aid and transforming the whole character of the climb. It was then that I started wanting to climb El Cap.

V. Day One

I tied into the new red rope and stepped off the ground, happy to have finished all the planning and sorting, the packing and driving; starting a climb is always a relief. Within a few feet I was absorbed in the delicately isometric tension of free climbing. El Cap felt clean and warm, coming to hand like an old lover.

Absorbed by the climbing and happy in the company of old friends Gordon Wiltsie, the mountain photographer, and Jay Jensen of the Rolling

J Ranch, I was content with 400 feet of progress to Sickle Ledge. We began to adjust to life in the vertical, where everything has to be tied down. A British climber kicked his shoes off the ledge one night and had to rappel back down barefoot. Anything that can, goes. A climber ties in at the bottom and stays tied in until the top; at night the rope runs into his sleeping bag. Lito Tejada-Flores once was clowning around, hopping along a ledge with his feet in the haul bag when his partner noticed that he wasn't tied in. Lito dove for the anchors.

Tied in, we brewed tea, passed the pipe, and sank into comfortable hollows on the ledge, congratulating ourselves on not being up on some cold and snowy north face; no winter climbing for these basking armadillos, thanks. At the moment, February seemed not so unreasonable a season for attempting El Cap. We were sitting on the end of a ten-day spell of fine weather.

I recalled a pervading fear of the early Valley climbers, that someday a gymnast would arrive on the scene and show us all for the frauds that we were. And one day she did. Beverly Johnson was a dropout socialite from somewhere in the East, though she wouldn't talk much about that, and she had been a hot gymnast before wandering into Yosemite to become the first woman to climb El Cap.

Just above this spot one morning Bev was leading a key pitch by making herself into a human pendulum on the end of her rope, running back and forth across the blank wall in a widening arc to reach the Stoveleg cracks. She was concentrating hard until something dropped into her field of vision and she looked up to see a Mexican climber falling past her. She turned to her partner Dan Asay, and the now-classic line was uttered: "You don't see that every day." Bev went back to her pendulum. A tough lady, she later led the first all female ascent of El Cap.

VI. Day Two

Tricky aid and small-hold face climbing gave way to bold, jammable cracks set in the stark and steepening face. We crossed the pendulums into the celebrated Stoveleg cracks, which shot 400 feet up to our next bivouac platform atop Dolt Tower.

The Stoe legs were all I'd hoped and heard—good jam holds in a fluctuating crack that meanders in and out of vertical, with smooth wall stretching away on either side. A good hand jam is a thing of beauty and the best, most bombproof hold in climbing. Making a fist in a tight two-inch slot, I will cheerfully hang out under an overhang. But it's strenuous, and I can free climb the Stovelegs only at the expense of cramps in my forearms;

the grip muscles are not in shape. The next hundred feet goes slowly, shaking out one arm at a time and sewing up the crack with protection. Just as the rope runs out I pull up onto a block wedged in a wider section of crack and slip inside this tight chimney to belay.

As darkness falls I'm still there. Jay and Gordon are somewhere above, but not quite up to Dolt Tower, either. I'm worn out and keep falling asleep standing up in the chimney with my forehead resting against the cool rock, only to jerk awake and find my knees cramped. But it could be worse. People have slept standing in their slings out on the wall. I think of my friends Pratt and Fredericks, who spent a night standing in a similar slot over on the Dihedral Wall. Above the possibility of retreat, they stood there soaked and shivering as the temperature dropped into the twenties. Friends back in camp worried as it got colder.

That night, Jim Madsen was desperate for a project, anything, and he took it on himself to check on his two friends. He hiked to the top of the Captain with a pack full of ropes, and in the morning began rappelling, alone, down the face to look for them. They decided later that he had simply rappelled off the end of his rope; the pair below, dried out and renewing their climb to the top, clung, for their last two days on the wall, to the belief that they had seen a deer fall by them. The wake for Madsen slowed down traffic on the Captain for the next year. The first death is the hardest, an end of innocence.

Yes, there are deaths on the wall, but very few. Three at once last spring doubled the toll for El Cap, and there are only two dozen in all in the fifty years of roped climbing in Yosemite. That compares pretty well with 300 a year in the Alps, where climbers have to contend not only with crevassed glaciers, avalanches, and sudden storms, but also loose rocks dislodged by the dozen other parties trying to climb the same route on the same day.

Soggy bivouac on El Cap Tower. Gordon Wiltsie photo

Yosemite climbing has none of those traditional Alpine problems; by contrast it is as simple and straightforward as the clean, smooth walls of the Valley. No repressed death wish for these casual Californians. With good weather, solid rock, and safe rope work, the only problem is sheer difficulty. The smooth rock is very hard to climb, and concentrating on it tends to clear the cobwebs out of the head, leading at last to that simple directness that climbers crave. Climbing alone makes sense.

VII. Days Three and Four

In spite of stiff legs, the third day proved much like the second, with more of that fine crack climbing that will make this route as much a classic of the new style as it was of the old. By 1978 there were only five aid pitches left on the Nose. I was fist jamming a perfect three-inch crack when the rain began.

It rained on and off all afternoon, making us fidget on top of El Cap Tower, and it came down steadily through the night. A burst of morning sunshine allowed us to set the ropes another 200 feet up the wall, but by noon we were hunkered down in our bivouac bags once more. From then on it poured. We gradually sank into that catatonic position cold people assume when they don't want to move and stir up the cold water they're sitting in. Shivering spasms moved us anyway, long before dark.

Night thoughts focused on our soaking wet ropes hanging above in the dark, just a freeze away from becoming stiff, useless cables that would strand us here until a thaw. Each time I woke up shivering I was relieved to hear it still raining. But being stranded on the wall was not the worst of the night's frigid nightmares. I vividly recalled a sunny February day many years ago when I had walked up to the base of the wall—the kind of bright day you have after a hard freeze. That morning there was a cracking noise high up the face, followed by a flash in the sunshine. A sheet of ice 1/4-inch thick by 30 feet across had broken loose from the upper wall and was swooping and sailing downward. Soon it cracked against the wall and broke into a cascade of fragments. Some of them were still two feet across when they landed on the ground, sending me running for shelter in the forest. That went on all morning. Then I understood why nothing grew within 20 feet of the base of the cliff, and I shuddered to think what could happen to a climber tied to the wall under such a barrage of guillotine flakes.

VIII. The Last Day

At dawn we started down, rappelling the double rope and then pulling it down behind us. We were tense. If the trailing rope wedged in a crack, it would have taken us hours to climb back up and free it. The rain kept coming, punctuated every few minutes by a flurry of snow; and we had

Doug Robinson

to wait, shivering, with our hands shoved in our groins, to get a grip back in our fingers before each rappel. Then, each time we moved on, water ran down the ropes and into our sleeves. My soaked feet felt like wooden blocks.

About halfway down one of our rappel anchors was submerged by a waterfall, and from that pitch on we were totally soaked. I started to think about Harding again, and my moves came almost mechanically out of shivers as the ground rose slowly to meet us.

Yeah, Harding. As he hammered in the last bolt and staggered over the rim that morning in the dawn of the big wall era he was struck by the irony of his conquest. "It was not at all clear to me," he noted, "who had conquered and who was conquered. I do recall that El Cap seemed to be in much better condition than I was." Amen.

Finally, in the middle of the afternoon, I touched down and it was over. El Cap, for me, is still there.

IX. Next rounds and Old Soldiers

What's the point of this style business anyway, deliberately making already steep rock even harder to climb by tinkering with the rules? It cannot be merely a desire to meet some Platonic ideal of pure form. Maybe the climber seeks to preserve the central experience of climbing, the feeling that comes only from riding the edge between kinesthetic joy and sheer terror. The way to stay there seems to lie in adjusting the style until you're putting out a maximum effort that still doesn't assure you of success. "We longed," said Robbins, "to tremble before unclimbed walls again." But since those walls could never again be unclimbed, the frontier had to shift from summits to style to keep that elusive, essential feeling from drowning in the mere mechanics of ascension.

But the golden age of the big Yosemite walls is past, and even the latest revolution in style, redoing the walls free instead of with aid, doesn't guarantee that element of mystery and fear that adrenalizes a new adventure; the leading climbers, when they can afford it, are looking beyond the Valley. Some think that the title "greatest granite monolith" may have been a bit prematurely awarded to El Cap, and that tucked away in the Arctic or in obscure corners of the Himalayas there just might lie even bigger walls, with the fascinating complication of severe weather and ice, waiting to be discovered. Indeed, some have already been found and are being explored—as often as not by Yosemite climbers.

Do climbers still dream about El Cap? Today thye sit back in their vans in the Curry parking lot, rows of overflows from the old campground, listening to the Grateful Dead and smoking that airplane weed, but their dreams are still El Captivated. The young dream of the Nose or Salathe, the two-season veterans dream of going back for some of the hard new El Cap routes like Mescalito or Magic Mushroom or Cosmos. The old hands have their dreams too, of Arctic weather walls, granite and ice together, Patagonia maybe, or the great granite spires in the Himalayan foothills—with ABC Sports contracts to match their mountains.

Robbins has taken up kayaking and tennis. Someone recently asked him if he played for fun or for the tournaments. He answered, "Fun?...Fun?" Bridwell recently scaled the face of Cerro Torre in Patagonia, a granite spire that fierce Antarctic weather makes about the most inaccessible in the world. The problem there isn't the vertical granite, it's the overhanging ice mushroom capping the spire and shedding megaton chunks.

The last time I saw Harding he drove up to the Buttermilk boulders near Bishop just as we finished climbing for the day. Actually his new girlfriend, apparently just old enough to have a license, was driving. Warren got out with half a gallon of wine (a familiar sight) and two wine glasses (a new touch of refinement). But like always, he started pouring it around.

POSTSCRIPT: If this 1978 perspective were updated today, the remarkable changes would not be that doing the Nose in a day has become a standard rite of passage for hot climbers, or that out of the 60-odd El Cap routes this one is still the popular classic. It would not be remarkable that teams of women cruise the big walls, or even that the Nose and Half Dome have been climbed in a day, not to mention two El Cap routes in a day. Those developments are evolutionary. No, the big news would have to be that Lynn Hill finally free climbed the entire Nose in 1993, something that no man, no other climber at all, has been able to repeat. Then, a year later, she free climbed it in a day.

It was a bittersweet year. Also in 1994 Beverly Johnson, who had gone on to become an environmental film maker, and whose high-spirited enthusiasm and great common sense still delighted us, died in a helicopter crash in the Ruby Mountains of Nevada.

Beverly Johnson relaxing in Camp 4. Gene Foley photo

Yahoo!

Return to skiing, to spring in the high country. Return every year. The Sierra is at least *one of* the very finest places in the world for this, and we like to take full advantage. I can lose myself in the experience, as you are about to see. . .

The piercing High Sierra light had just gone to gold as I swung into another kick turn on the steepening slope of Half-moon Pass. To the west the sun was dropping fast into the upper layers of San Joaquin Valley haze. It would be dark soon, and I squinted again at the gap marking the pass in the snowed-over ridge above. It was a little closer this time.

Leaning into my pack straps, I panted a rhythm up the slope, leaving in my wake the long diagonal signature of ascent. The deep snowpack revealed no trace of the irregularities of shape and color so familiar in the summer Sierra, accentuating instead the graceful, even sensuous contours of what would otherwise be a ragged landscape. My partner and I had just enough time, I thought, to reach the top and finish our Sierra crest tour with a fast descent into Rock Creek Canyon. Hot food, friends, and a crackling fire awaited us at Rock Creek's secluded cross country resort.

At the top I realized immediately that something was wrong. It was not Rock Creek below me, so that wasn't Golden Lake back there, and this could not be Half-moon Pass. I looked around. The stark, white alpine landscape swept away north and south like colossal storm surf, each wave tipped with spiky gray granite—the crest of California. I had been ski mountaineering since the early sixties and thought I knew the crest pretty well. Could I be lost?

We had started two weeks earlier, skiing away from Highway 395 near Bridgeport into a blizzard. There were four of us then, all experienced and none particularly dismayed by stinging wind and iced-up beards. Along the way, the demands of homes and jobs had whittled away at our ranks, until now only Tim Lemucchi was still with me, just kick turning onto the last switch back in the dusk below. For three hours he had been skiing uphill as fast as his considerable strength could take him, a chicken dinner in Rock Creek on his mind. Boy, was he going to be surprised. Getting lost wasn't something we had counted on six days before as we lounged in the hot tub outside Lemucchi's condo in Mammoth, plotting the second leg of our journey. We had double-staged into town to resupply, taste the French cooking at Roget's, and soak our pack-weary muscles. After a week in the wilderness, Mammoth seemed like Newport Beach with down jackets—all hustle, jive, and stretch-tight pants. Across the tank a couple of downhillers bitched about their thighs, still burning from a day in steep Mammoth Mountain powder chutes reachable only by laborious side-stepping up from the top of a lift. We had to smile, thinking how much more accessible those gullies would have been to us on our skinny touring skis fitted with removable climbing skins and heel free, three-pin bindings. We were just "pinheads" to these hotties, but their serious powder-hound voices out of the mist represented a Mammoth we could relate to. I drained a beer in a silent toast.

For most of that first week we'd had fitful snow conditions—a lot of breakable crust, often unskiable. We would look out over a beautiful downslope, sigh, and go back to traverses and kick turns. Survival skiing.. Only once did the snow lighten up, in deep woods north of Donohue Pass where new powder had not been wasted by high winds. That morning, after taking my turn at breaking trail, I peeled off the end of the line, took the skins off my skis, and dropped my 50-pound pack. The terrain was quite steep, but with a foot and a half of powder to cushion me, I could drop over benches

and career off the sides of ravines while going slowly enough to miss the trees. After 800 feet of yahooing I remembered my friends disappearing toward the pass and my pack by the trail, and I went back up. It was my best powder run of the year; not too bad for April.

When we got to Mammoth, Paul Allen had to leave us and rush back to work. Allen is a mining executive—or was, until a couple of years ago when his company forcibly retired him for no

A. P. Marsten

other crime than turning 65. Allen was mad as hell. But the next day they turned around and hired him back as a consultant. Now he consults for five other companies, is busier than ever, and often flies in from Houston or Tokyo to join a ski tour.

Allen's departure left A. P. Marsten soaking alongside Tim Lemucchi and me. I had met Marsten while ice climbing several years back, and in the course of pursuing that arcane branch of mountaineering we had traveled to Canada together to bag the second ascent of the Wenkchemna Ice Tongue. But a chronically dislocating shoulder, which can be troublesome if it is the one supporting your weight hanging from an ice axe, prompted him to take up ski mountaineering instead, and we had since been on several long tours together. The previous spring we had spent three weeks traversing the southern half of the crest.

Tim Lemucchi

Lemucchi had been with us. He has been leading an increasingly athletic life, which is saying something, since it didn't start out exactly sedentary. Tim was a half miler in high school, a member of the feared East Bakersfield Blades; we had heard about them on track teams as far away as the San Francisco suburbs. At Stanford, on his way to a law degree, he was a junior varsity halfback. Back home in Bakersfield he soon became a courtroom opponent to be reckoned with— until ski season rolled around and he cleared his calendar to be in the mountains. At 45, his mile time is 45 seconds faster than it was in high school. "So where's the limit?" he wonders.

The limits keep rising. The Sierra crest was first skied by following the John Muir Trail, which traverses a lot of alpine country but also drops into the forest for long stretches. Deep woods make nice summer hiking, but on skis, with melted moats around trees and irregular patterns of melt and freeze in the broken shade, the going can be difficult. Navigating under an evergreen canopy isn't easy, either. Haute Sierra touring evolved partly out of the expediency of seeking more open terrain, but in the last ten years it has become a game to find ever-higher routes along the crest. Now we traverse the sides of high bowls and weave a line of travel among the peaks.

Of course, travel in the alpine zone has its hazards. A third of the earth's atmosphere is below you, and the thinner stuff above is often very cold and blowing hard. The sun can burn like a torch, the slopes can be steeper than anything at Squaw or Mammoth, and, of course, this is avalanche country. Haute touring is not just skiing, it's mountaineering. Not for beginners.

We were proud of having pushed the line a little higher on the first part of our trip by staying right along the crest from Virginia Lakes to Saddlebag Lake. The next section south from Mammoth to Rock Creek Canyon posed another challenge. It was not the highest part of the crest, nor the most remote, but its intricate terrain had long resisted attempts to find a high traverse route, sending several parties skittering down canyons into the forest. I had spotted what appeared to be two small passes on the map. If we could get over both of them, we could link a known traverse line from the north with one we knew continued all the way to Rock Creek. But those notches were still just a gleam in the map reader's eye. Unfortunately my topographic map had a colored stripe running right along the Sierra crest, indicating the boundary between Inyo and Fresno counties—political trivia as far as mountaineers are concerned. To citizens of what we like to call the Sierra Nevada Free Zone, the only meaningful jurisdictions are those imposed by climate and geography. I could see contour lines crowding together as they ran up under the stripe, showing obvious steepness on both sides of the ridges, but thanks to that boundary line there was only one way to find out what was at the very top.

Lemucchi, however, was fast hatching another plan. The tub we sat in was hemmed in by fencing and barbed wire—protection against wandering ski bums—and gave only a narrow glimpse of winter sky. He had begun to yearn for a wild hot spring, and before we knew it Marsten and I had been talked into a digression way off the crest, miles to the west, thousands of feet down, and all of it through the densest of red fir forest. We would begin, then, with a visit to Reds Meadows hot springs.

The next afternoon we slid back into the wilderness, skiing by the Mammoth lifts so late after last-minute shopping that even the ski patrol had finished hallooing through the woods and retreated to the Village Inn for the popcorn hour. The snow had been baked to mush by spring afternoon sun, so that even on skis we sank a foot in places. Thick woods growing on a steep-sided ravine made for exacting course work. I dropped straight into the ravine bottom between huge red firs, accelerated across the snowed-over creek, and sat my weight back on my skis at the exact moment the angle changed to keep from flying over my ski tips and burying my head in the opposite bank. My reward was losing fifteen feet of altitude. I exhaled, kick turned, and picked another line through the trees. Dusk was falling in the deep woods. At full dusk we gave up our vision of dinner at the hot springs and shoveled a tent platform out of the steep hillside.

Soon a steak was sizzling in the open doorway of the big dome tent, a salad was torn up, and a bottle of fine cabernet uncorkedChateau Montelena 1974. the rough-and-tumble off Mammoth Mountain hadn't bruised it at all.

In the morning we found that even the Reds Meadows hot springs aren't wild anymore. The water is piped into a cement tank, and to get at it we had to wrestle off a steel-plate cover. But the springs were piping hot, and the water mingled so pleasantly with morning sunshine that we lingered way past noon and made it only three more miles to camp at Red Cones. The Cones, a pair of old volcanoes, are even-angled and steep. We dropped our packs and spent the last two hours of daylight skiing good snow through open forest and the steep drops off the cones. Then we dove into the tent for another fine little alpine feast.

The side trip brought back memories of an April afternoon in 1970 when Carl McCoy and I skied past the Red Cones under a lowering sky. McCoy, third son of the McCoys who founded Mammoth Mountain ski area, knew the territory like his own back yard—which it was—but in the dense forest the Cones were our only clue that we were finally near Reds Meadows. We pushed on without a word, intent on a sealed plastic bucket we had left there high in a tree earlier that winter. Inside was enough food to get us to Yosemite Valley—if we didn't eat it all at once. It had been a month since we had left Whitney Portal, 200 zigzag miles south, and we had gone the last three days on tea, vitamin B, and the hope of reaching our cache. We spent the next two days in front of the wood stove in a boarded-up cabin owned by a friend of McCoy's, watching snow blow in through the chinks and waiting for our stomachs to unbloat so we could stuff them again.

Five days later we made it to Yosemite to celebrate the second-ever traverse of the Sierra crest on skis. We hadn't heard about Orland Bartholomew's trip until our preparations were well under way, and we didn't get any details until much later, but it turns out that he had had food troubles near Red Cones, too. Bartholomew, one of the Sierra's first snow surveyors, skied up to an old cabin where he had cached his food, only to find two trappers eating it. When Bartholomew pointed out their error, the trappers snowshoed out to Mammoth and brought back fresh supplies. Bartholomew pulled into Yosemite at the end of April to complete the first ski traverse of the John Muir Trail. It had taken him a hundred days, and he had done it all alone. The year was 1929.

In the morning, in the meadow below Red Cones, Lemucchi, Marsten, and I were loafing over coffee when Marsten suddenly announced he was leaving. He was going to ski out over Mammoth Pass, conveniently nearby. Now A. P. Marsten is an oil heir from an old San Francisco family, and while he has often proven himself to be a fine ski mountaineer, he has been known to disdain hard work. Lemucchi and I ribbed him unmercifully, but he was adamant. He dumped his share of the community gear on us and departed. We found out later that something approaching the psychic was going on: when he got out A. P. found out that there had been a medical emergency in his family that morning.

Then we were two. Lemucchi and I zigzagged up Deer Creek all afternoon, each in the cocoon of his thoughts, and camped short of the crest. Sitting on our packs the next morning in shirt sleeves, we took in the scene. Mammoth Mountain was already below the skyline and fading from prominence; there wasn't a skier on its whole southern exposure. It was only half a day's ski away. We had been three days on a great circle route to get here and didn't care. It had been a kind of Mediterranean digression for ski mountaineers to travel among lush red fir forests and bask in hot water. But then we faced south, squinting over Duck Pass to the granite spine of the Sierra, at the still questionable line of our desire weaving among the peaks.

Beautiful skiing on corn snow—nature's version of the county fair snow cone—took us down to Duck Pass. Myriad ski tracks came up the Lakes Basin from Mammoth, shuffled awhile on the pass, and returned. We crossed them at right angles and climbed the far side. We were on our high line at last.

We sneaked around the top of a long bowl and pulsed over the first of the unknown notches, short but steep, beyond. It was our third pass of the day, if you count Duck Pass, which for us was really a hollow, so down the other side we stopped for lunch. Afterward the corn snow had softened to that perfect inch-and-a-half depth sometimes called cheater snow. We abandoned our packs and hiked up the hill to take short runs through a scattering of bleached gold, snow-blasted timberline snags.

We were a little late across Franklin Lakes that afternoon, approaching the unnamed high notch that would be the key to this passage. If we could get up it. The corn had long since frozen when I dropped my uphill hand out of the wrist loop and gripped the pole a foot lower, at the wad of strapping tape that marked steep climbing position.

The pitch above was short, just a few hundred vertical feet, but it riveted our attention. The slope ran from 40 to 45 degrees, steeper than the top half of the fearsome Cornice Bowl at Mammoth. Old corn snow had frozen into a coarse-grained, lumpy surface that would be an effort to cling to even with the sharp steel edges of our modified cross country skis. But it was the rocks that really bothered us. Sticking out of the snow like shark's teeth, they could make a slip extremely unpleasant. Each step up toward the pass became an exercise in edgy precision. Such moments swallowed an hour.

The evening ritual unfolded nearly as usual. I leaned out the door to hack snow with an ice axe, filled a pot, and slapped it on the propane cartridge stove. I had to hang on to the pot and stove, though, as bubbles of wind ripped between the tent and its icy platform. When we finally got hot water I made tea, adding dried lemon slices, honey, and a dollop of 151-proof rum. We drank that down and started another round with more snow. Dinner was a little simpler, bulgar wheat with tuna and dried vegetables.

Dawn brought calm air, but I couldn't relax at breakfast. I'd had an unsettling glimpse the night before of the far side of the notch we were perched on. It's north face was no steeper than yesterday's climb but was about three times longer. I was afraid it would be frozen solid. If so, we would not be able to ski down it, and chopping out steps with the ice axe would take nerve-wracking hours. Perhaps it was just as well that the cartographers had seen fit to hide this place under a political boundary line.

But geography came to the rescue. The north face caught less sunshine, so it didn't go through as much daily melting and nightly freezing. The snow was softer than the flinty crust we had struggled with coming up the other side. Facing the slope and backing downhill, I kicked a line of pigeonhole steps with the toes of my boots. Holding a ski vertically in each hand, we sank one tail at a time a foot into the snow to provide an anchor. In an hour we were down far enough to ski again, happy to be spared an ordeal Orland Bartholomew had once faced on his solitary tour, chopping steps all afternoon to get down off an icy pass. He had used the only tool he had, his double-bitted axe.

It felt good to cut loose on a mile-long traverse, ankles burning as they held an edge on the crust. Then it turned to powder, and I started cutting half turns, leaving a dipsy-doodle wake across the slope. When the powder got deep we gave up the most efficient line, submitted to gravity, and bombed down into the upper reaches of Convict Canyon.

It was a cold day. Done up in full parkas and hoods, we cut switch backs up to the comparatively low-angled notch into McGee Creek, happy not to be scraping edges on another steep headwall. From just over the notch we looked back to see high cirrus, those wispy ice clouds of the upper atmosphere, being absolutely shredded by the rotor of the Sierra wave. The rotor is an awesome band of turbulence that forms in the lee of the crest when winds blow especially hard across it. The local hang glider pilots speak of it with respect. "Rip your kite apart," they say, opting for a six-pack instead of flying for the day.

We camped at the head of the canyon, right on the creek, I think, though it was hard to tell. There were even a few trees around. The night was

Working the steep above Rock Creek. Marty Hornick photo

perfectly still, with unwavering bright stars, as they can only be when you're up high in winter.

In the morning we took off with a seven-league attitude, dreaming of wine, wives, and a landscape less white. Honed by two weeks of effort, we were lean machines, able to put our heads down and pant away a thousand feet without breaking stride, indifferent to thin air, dragging packs, and steep climbs. We hardly paused on Steelhead Pass and cruised through Pioneer Basin. Below, in deep woods, we turned sharply to the left and followed the creek bed up to Golden Lake. There above the lake was Half-moon Pass, the last one. Just over the pass lay Rock Creek Canyon, the end of the line, where Marsten would be waiting in a toasty cabin with a chicken dinner baked in rum-butter sauce as he'd promised. We put our heads down for one last pull.

Lemucchi's first clue that something was amiss was the sight of me sitting on my pack on the crest of the ridge, laughing. Betrayed by the forest again, I thought. I never have any trouble finding the route as long as I stay up in the alpine zone where I can see. But down in the forest I can get so turned around that I end up looking for moss on the north sides of trees like anyone from the city. There it was on the map: I had turned left a quarter mile too soon, up the wrong creek. It amused me how much the basin above resembled Golden Lake. But there was the real Golden Lake, down in front of me, with the real Half-moon Pass beyond. How to get there without going clear back and around was the problem now. And dark was coming on.

The first step was to breach the cornice. It was massive, cantilevered out fifteen or twenty feet in places over the leeward side of the ridge. I couldn't get close to the edge for fear of snapping off a few tons and riding the pieces down. But by the time Lemucchi hit the ridge top I had found a safe way through an uncorniced section a hundred yards away. The gully below was very steep and incredibly soft. It was too narrow to ski, so we had to take off our skis and wallow. We were up to our waists at every step, floundering, trying to throw ourselves downslope. By the time we got back on our skis it was nearly too dark to see. We set up the tent on Golden Lake, and I rifled the garbage bag to wring out some old tea bags for one more night's camp. Lemucchi wasn't saying much.

We woke up thinking about food. Avoiding the direct line across the real Half-moon Pass, we took an easier way out over Mono Pass. On the descent, we passed a couple just skiing in from Mammoth on the low route, the first people we had seen all week. The going got steeper, and deeper, until we found ourselves cranking hard, wrestling our packs through each turn in a foot of overcooked oatmeal snow. Still, we managed long lines of turns before we pulled up, panting with exhaustion. A shudder of delight ran up my spine, and I toppled backward into the snow laughing.

The snow was cool on my sweaty neck. I let the moment lengthen, listening to the beat of my heart in the perfect stillness. Below, the twentieth century awaited us: the night wind would take care of our tracks.

Haute touring is still a fringe sport. There are hardly any more of us now than there ever were. But we don't care; we revel in the solitude. The Sierra in winter is as close to true wilderness as anything left in the country, and it is a privilege to have the run of it.

We found Marsten's cabin empty, the stovepipe cold. Cursing our friend, we skied across the lake and down the road to Rock Creek Winter Lodge. There, standing in a bright circle of friends in front of the lodge, we drank Anchor Steam beer, kicked at the melting snow, and started polishing the tales of a fresh adventure.

Photos by Vern Clevenger

A High Route fit for the Sierra

There are climbers and skiers who hate to repeat a route.
Like Alan Bartlett, who will drag both friends and clients to obscure formations with an eye toward adding to his life list for,
say, Joshua Tree. He probably holds the world record there,
and has opened up many an adventure for his companions
along the way. Personally, I take the opposite tack. I look forward to repeating classic routes that have becom old friends.
Maybe I'm just easily amused. But a simple-minded enthusiasm for a fourteenth ascent of the Moon Goddess Arete, or skiing yet again from Mammoth to Yosemite, has helped me to really enjoy a long guiding career. Along the way I've lost track
of how many times I've skied the Sierra High Route. It feels
like maybe a dozen. Certainly not the 22 crossings of David
Beck, one of the High Route's originators. One spring I
guided the High Route twice. Between trips, to get home, I
skied back across, alone, in a single 22 hour push. Just for fun.

The buzz lately is that backcountry skiing is beginning to
grow again. We'll see. I predicted that nearly twenty years ago
in *Outside* magazine, and it didn't happen. Now there are two
magazines devoted to backcountry skiing, and *Outside* is calling
this trip "The best ski tour on the planet." Either way, it's high
time to just carve up some more of the finest spring snow on,
uh, the planet. Time to get back out there for more of those
nights on the ground, days in the open.

There are teasing glimpses all morning as I ski sweeping turns
through the open forest off Watkins' shoulder, but abruptly the trees give way
and there is Half Dome. It seems bigger than life from where I stand, looking
straight across Tenaya Canyon at the great sheared face.

Doug Robinson

This view of Half Dome is a fitting climax to what has become everyone's first trans-Sierra ski tour. The word has gotten around that the 50-mile crossing from Mammoth is not only the easiest of the dozen or so tours across the crest of this range but, well, a classic. It's a little like the standard route up the face of Half Dome over there across the canyon, which is known throughout the climbing world as the easiest climb in the hardest grade—memorable granite passages and fine position—a rite of passage into big wall climbing.

The first time I skied to a stop up here across from Half Dome was with several other climbers who well knew the ledges and crack systems of that great wall. The challenge for us on that trip had been getting here on fragile wooden touring skis; it was 1972, and our first venture away from alpine touring equipment into the unknown new world of nordic skiing. Since then I have skied this route maybe a dozen times. Once was with two companions who had never before seen Yosemite Valley. Imagine coming suddenly and on foot onto the rim of this awesome valley, emerging from the backcountry of the Sierra Nevada at its wildest season after skiing clear across the range from the east. Only such an approach can still give any idea of what Joseph Reddeford Walker and his party of fur trappers must have felt in 1833 when they rode abruptly onto the rim of the Valley on their way west out of the Great Basin. On another trip I was with a guy who loved the winter wilderness but had spent only four days on skis before launching across the Sierra. Will discovered that by keeping his skins on for the steeper descents they worked like training wheels; barely able to turn, he could still traverse a dream.

To ski trans-Sierra, clear across the Range of Light: who would think it possible during those first awkward moments on touring skis, trying to kick and glide around a flat meadow? Yet the name says that this is a sport of skiing across country. So who could resist dreaming, while peeling off damp long johns that same evening, of being able to climb the face of the range on skis, set up housekeeping right on the snow, and cut turns off the crest, gliding out to civilization a week later on the other side of the mountain barrier? This is the mountain range that cannibalized the Donner Party, a 400-mile crest that throughout the winter is still without an open road pass nearly from Lake Tahoe to Los Angeles.

As backcountry skiing grew up in this country—and all through the seventies it was doubling in popularity every year even without hut construction—more skiers learned that with a couple of years of enthusiastic practice (and a good guide), they too could ski trans-Sierra. Which led to a question that growing numbers have asked, while standing up here on top of the Snow Creek switch backs above Yosemite: What next?

One could set sights on the best-known ski tour in the world, the *Haute Route*, which winds along the crest of the Alps for a week's traverse from Chamonix, France to Zermatt, Switzerland. But escalating expenses make that tour seem further away every year. I mean, a French hut can cost twice as much as a Motel 6. Soon it may be cheaper to ski in the Himalaya than the Alps.

Cindy Pierce on the steep climb to Milestone Col.

"If there was to be an *Haute Route* in the United States," wrote David Beck in his classic 1980 guidebook *Ski Touring in California* (now long out of print), "this would be it." David was referring to a challenging new tour down by Mt. Whitney called the Sierra High Route. It's an appealing idea that the hardest of all the Sierra crossings should share with the easiest the distinction of being the most beautiful. But was it true? David, after all, had helped to pioneer this local High Route, following Nick Hartzell's lead in 1975. He had, to his credit, also skied the original *Haute Route* through the Alps, and on pin bindings no less. So who knew? This Sierra High Route could be pure California hubris, or a new secret classic. There was, of course, only one way to find out.

But I was busy. By the spring of 1980, ski mountaineering guiding was thriving, and I already had a group of seasoned skiers lined up with plans to ski half of the highest crest of the Sierra, a hundred miles down range in two weeks. Then the wheels started turning. It was easy, on paper, to turn west just short of Mount Whitney and finish off along the Sierra High Route for another week. Jumping onto the High Route just before it cleared the crest, we could also avoid most of the initial 6000-foot climb as it pulls unmercifully up out of the eastern desert. Since we would already have two weeks on the trail behind us, the crucial link was talking two friends into meeting us with fresh supplies of food, fuel, and an entire chocolate cake.

The plan worked perfectly. We got to Anvil Camp within five minutes of our resupply in the middle of April, and that evening David Beck himself arrived guiding a ski tour over the route. Anvil Camp sits in one of the rare groves of Foxtail pines in the Sierra and commands a view of the Owens Valley, a ten-mile-wide strip of high desert sandwiched between the eastern escarpment of the Sierra and the dust-dry White and Inyo mountains to the east. The 4500-foot uphill trudge from roadhead to Anvil Camp was one we were happy to leave to the imagination.

Peter Nemes cranks a tele with a full pack

We were on the Sierra High Route at last. Our first day began cold and ended by snowing. On the climb to Shepherd Pass the snow stayed frozen and kept getting steeper, until we found it prudent to take off our skis and follow a line of old steps fossilized in the hard crust. Up ahead, a member of Beck's party stopped to take a photo, balancing his pack between his knee and the frozen headwall. The pack escaped and at first it slid, then rolled, and finally cartwheeled toward us, hundreds of feet below its chagrined owner, who then acquired the distinction of climbing Shepherd Pass twice.

The top of the pass, although 12,050 feet high, is not the usual notch in a ridge but the edge of the vast Tyndall Plateau. West off the top is as gentle as the east side is steep, and miles wide, dropping only gradually to a ragged timberline, then more steeply into the Kern River drainage beyond. Past that, we might have picked out the line of our High Route weaving among the peaks of the Great Western Divide, but it was too windy to linger for a panorama. Gusts of up to fifty miles an hour blew straight in our faces. I set my pack down on top of my skis to keep them from blowing back over the pass, and put on every stitch of clothing I had along.

The skiing was miserable. Even leaning into the wind, we still couldn't glide down the gentle incline against those gusts. And the snow surface didn't help. It was frozen solid despite the bright sun, and had been pitted by weeks of thaw until its tortured surface resembled volcanic lava. Our ankles burned from the effort, we were too cold to stop for lunch, and when snow started to fall on the rim of the Kern River, we thankfully dove into the tent.

It snowed the next day too, from cloud so thick we could only see one bench at a time as we zigzagged up Milestone Creek. We climbed on skins, which were new to us after thousands of miles using only waxes. Originally sealskin, these useful tools are now just a napped fabric resembling stiff corduroy. A reusable glue backing fixes a thumb-wide strip down the center of each ski; with the nap facing toward the rear they will glide forward but not back. Skins climb better than wax and remove more easily than klister. Furthermore, they actually weigh less than the assortment of waxes we would have used during a week on the trail. Once the excitement of the new technology wore off, we ended up using skins half the time, on the long steep climbs, but preferred to stay on waxes for the miles of rolling terrain like the Tyndall Plateau and the Tablelands.

By 1980, skis had changed too. Ten years earlier we were on alpine skis with convertible bindings. Five years back Beck pioneered this traverse on lighter wooden nordic skis with segmented metal edges. Since then the blossoming of nordic-style ski mountaineering had caught the attention of mainline ski makers, so on this trip we were skiing on some of the first of the fiberglass Karhus. They were both lighter and stronger with a foam core, full metal edges and the flex of a good powder ski. Those skis would dominate Sierra ski mountaineering for the next decade.

The clouds lifted, wavered, and dropped again. Not knowing how much new snow might be creating an avalanche hazard on the steepest slopes under Milestone Col, which is the highest notch of the trip at 13,300 feet, we stopped and set up the tent. Then, of course, it cleared—the perfect excuse to check on avalanche conditions and make use of the new powder. Tom Allen and I charged up the slope, literally running at times, we felt so light without our packs. The new powder was ankle-deep, cold and very light. We hit a small ridge within the bowl and kept climbing. After 500 feet we couldn't stand the suspense, so we turned off the ridge and skied. It was perfect. Tom telemarked, I skied paralleled, and the powder flew. We went from tight turns into wide swooping arcs and all too soon were back in camp.

David Beck was standing on the outskirts of his camp, nursing a steaming mug and musing under his breath about the frozen crust beneath the new load of powder—weighing adhesion against the chance of the powder's sliding off the traverse the next day. I was glad to be able to tell him that as far as I had gone it was stable. I had even found a 30-foot test slope, a very steep little knoll facing the same direction relative to both the sun and the wind as the headwall of the pass, and ski-cut across the top of it. No slide.

Still, in the morning we stuck close to the rocks to bypass the steepest slope. Even with each of us carrying an avalanche radio beacon and with David's faithful avalanche dog, Guinness, trotting along in dark glasses, we couldn't be too careful.

"It's like camping in a God-damned icebox," Tim Lemucchi said as we skied back into camp that night. But he said it with a grin, and he too hung around outside the tent right along with the rest of us until the lingering alpenglow on Mount Whitney turned to ash. When we finally dove into the tent, it was two below zero.

Inside, the evening ritual was well underway. Snow was melting on one stove, tea steeping on the other. We settled into the built-in backrests of our Octadome in a circle facing the teapot, which was soon poured out with dried lemon wedges, honey, and a dollop of 151 rum—experienced mountaineers are quick to take advantage of any weight-saving supplies, even dehydrated alcohol. We too were dehydrated. Ski touring is one of those "water, water everywhere..." situations. We went through three rounds of tea and two of soup before the main course, and melted a liter each the next morning to carry for the day.

The greatest contrast to the European *Haute Route* is highlighted this evening: the accommodations. Alpine huts are really more like high altitude hotels. In the first anteroom ski boots come off and are replaced by a pair of hut slippers from the rack. From there you step into the dining room to order a beer or a glass of white wine. After dinner it's upstairs to a dorm room complete with blankets. You don't even need a sleeping bag. In fact, all you carry for a week of skiing along the top of the Alps is lunch, parka, camera and wax.

So much civilization in the evening, however, can mean 70 people on the trail with you the next morning, which diminishes the wilderness experience. Traffic had cut a trench along the route when I skied the *Haute Route*, so there's not much question about where you're going, and any powder that has fallen is likely to be skied up. One morning, though, as we shuffled out of the *Vignettes Hut* before dawn, there *was* new snow. Also a line of skiers already disappearing ahead of us into the dark. I gradually worked my way to the head of the line and took over the trail breaking. The stuff was light, six or eight inches of it. I had put away most of the 3000-foot climb to the

Pigne d'Arolla and was already beginning to savor my first tracks when a helicopter landed above me and disgorged a bunch of fat, Euro "powder pigs."

Remembering that burst my bubble, and I found myself back in California, mulling my camp up the Great Western Divide. On the fourth morning we crossed the shoulder of Milestone Mountain, which was more like sneaking over a ridge than going through a pass. On the other side, noonday sun was turning the six inches of new snow in Milestone Bowl into mush, so even the likes of David Beck were tripping and dripping, and shrugging off wetness by falling back on the old standby, traverse and kick turn. Halfway down the bowl I caught up with Andrea Mead Lawrence. She was the only member of David's group who had not skied trans-Sierra before, but she had been admitted to the tour anyway because of her credentials: she is the only American to have won *two* gold medals in Olympic skiing. Andrea was using the tour to quit smoking. "I sure wish I had my downhill skis..." she began, and it was easy to imagine the tracks she would lay down even in that crud. But I could see that she didn't really care about not having other skis, and that just being up on the crest of the range in that sweet, sharp air was more than enough.

That night no one was taking runs above camp. The snow had turned to breakable crust, and we were relieved to get there and step off our skis before falling down—again.

The next day, our fifth on the High Route, was the kind of perfect mountain day that lives with you forever. We struck camp purposefully and in an hour were on the notch by Triple Divide Peak, where it was too windy to linger. Dropping onto the north side of the ridge again brought a swift and dramatic change in the snow. In Milestone Bowl and on the sunny southern exposures the new snow had been rotting away to unskiable mush before our eyes, but here on north slopes, shielded from the sun, lay quiet fields of perfect powder. We skied down from the notch through a band of breakable crust and into the powder. After we got below the wind, we stopped and were sitting on our packs eating dried mushrooms when Andrea's son, Matthew, skied down to join us. There was a lot of grinning and head shaking about our good fortune to be in that high, unlikely place.

The day was just getting rolling. The snow had turned perfect, and now the terrain was opening out to match. When other trans-Sierras would be ducking down into the forest, our Sierra High Route was going into overdrive. We skied down another 500 feet of perfect snow, went left under a rock band, and began a long gradual traverse toward the notch in Glacier

Ridge. We were beginning to see the Whaleback, a graceful spine of grey granite breaking the endless sea of snow, its glacier-polished flanks shimmering with melt water.

Along the traverse the snow got deeper and then irresistible. We threw off our packs and reveled in it, running up the slope to ski back down. I lingered so long that by the time I reached the notch, the figure out in front was already a speck, breaking trail across the vast upper rim of Deadman Canyon. David Beck's group skied down and camped while we pushed on over yet another high notch, our third for the day and the next-to-last of the route. Near the notch I looked back to see David's tents ranged on a small flat. A lone figure broke from the camp and began cutting telemarks down the canyon. The terrain rolled before him as gently as a cloud, and his skiing had a similarly unearthly quality. He rounded each turn nearly to a stop before submitting himself again to gravity. He finally stopped 1500 feet down to remount his skins. The show was over. We went on over the ridge to set up our tent in the dark. It was that kind of a day.

Re-entry after so long above timberline was a feast for the senses. It went from the pine fragrance of the first trees to bluebirds welcoming us to the road and the hushed shade under giant sequoias. That evening, driving toward our victory dinner at Tim's restaurant in Bakersfield, we had all the van's windows open for the fragrance of orange blossoms that rolled in out of the darkness.

David Beck was right about this tour. It *is* the Sierra High route. David Smiled. "Yes," he said, it's an elegant trip. It sneaks through, finding a high line without forcing its way. It never lapses into mountaineering, but you're glad to have the rope and ice axe along. There is good snow late in the spring, and as you go west the tour gets better—just where others would be petering out into the forest." A few months later it was David's turn to be surprised by me, for my original skepticism had given way, and even I was calling the tour "The High Route of the Americas."

It might very well be. I keep thinking back to that unnamed high notch between Cloud and Deadman Canyons. Over the notch were a series of granite bleachers where everyone was lounging, eating lunch and staring off to the horizon. So calm and warm a day on a high pass is rare, an event to be savored, and most of the skiers had been there an hour. Even A. P. Marsten, who is usually so voluble in his appreciation, had fallen silent. Deadman Canyon was nearly identical to Cloud Canyon, behind us—a huge glacial cirque rimmed by spikes of solid granite, but offering a gently rolling

ski line across its top to yet another unnamed notch. Beyond was a glimpse of the high open plateau of the Tablelands, where we would be tomorrow. The skiing from there down into giant sequoia groves was hidden, and beyond, a cloud bank filled the entire central valley of California, hiding oil rigs and cotton gins, the lowriders of Bakersfield and the smog layer that usually conceals what passes for civilization. Beyond the fog, way out on the horizon, floated the coast range of California, something I had seen before from the Sierra but could never count on the way John Muir had. Behind us the crest of the Sierra ran to the north showing a sharp relief that can only be seen from a spot this high, yet far enough away to appreciate the full scope of it sweeping along the horizon. We could pick out familiar peaks and passes—the route we had been following for nearly three weeks. Sequoia National Park spread out to the south of us, and Kings Canyon raced away north; the only sign of civilization in the entire panorama was a thin line of ski tracks behind us.

Here was a more astonishing prospect than even Half Dome jumping up from the forest: a clear view halfway across California, exactly as it would have appeared when Pueblo de Los Angeles had only one dirt street and Snowshoe Thompson was just another kid learning to ski in Norway.

The High Route, indeed.

Doug Robinson

Forgetfulness and Bliss:
the Endorphin Effect

The final return is to the intrigue of the visionary. This one leads to the future.

Everyone knows by now that endorphins are behind runners high. Simple. Well, I hate to be a spoilsport (actually, I kind of like it), but it is far from being that simple. The whole answer is richly complex, as subtle and elusive as consciousness itself, and its component parts have not yet all been discovered. The endorphins are a crucial part of that eventual picture, but ultimately only one part among many. Here, then, is an early stab at understanding how the endorphins work to help frame our perception of action in the wilderness, written with the excitement of the period when this whole topic was hot and new.

"If you remember it you weren't there"
—quoted by Thomas McGuane

There is something forgetful about the wilderness. Saturday's high mountain times can slip away from memory by Wednesday. You go back anyway—sometimes it seems to be on faith—only to be overwhelmed anew by a fresh intensity of experience. The mountains smell so fresh, and your body reaches a rare harmony of motion along the trail. There is no way to forget this. Yet halfway through the dark drive home the memory has vanished.

The more intense the experience of the mountains, the sooner it seems forgotten. Actually, it's only intensely *active* times that seem to be the first to vanish. The contemplative ones remain. Lying in the meadow comes back sharp and clear; the smell of heather, the gurgle of the creek, the shape of grass hummocks under your back remain vivid. But the wildly physical pell-mell run down the hillside that led into the meadow, what is left of that? Just sweat—and even that evaporates and is gone.

If I sometimes remember hikes in toward the peaks, often the climbs themselves will be gone. More than once I've gotten onto the third pitch of a climb before remembering that I had done it before. It feels a little silly, a little odd.

Some will object. Steve Roper, who writes guidebooks out of his photographic memory, will say that it's just me, and roll his eyes. People are different, that's for sure, but that's not the whole story. It doesn't explain why so many others have felt this way too. It doesn't explain how the amnesia seems to increase along with the physical intensity of the experience, or why you might clearly recall the view from a belay ledge but not the climbing that led to it.

Medical researchers would quickly notice that we have separated experience from the memory of it according to what they call stress. We don't usually consider our strenuous fun in the wilderness as stress, but it does fit into the medical definition. Strenuous is stressful and soon forgotten. Contemplative is calm; its memory lingers.

Stress and amnesia keep company in the lowlands too. Consider the way the victim of a car crash won't remember the moment of impact, or sometimes the whole day leading up to it. Not so long ago this wasn't even considered a medical mystery, just tricks played by the mind. But in the mid-seventies some researchers—who as usual were looking for something else—stumbled onto a clue that would eventually lead back to forgetfulness. They were studying morphine, trying to find out how it works in the brain, what circuits it closes to relieve pain. Their motivation was obvious, since pain is of more than passing interest to medicine. But a glance at the textbooks in use before 1970 showed a phrase so typical it might as well have been made into a rubber stamp: "Mechanism of action unknown."

The early 70s brought an interesting discovery: Morphine doesn't club the whole nervous system the way a general anesthetic like laughing gas does; rather it works directly on a few select groups of nerve endings that seem to be tuned specifically to receive its anesthetic message. Those nerve endings the researchers named opioid receptors.

Now the trouble with finding opioid receptors clustered in the human brain is that their existence leads to other, more disturbing, questions. Like why are they there? Why do we have a specific reaction to opioids built into our brains? Finding such receptors is an open invitation to look for some natural process that uses them. None had been discovered in 1970, so, back to the lab.

In 1975 beta-endorphin was found. Not only did it fit those opioid receptors like a glove, but it turned out to be a human hormone and 20 to 50 times stronger than morphine, which until then had been the best pain killer known to man. Most of our beta-endorphin is made in the pituitary, the body's master gland folded deep inside the brain. Finding it wasn't easy. One lab in La Jolla, for instance, collected the pituitary glands from five million cow brains over the years, just to extract enough beta-endorphin to keep the research going. After all, anything that much stronger than morphine wouldn't be sloshing through our systems by the bucketful, or not much research would get done. If the opioid receptor is like a lock, then beta-endorphin fits into it like a key, and before long all manner of remarkable effects were being traced to it. One lab reported a "retrograde amnesia mechanism," which sounds suspiciously like that mountain memory loss.

Bruce Robinson bouldering in the Wind Rivers

The opiates are revered medically, of course, as the world's best pain killers. Morphine was the ultimate anesthetic until beta-endorphin came along, and it's still the practical one. Although beta-endorphin has come down from an early price of $3000 per milligram to today's bargain $180, doctors won't be reaching for it in the emergency room just yet. Beta-endorphin is still a research tool.

Researchers are now suggesting that beta-endorphin is an automatic, self-administered anesthetic that responds to either pain or stress. Pretty handy for the body to be making its own pain killer. We can see this happening in the mountains too.

Blood is sure to draw attention, even when there is little attention to spare. Drops of blood appear on the rocks right next to a jamcrack. But the crack is vertical, the rock smooth, and strength is ebbing. Higher are more bright drops on the granite—fresh. Finally the ledge. I pull onto it panting and shaking, raise a hand to wipe sweat out of my eyes, and then I see: the blood is mine. I've gashed my hand somewhere below, without even feeling it. This has happened a dozen times to me, and to every climber I know. Surely there is a dose of beta-endorphin—stimulated by the stress of climbing and on hand well before the injury—behind this familiar climbing story.

Last winter I saw beta-endorphin at work in a couple of skiers with torqued ankles. Take Allan Bard. It was hardly unusual for him to be yahooing his skinny skis through the woods on the windward side of a Mammoth Mountain blizzard day. It *was* unusual that he got caught. First an edge, then a whole ski crosswise in the trees abruptly terminated his considerable momentum. When Allan got up and nothing in his ankle rattled, he jumped back on it and skied, hard, right up until the lifts closed hours later. Then he walked nearly normally to the car. But after a half hour ride into town, Allan hobbled into his house, and he limped around moaning for the rest of the evening.

That got me thinking. Allan had felt his ankle go twang the instant that it happened; he had been really pleased to get up and ski away (and happy not to waste his expensive lift ticket). If instead he had twisted it, say, stepping off a curb, beta-endorphin would have welled up in his system to take the edge off the pain. Still, most people in that situation would hurt enough to sit in the gutter while they waited for help. But when Allan went down in the powder in the woods he had been skiing hard all day, and shaving a fine line past the trees at that, so he was already in a high state of stress, with plenty of beta-endorphin in his system before he fell. No wonder, then, that on a double dose of God's own finest painkiller, Allan got right back up and skied, never knowing until he slowed down that evening just how badly he was hurt.

When Tom Bates went down the next afternoon, I had a better idea what was happening. He came off the apex of Dave's Run, one of the expert-only headwalls that line the top of the mountain, sliding and then bouncing in a sickening acceleration of flying powder and flailing limbs. After collecting the gear spread in his wake, I found Tom tentatively fingering his ankle. "It doesn't feel too bad..." he began, but this time I knew how little that meant. We skied gently down to the car, and sure enough he was hobbling for weeks afterward.

Researchers would not have been surprised at such turns of events. They had already noticed the resemblance between increased doses of beta-endorphin and the usual stages of general anesthesia. In other words, inject enough beta-endorphin into a person—and remember, it takes very little—and it is possible to perform radical surgery without bothering him at all. But it's the reaction to lower doses that is really intriguing. During the early stages of general anesthesia, people get animated. They act, well...high. Anesthetics, alcohol, morphine: they all start out at low doses acting like stimulants. Apparently the first thing they numb is a person's inhibitions. Literally, they dull nerve circuits in the brain whose primary function is keeping a lid on things. The textbooks keep mentioning qualities like euphoria. Not your typical medical language, but it sure resembles the stuff of a spontaneous joy shout for no better reason than a breathless run in perfect powder.

Survival Skiing. Gordon Wiltsie photo

To people going for it outdoors, beta-endorphin has always, ever before it had a name, been a euphoriant. Long before morphine became a medical pain killer, the opium poppy was explored for its dreamy buoyancy. And way before that, early man must have haphazardly noticed the euphoric after-effects of a healthy dose of stress. Not that he would have been chasing it the way his post-industrial descendants chase after runner's high, around and around the Marina Green on a San Francisco lunch break. But surely he would have noticed the deliciously heady sensation that followed a hair-raising escape from one of the local big-fanged cats, or wrapped himself in the transcendent oblivion that precipitated from a long walk home in the freezing dark. Runner's high, climber's euphoria, and that little irrepressible shudder of excitement that sweeps over you for no other reason than finding yourself so much alive and hard at work on a mountain trail—all seem to be due, at least in part, to a rising level of beta-endorphin in the body.

The beta-endorphin in turn comes from stress. Stress has gotten itself a bad reputation as the tension behind so many urban ulcers and heart attacks. But just as prominent and a lot more fun is the positive side of stress, exemplified by the relaxed and cleansed feeling after a hard day in the mountains. High altitude and cold are so common we take them for granted, but they also fit under the umbrella definition of stress. Indeed, the evening chill in the mountains is often said to be "bracing," another part of the "tonic" of wilderness that leaves us feeling more alive without quite knowing why. Many facets of a day in the mountains come together to encourage that extra degree of relaxed alertness that we feel in the wilderness, lack in the city, and go back searching for without understanding.

Upper Headwall of the Dark Star Buttress, first ascent. Photo by Gordon Wiltsie

It's tempting to call beta-endorphin the whole explanation for people getting high on mountains. But studies of people under stress, typically runners, show that when the endorphin level is rising in the body, the levels of adrenaline-related compounds in the body are running right along with it. There is even some recent evidence that both are released simultaneously from the same nerve endings. So the newly discovered stress response of endorphins appears to be working in close harmony with the classic stress response of adrenaline. If beta-endorphin accounts for the relaxed and euphoric feelings, then increases in the adrenaline family of hormones probably explain such stimulated effects as sharpened awareness and even heightened consciousness. How are they linked? No one is sure yet. And why? A preparatory dose of pain killer might be handy in case stress leads to injury—there's no time to nurse a sprained ankle with a tiger on your tail. There are other guesses, intriguing speculations, but as yet no firm connections.

I keep returning to those studies of runners. One after another they show nearly double beta-endorphin levels in the runner's bloodstream while he is working out. Perhaps this is the best news of all, that these reactions are not limited to the rarefied atmosphere of wilderness, but are as close as your favorite physical form of stress. I feel it these spring afternoons pounding over hills on the coast road. After half an hour I've run myself happy; thoughts float free, associating, legs are on automatic. It is a very physical form of joy, and it begins to fade after I quit moving.

These intensities, evidently, are to have but not to hold. Even this quality was anticipated by the original be-here-now advocates, the Zen Masters, as a sign of right attitude toward experience. It's all right, let it go. Suzuki Roshi says in "Zen Mind, Beginners Mind:" "Zen activity is activity which is completely burned out, with nothing remaining but ashes."

Two Afternoons in the Sixties

Here is a sneak preview of the unpublished book, "The Alchemy of Action." The book grows out of two pieces included here, *The Climber as Visionary*, and *Forgetfulness and Bliss*. In outline, it begins with the strong experiences of runners high and climbers euphoria, and the question of where they come from. It explores the volatile world of adrenaline and then goes on to an updated view of beta-endorphin (it was hard to refrain from re-writing *Forgetfulness and Bliss*, in light of how much more has been learned since it was published). It brings in clinical information from physiology and biochemistry, from the brains of lab rats and the blood of finishers in the Western States 100 trail run, but only when that data can be anchored to the reality of strong, human experience. Then the discussion takes a surprising turn, hinted at in *The Climber as Visionary* and now buttressed by much more specific information which the book goes on to lay out. Here is the chapter that turns that corner, hinged on a pair of experiences—on the street and in the University library—during the sixties.

By the mid sixties my flirtation with climbing had turned into the ruling passion of my life. All summer and most weekends I was off in Yosemite, or beyond there, back in the wilderness among the high peaks of the Sierra Nevada. And I was starting to guide.

In the autumn I went down to the city to study at San Francisco State. Like a lot of students I ended up living in the Haight-Ashbury, and as the sixties wore on our neighborhood transformed from a student ghetto into a cultural revolution. To stay active I often walked over the hills of the city to get to school, or ran downtown and put on a black bowtie for my job of pumping gas at Standard Oil. They had a dress code, which led to my being the only person in the Haight with a crew cut.

One afternoon between classed I wandered into the library to read Kerouac. His "Dharma Bums" was a vivid and barely fictionalized recounting of climbing Matterhorn Peak north of Yosemite with the Zen poet Gary Snyder, plus hanging out in Berkeley cottages drinking red wine and doing the kind of high-octane free association that had set the philosophical underpinnings for the current Haight-Ashbury scene. That had only been a few years before; the influence was still hot.

Kerouac's descriptions were so vivid that you could stumble in his prose where I knew there were real rocks in the trail to Matterhorn Peak. Some of my climbing friends who had tripped their way through Kerouac in Yosemite were now sitting in meditation at the Berkeley Zen Center and living in those same back garden cottages.

So I was overjoye—øthough not too surprise—øto run into one such friend at the 1966 Human Be-In in Golden Gate Park. In Yosemite Chris had been a mentor to my crack climbing technique; now he led me up a tree and pulled out a joint. When we came down I hopped up onto a fence to look out over the stage where Allen Ginsberg was chanting to the tidal surge of my generation, which was perhaps more in synch than it would ever be again, as the sun dropped through Eucalyptus trees into the sea. When I turned around Chris had vanished into the crowd and I was higher than I had ever before imagined.

Ginsberg concluded and I fell in with the crowd streaming through the twilight park back toward the Haight. I followed along, feeling lost even on paths that I knew well from running them every week. I seemed to be having some trouble keeping my feet on the ground. There was this sense that my legs would just keep rising behind me as my head tucked forward and I relaxed into slow rolls through deep space. But not quite; the next instant I snapped back to the present, awe-struck by this river of humanity flowing by all these vivid tones of green as the park slipped toward darkness.

Things kept changing fast. I would gulp down an occasional flash of panic by power walking through the crowd, then feel like raging consciousness might at any moment drag me head first off the path to collapse onto the lawn, crying. Wild, rapid surges of thoughts and feelings were sometimes only kept grounded—held nearly in control—by picking a person 20 feet ahead of me on the path who I sensed could help if I suddenly began to diffuse. But by the time I had caught up, it would all have shifted again to shuddering joy and certitude.

It wasn't until several years and much study later that I concluded that the joint I had been handed up in the tree that historic afternoon must have been dosed with DMT. That swift and potent hallucinogen, which like LSD had at the time not yet been declared illegal, had earned the nickname "businessman's lunch" for coming on so fast and hard, only to vanish equally rapidly an hour or two later. We will meet it again, deep in the brain.

"On the Road" proved less compelling to me than Kerouac's Sierra wanderings had been. After forty pages I put it up and, turning along an unfamiliar aisle of the library, took down an academic-looking volume called "The Hallucinogens." "Hallucinogen" turned out to be an earlier term for the Psychedelic group of compounds, and the book in my hands was their encyclopedia. But both terms were just part of a struggle to characterize a state of mind that kept—well—sort of expanding beyond its definitions. "Psychotomimetic" was another abandoned term. Any street chemist in the Haight could tell you that the experience went beyond the mere mimicry of madness. Our neighborhood was growing notorious on the premise that these chemicals unlocked ecstasies that united people in visions of universal love. On the other hand the doctors at the Free Clinic, never more than a few steps away from a fat syringe of Thorazine, were quick to remind us that if a personality was teetering on the brink, it could easily be nudged, temporarily at least, into madness. There was a lot of latitude in those compounds, and the struggle to name them only highlighted unknown factors in a situation that was becoming more baffling even as it got more intriguing.

This book of Hallucinogens was an interesting mixture. It was full of roots and berries, and the recipes of Shamans alternated with reports from white-coated lab workers giving LSD to spiders to see what tangled webs they'd weave. (They did better on acid than on caffeine.) It grouped the compounds into chapters by some system that was at first obscure, than illuminating, and which finally led me to a great revelation.

Photo by Gordon Wiltsie

I was a chapter away from the "businessman's lunch" I'd eaten in the park—DMT—just the next block over chemically speaking, and window shopping among much more familiar compounds like mescaline. I turned the page and there it was. At the center of a chart was adrenaline, with its now-familiar molecular map. Arrows radiated out, showing adrenaline's possible transformation in intriguing directions. One of the arrows led to mescaline. And the steps in between could be guided by common brain enzymes.

Doug Robinson

A simple observation, to look back on it. But then the good ones always are. Just put the two compounds next to each other on the page and the family resemblance is obvious even to a non-chemist. "The Hallucinogens" was written, in part, by Dr. Humphrey Osmond, a psychiatric researcher and a friend of Aldous Huxley, who in the early fifties had been the first to notice the kinship of adrenaline and mescaline. Pointing that out had led to a whole field of research in brain chemistry. And the implications of that relationship have rocked psychiatry, to the extent that forty years after the similarity was first noticed, it still forms the basis for one of the two leading theories of schizophrenia.

I was transfixed. This little chart confirmed an old intuition, one that went back to my first psychedelic experience. It was a comparatively mild high from smoking marijuana, but it gave me the immediate sense that I was on familiar ground. Oh yeah, I realized, I know this place. I've run myself into this state. I've gotten to this intensity of perception, these racing thoughts, from skiing and climbing, even hiking.

Now Dr. Osmond's chart was showing me a clear link between the high experiences that flowed naturally out of my climbing days so charged with adrenaline, and the chemically-induced ones that felt so similar. That striking similarity led my thoughts beyond mental illness (or more likely, pulled up short of it) to suggest possibilities hovering along the outer reaches of healthy consciousness, implications for the chemistry of enlightenment. The same compounds could lead either toward madness or great insight, depending more on the circumstances— the state of mind and body—of the host than the shape of the chemical pathways.

Origins of the Writings

Every piece reprinted here has been revised. Most were changed by only a few words, while several more had a paragraph or two reworked. Three pieces have been extensively rewritten. Five pieces, as well as all the introductions and postscripts—a good quarter of the writing—appear here for the first time.

"Bringing Light out of Stone" was written to introduce this book.

"Five," copyright ©1989. First appeared in *Trips*, July 1989.

"Wanderers of the Range of Light," copyright ©1986. Reprinted by permission of *Rock&Ice* #16, September-December1986.

"Tuesday Morning on the Lyell Fork with Eliot's Shadow," copyright ©1968. Reprinted by permission of *Ascent*, 1968

"Camp 4" copyright ©1969. First printed in *Mountain* #4, July 1969

"The Climber as Visionary," copyright ©1969. Reprinted by permission of *Ascent*, 1969

"Four Feet over Sierra," copyright ©1974. Extensively revised and reprinted by permission of *Powder*, 1974.

"Truckin' My Blues Away," copyright ©1970. Originally appeared in *Mountain* #9 1970.

"Mountaineering Just Means Glad to be Here" has never appeared before.

"All that Evolving," the title poem, copyright ©1976. First appeared in *Simple Foods for the Pack*. San Francisco: Sierra Club, 1976. The other poems in this section appear here for the first time.

"Ice Nine," copyright ©1977. Reprinted by permission of *Outside*, Dec 1977.

The Pinheads Meet the Yo-Yos," Originally titled "Skiing the Skinny Boards," copyrightÊ©1986. Reprinted by permission of *L.A. Times Magazine*, February 9, 1986.

"Technique and Technology," headquote copyright ©1975. Reprinted by permission of Yvon Chouinard, Chouinard Equipment trade catalog, 1975.

"The Whole Natural Art of Protection," copyright ©1972. Reprinted by permission of Yvon Chouinard, Chouinard Equipment trade catalog, 1972.

"Half Dome Comes Clean" was written for this book.

"Tool Man," originally leading the chapter "Style and Ethics," copyright ©1978 by Yvon Chouinard in *Climbing Ice*. San Francisco: Sierra Club 1978. Reprinted by permission.

"Dances with Gravities," originally leading the chapter "Keeping Your Head About You," copyright ©1978 by Yvon Chouinard in *Climbing Ice*. San Francisco: Sierra Club 1978. Reprinted by permission.

"Running Talus," copyright ©1975. Reprinted by permission of Yvon Chouinard, Chouinard Equipment trade catalog, 1975

"Moving Over Stone," copyright ©1988 Range of Light Productions.

"Oklahoma Rock," copyright ©1985. Reprinted by permission of *Outside*, Sept. 1985.

"Hang Gliding—The Olympics of Lift," copyright ©1981. An abridged form was published by *Outside*, Nov 1981.

Chiura Obata, the artist who painted the art featuring on the cover, painting Evening Glow in Vidette Meadow, King's Canyon National Park, August 1948, at Sierra Club base camp. Photograph by Cedric Wright. Courtesy of Susan Herzig & Paul Hertzmann, Paul Hertzmann, Inc., San Francisco

OTHER MOUNTAIN N'AIR BOOKS